Lecture Notes in Computer Science 1590

Edited by G. Goos, J. Hartmanis and J. van Leeuwen

Springer
Berlin
Heidelberg
New York
Barcelona
Hong Kong
London
Milan
Paris
Singapore
Tokyo

Paolo Atzeni   Alberto Mendelzon
Giansalvatore Mecca (Eds.)

The World Wide Web and Databases

International Workshop WebDB'98
Valencia, Spain, March 27-28, 1998
Selected Papers

 Springer

Series Editors

Gerhard Goos, Karlsruhe University, Germany
Juris Hartmanis, Cornell University, NY, USA
Jan van Leeuwen, Utrecht University, The Netherlands

Volume Editors

Paolo Atzeni
Università di Roma Tre
Dipartimento di Informatica e Automazione
via della Vasca Navale, 79, I-00146 Roma, Italy
E-mail: atzeni@dia.uniroma3.it

Alberto Mendelzon
University of Toronto, Department of Computer Science
6 King's College Road, Toronto, Ontario, Canada M5S 3H5
E-mail: mendel@cs.toronto.edu

Giansalvatore Mecca
Università della Basilicata
via della Tecnica, 3, I-85100 Potenza, Italy
E-mail: mecca@dia.uniroma3.it

Cataloging-in-Publication data applied for

Die Deutsche Bibliothek - CIP-Einheitsaufnahme

The World Wide Web and databases : selected papers / Workshop WebDB '98,
Valencia, Spain, March 27 - 28, 1998. Paolo Atzeni ... (ed.). - Berlin ;
Heidelberg ; New York ; Barcelona ; Hong Kong ; London ; Milan ; Paris ; Santa
Clara ; Tokyo : Springer, 1999
(Lecture notes in computer science ; Vol. 1590)
ISBN 3-540-65890-4

CR Subject Classification (1998): H.5, H.4.3, H.2, H.3, C.2.4

ISSN 0302-9743
ISBN 3-540-65890-4 Springer-Verlag Berlin Heidelberg New York

Typesetting: Camera-ready by author
SPIN: 10704656   06/3142 – 5 4 3 2 1 0   Printed on acid-free paper

Foreword

This volume is based on the contributions to the International Workshop on the Web and Databases (WebDB'98), held in Valencia, Spain, March 27 and 28, 1998, in conjunction with the Sixth International Conference on Extending Database Technology (EDBT'98).

In response to the workshop call for papers, 37 manuscripts were submitted to the program committee. The review process was conducted entirely by e-mail. While the quality of submissions was generally high, only 16 papers could be accepted for presentation within the limited time allowed by the workshop schedule. Authors of workshop papers were invited to submit extended versions of their papers for publication in these post-workshop proceedings. The 13 papers appearing in this volume were submitted and selected after a second round of reviews.

We would like to thank the program committee of WebDB'98, all those who submitted their work, all additional reviewers, and the conference officials of EBDT'98 for their invaluable support. Special thanks go to Paolo Merialdo, who actively participated in the organization of the workshop.

February 1999   Paolo Atzeni, Alberto Mendelzon and Gianni Mecca
WebDB'98 Post-Workshop Proceedings Editors

Workshop Organization

Workshop Co-Chairs

Paolo Atzeni	(Università di Roma Tre, Italy)
Alberto Mendelzon	(University of Toronto, Canada)

Program Committee

Paolo Atzeni	(Università di Roma Tre, Italy)
Sophie Cluet	(INRIA, France)
Jon Kleinberg	(Cornell University, USA)
Alon Levy	(University of Washington, USA)
Udi Manber	(University of Arizona, USA)
Giansalvatore Mecca	(Università della Basilicata, Italy)
Alberto Mendelzon	(University of Toronto, Canada)
Eric Neuhold	(GMD-IPSI, Germany)
Oded Shmueli	(Technion, Israel)

Organizing Committee

Paolo Atzeni	(Università di Roma Tre, Italy)
Giansalvatore Mecca	(Università della Basilicata, Italy)
Alberto Mendelzon	(University of Toronto, Canada)
Paolo Merialdo	(Università di Roma Tre, Italy)

EDBT Workshop Coordinator

Oscar Pastor	(Universitat Politècnica de València)

Sponsoring Institutions

Universitat Politècnica de València
The EDBT Foundation
Università di Roma Tre

Table of Contents

A Unified Algorithm for Cache Replacement and Consistency in Web Proxy Servers

Junho Shim[1], Peter Scheuermann[1], and Radek Vingralek[2]

[1] Department of Electrical and Computer Engineering
Northwestern University, Evanston, IL 60208, USA
shimjh,peters@ece.nwu.edu
[2] Lucent Technologies, Bell Laboratories
600 Mountain Ave., Murray Hill, NJ 07974, USA
rvingral@research.bell-labs.com

Abstract. Caching of Web documents improves the response time perceived by the clients. Cache replacement algorithms play a central role in the response time reduction by selecting a subset of documents for caching so that an appropriate performance metric is maximized. At the same time, the cache must take extra steps to guarantee some form of consistency of the cached data. Cache consistency algorithms enforce appropriate guarantees about the staleness of documents it stores. Most of the published work on Web cache design either considers cache consistency algorithms separately from cache replacement algorithms or concentrates only on studying one of the two.

We argue that cache performance can be improved by integrating cache replacement and consistency algorithms. We present an unified algorithm LNC-R-W3-U. Using trace-based experiments, we demonstrate that LNC-R-W3-U achieves performance comparable (and often superior) to most of the published cache replacement algorithms and at the same time significantly reduces the staleness of the cached documents.

1 Introduction

The response time of Web clients is often improved by caching Web documents at nearby caching proxies [2, 5, 8, 9, 17, 20]. The design of most Web caches relies on a replacement algorithm to dynamically select a suitable subset of documents for caching so that some performance metric such as *hit ratio* [2] or *delay savings ratio* [5, 20, 17] is maximized. Caching copies of Web documents at proxies leads to inconsistency when the original documents on the server are updated. Therefore, most caching proxy implementations rely on a consistency algorithm to ensure a suitable form of consistency for the cached documents.

Cache consistency algorithms for client/server database systems usually enforce *strong consistency* (i.e. no stale data returned to clients) [14]. In the context of WWW, strong consistency can be either guaranteed by having the caching proxy to poll servers each time a client hits the cache or by maintaining a state on each server with callbacks for all the proxies caching the server's documents.

The former approach leads to an overhead which practically eliminates the benefits of caching, while the latter approach is not supported by any of the currently available Web servers. Consequently, all caching proxies known to the authors guarantee only some form of *weak consistency* (i.e. clients may receive stale data) [9, 11, 12, 15]. A typical implementation of weak consistency assigns to each document (or group of documents) a *time-to-live* (TTL) interval [1, 7, 11, 12]. Any client request for a document which has been cached longer than TTL units results in document validation by sending HTTP conditional (If-Modified-Since) GET request to the server. The server responds with the requested document only if it has been updated. A common guideline for setting TTL for a document is based on the observation that documents which were not updated in the past will not be updated also in the future [6].

However, to the best of our knowledge, the value of TTL has not been considered explicitly by the cache replacement algorithms reported in literature. Consequently, frequently updated documents which must be continuously validated are as likely to be cached as infrequently updated documents which require only seldom validation. At the same time, the TTL estimates provided by the cache consistency algorithm can help the cache replacement algorithm to select eviction victims so the performance is maximized. For example, if a cache contains two documents of approximately the same size which are loaded from the same server and referenced by clients with the same rate, then the cache replacement algorithm should select for eviction the more frequently updated document (i.e. the one with a smaller TTL) because more references can be satisfied directly from the cache without validation and thereby providing a better response time to clients.

We describe a new unified cache maintenance algorithm, LNC-R-W3-U, which integrates cache replacement and consistency procedures. The LNC-R-W3-U algorithm is an extension of the LNC-R-W3 cache replacement algorithm introduced in [17] and maximizes a performance metric called *delay-savings-ratio*. Like its predecessor, LNC-R-W3-U takes into account document size and network delays in order to make cache replacement decisions. In addition, the LNC-R-W3-U replacement procedure considers also validation rate of each document. Our algorithm estimates time-to-live intervals for cached documents using a sample of K most recent Last-Modified timestamps. It has been shown that more reliable estimates of reference rate to documents improve cache performance in presence of transient data access [16–18].

Finally, using trace-based experiments, we demonstrate that LNC-R-W3-U achieves comparable (and often superior) performance to most of the published cache replacement algorithms and at the same time significantly reduces the staleness of cached documents.

2 Design

2.1 LNC-R-W3 Algorithm

The LNC-R-W3(Least Normalized Cost Replacement-WWW) cache algorithm was designed as a cache replacement algorithm which selects victims for replacement using not only the reference rate to the document (as exemplified by LRU), but also the document size and the network delay resulting from downloading the document from the server [17]. LNC-R-W3 also exploits a frequently observed fact [10, 17] that Web clients exhibit strong preference for accessing small documents.

LNC-R-W3 aims at maximizing the fraction of communication and server delays which is saved by satisfying the references from cache instead of a remote server. The corresponding performance metric is called *delay-savings-ratio* and defined as

$$DSR = \frac{\sum_i d_i \cdot h_i}{\sum_i d_i \cdot r_i} \tag{1}$$

where d_i is the average delay to fetch document D_i to cache, r_i is the total number of references to D_i and h_i is the number of references to D_i which were satisfied from the cache. All sums are defined over all referenced documents.

Once the available cache space is exhausted, the LNC-R-W3 algorithm selects for eviction the documents with the least value of *profit* defined as

$$\mathrm{profit}(D_i) = \frac{\lambda_i \cdot d_i}{s_i} \tag{2}$$

where λ_i is the estimated rate of reference to document D_i, d_i is the average delay to fetch document D_i to cache and s_i is the size of document D_i.

Both estimated reference rate and average delay are smoothed by averaging the last K reference times to document D_i or delays to fetch document D_i. Smoothing of the reference rate helps to prevent flooding the cache with useless documents in presence of workload with transient phases. The motivation for reference rate smoothing is drawn from observing inadequacy of LRU performance in database buffer managers [16]. Similarly, smoothing of the delay to fetch a document helps to counteract the variance of network delays and server latency. Both averages are computed using a sliding window of last K samples. The average delay d_i is directly computed as an average of the sample of K delays. The estimated reference rate λ_i is defined as

$$\lambda_i = \frac{K}{(t - t_K) \cdot s_i^b} \tag{3}$$

where t is the current time, t_K is the time of the K-th most recent refence (i.e. the oldest value in the sliding window) and b is a constant.

The first factor in (3) simply calculates the average reference rate using the sample of K reference times. Unlike other statistical methods for signal smoothing such as moving average, the above method enables aging of reference rate of non-accessed documents by incorporating the current time t into (3). The second factor weights the computed average by a hyperbolic function of size of the document. It has been observed that there is a strong relationship between the document size and its reference rate which closely follows the Zipfian Law [10, 17]. Thus knowing size of a document also provides information about its future reference rate. The constant b is the skew factor of the dependency. In [17] we determined the value of b as 1.30 based on statistical analysis of our traces.

Whenever fewer than K reference times are available for a document D_i, the estimated reference rate λ_i is determined using the maximal number of available samples. However, such an estimate is statistically less reliable and thus the documents having fewer reference samples are more likely to be selected for replacement by LNC-R-W3. To prevent starvation of newly referenced documents, LNC-R-W3 keeps the sliding windows with the collected samples even after the corresponding documents get evicted from the cache. The mechanisms for garbage collection of the sliding windows are described in [17]. In [17] we experimentally determined the optimal setting of K to be between 2 and 3. Smaller values lead to poor cache performance due to transient trends in the workload and larger values result in excessive overhead for keeping the sliding windows.

2.2 LNC-R-W3-U Algorithm

Similarly to other published consistency algorithms, the LNC-R-W3-U(LNC-R-W3-Unified) cache consistency algorithm guarantees weak consistency by assigning TTL interval to each cached document and performing validation check before returning to client any document cached longer than TTL units. The consistency algorithm must balance performance and consistency. The best performance is achieved when the validation rate approaches zero, i.e. a document found in the cache can be always returned to a client without any validation. However, the returned documents can be arbitrarily stale. On the other hand, the best consistency is achieved when the validation rate is infinite, i.e. a validation must be made before satisfying any request from the cache. The resulting performance is poor because clients must always wait for a round-trip message to the server.

The LNC-R-W3 cache replacement algorithm would benefit from knowing which documents are frequently validated and avoid caching them. Consequently, more cache space is available for caching of less frequently validated documents which in turn leads to a better performance because more references can be satisfied from the cache without validation. At the same time, the cache consistency algorithm would benefit from using the extensive bookkeeping provided by the LNC-R-W3 cache replacement algorithm. More accurate estimates of documents' TTL intervals lead to a better consistency and possibly reduced number of validations.

Similarly to LNC-R-W3, our new algorithm aims at maximizing delay-savings-ratio (DSR). However, we explicitly include the costs of cache consistency maintenance in the new definition of DSR as follows :

$$DSR = \frac{\sum_i d_i \cdot h_i - c_i \cdot u_i}{\sum_i d_i \cdot r_i} \tag{4}$$

where d_i is the average delay to fetch document D_i to cache, r_i is the total number of references to D_i, h_i is the number of references to D_i which were satisfied from the cache, c_i is the delay to perform validation check on document D_i and u_i is the number of validation checks made for document D_i. All sums are defined over all referenced documents. The cache replacement algorithm has no control over parameter u_i which is determined by the cache consistency algorithm. However, the cache replacement algorithm may choose to evict document D_i from cache and thereby eliminate the consistency costs entirely.

In order to maximize the delay-savings-ratio from (4) the LNC-R-W3-U cache replacement algorithm uses a modified version of profit to select victims for eviction:

$$\text{profit}(D_i) = \frac{\lambda_i \cdot d_i - \mu_i \cdot c_i}{s_i} \tag{5}$$

where λ_i is the estimated reference rate to document D_i, d_i is the average delay to fetch document D_i, μ_i is the average validation rate for document D_i, c_i is the average delay to perform a validation check for document D_i and s_i is the size of document D_i. Profit of document D_i gives the expected delay savings from caching single byte of the document.

The document statistics λ_i, d_i and s_i are maintained in exactly the same manner as in LNC-R-W3 described in the previous section. The average delay to perform a consistency check c_i is obtained by averaging the last K delays to get a response for conditional GET for document D_i. In absence of the Expires timestamp in document D_i, the average validation rate μ_i is calculated from a sliding window of last K distinct Last-Modified timestamps as

$$\mu_i = \frac{K}{t_r - t_{u_k}} \tag{6}$$

where t_r is the time when a new version of document D_i was received by the caching proxy and t_{u_k} is the Kth most recent distinct Last-Modified timestamp of document D_i (i.e. the oldest available distinct Last-Modified). We assume that the update rates of documents are stable. Therefore, it should suffice to validate each document with the same rate as it was updated in the past.

If, on the other hand, the Expires timestamp is available, the validation rate is calculated in a similar manner, but using the Expires timestamps instead of Last-Modified timestamps whenever possible. The most recent Expires timestamp substitutes t_r in (6). We assume that servers know when their documents will be updated if they decide to provide Expires timestamps to their clients. Consequently, LNC-R-W3-U uses the server provided information to determine validation rate, rather than trying to estimate it from the past modification timestamps.

The LNC-R-W3-U consistency algorithm sets TTL for a newly received document D_i as either

$$TTL_i = \frac{1}{\mu_i} \qquad (7)$$

if the Expires timestamp is not available or

$$TTL_i = Expires - t_r \qquad (8)$$

otherwise.

Whenever document D_i has been cached longer than TTL_i units, the consistency algorithm validates document D_i by sending a conditional GET to the server. Whenever a new version of document D_i is received (which may be a new, previously uncached document or a new version of a validated cached document), LNC-R-W3-U updates the sliding windows with the last K distinct Last-Modified timestamps and the last K validation delays and recalculates c_i and μ_i. The pseudo-code of LNC-R-W3-U is shown in Fig. 1.

In [18] we show that it is NP-complete problem to find the optimal subset of documents for caching so that the delay-savings ratio from (1) is maximized. We also show in [18] that LNC-R-W3 can approximate the optimal algorithm in a constrained model when cache fragmentation is negligible, the reference rates to all documents are a priori known, fixed and statistically independent and K approaches infinity. The delay savings ratio from (4) subsumes the definition in (1) as a special case where all $c_i \cdot u_i$ are equal to 0. Therfore, optimal cache replacement algorithm maximizing the delay savings ratio from (4) is NP-complete. Finally, it can be shown that given a fixed cache consistency algorithm which determines validation rate μ_i and c_i for every document, the LNC-R-W3-U cache replacement algorithm approximates the optimal algorithm in the same constrained model. Since the proof is almost identical to that in [18], we omit it here.

3 LNC-R-W3-U Implementation

The LNC-R-W3-U algorithm is implemented as a set of C library functions which may replace the cache replacement and consistency checking components of any Web proxy servers such as Netscape [15], CERN [7], and Apache [1]. We are currently integrating the LNC-R-W3-U library with the Apache code. The LNC-R-W3-U algorithm needs to keep with every document four sliding windows: one with the last K reference times, one with the last K distinct Last-Modified times, one with the last K delays to fetch a document and one with the last K delays to perform a validation check for the document. Storage of timestamps with a second precision requires 4 bytes in most UNIX implementations. Consequently, the bookkeeping overhead for a single document is $16 \cdot K$ bytes. For the optimal value of K determined in [17], $K = 3$, the resulting overhead is in 48 bytes per document.

Although 48 bytes overhead is relatively small compared to the average document size of 2.6 KB found in our trace and identical to the average URL string

D_i : a document requested from the client
t : time when D_i is requested
avail : available free space in cache

case
  D_i **in cache:**   // **cache consistency check**
    t_r : time when a new version of D_i was cached
    TTL_i : time-to-live of D_i
    if ($TTL_i < t - t_r$) {   // TTL_I expires
        HTTP Conditional GET(D_i) request to the server
        update c_i : average delay to perform Conditional GET(D_i)
        update μ_i : average validation rate of D_i
        update λ_i : estimated reference rate of D_i
    }
    else {   // TTL_I not expires
        update λ_i
    }

  D_i **not in cache:**   // **cache replacement**
    HTTP GET(D_i) request to the server
    s_i : size of D_i, d_i : average delay to fetch D_i to cache
    μ_i : average validation rate of D_i

    if (D_i has Expire timestamp)
        TTL_i = Expires - t_r
    else
        $TTL_i = \frac{1}{\mu_i}$

    if ($avail \geq s_i$) {   // enough space
        cache D_i and update λ_i
    }
    else {   // replacement required
      for $j = 1$ to K
        D_j = list of documents with exactly j reference samples in
           increasing profit (defined in (5)) order
      D = list of documents arranged in order $D_1 < D_2 < \ldots < D_k$
      C = minimal prefix of D such that $\sum_n s_n \geq s_i, 1 \leq n \leq k$
      evict C out of cache and cache D_i and update λ_i
    }

Fig. 1. Pseudo-code of LNC-R-W3-U algorithm

size which must also be cached with every document, we apply standard compression techniques to the sliding window representation in order to reduce the overhead by almost factor of 4. Since most documents do not require more then 256 seconds to fetch or validate, we use only a single byte store the fetch and validate delays. The reference time and validation time sliding windows must keep the full timestamp in order to be able to take a difference with an absolute time in (3) and (6). However, it is possible to keep the full timestamp only for the oldest sample in each window and encode the remaining $K - 1$ samples as differences with the respect to the oldest timestamp. Therefore, we reduce the sliding window overhead down to $2 \cdot (4 + (K - 1)) + 2 \cdot K = 4 \cdot K + 6$. For $K = 3$ we reduce the overhead to 18 bytes per document. URL strings cached with every document may also be compressed to save the space while preserving the mapping to the original string by e.g. the hashing technique used in [1].

Finally, both estimated reference rate λ_i defined in (3) and average validation rate μ_i defined in (6) depend on the value of current time. For performance efficiency, the values of λ_i and μ_i are updated only upon access to document D_i or at fixed time intervals in absence of any accesses to document D_i for a long period of time. Additional implementation enhancements can be found in [18].

4 Experimental Evaluation

4.1 Experimental Setup

Trace Characteristics We evaluated the performance of LNC-R-W3-U algorithm using Web client trace collected at Northwestern University. The trace represents a seven day snapshot (November 97) of requests generated by clients on approximately 60 PC's in a public lab at Northwestern University. The trace contains about 15K requests for the total size of 18 MB of data. Browser cache hits and non-cacheable requests (e.g. URL's containing "bin" or "cgi-bin") were filtered out from the trace. Requests of all browsers were re-directed to a proxy where for each referenced URL, we recorded the time when the request for document D_i arrives at the proxy, the time when D_i is actually received, the time when proxy issued conditional GET for D_i, the time when response for the conditional GET was received, the size of D_i, the value of Expires timestamp of D_i (if available) and the value of Last-Modified timestamp of D_i.

We found that approximately 89% of documents in the trace contained Last-Modified timestamp, approximately 7% of documents contained Expires timestamp and 90% of documents contained either Last-Modified or Expires timestamp.

We regard a document as updated if its Last-Modified timestamp changed at least once within the 7 day period studied in our trace. If a document was updated within the 7 day period, but was not subsequently referenced, we have no means of ascertaining that the update occurred and thus such updates are not captured in our trace. We found that approximately 6% of all documents were updated and less than 2% out of these changed every day. (Fig. 2).

documents with Last-Modified	89%
documents with Expires	7%
documents with Last-Modified or Expires	90%
updated documents	6%

Fig. 2. Update Trace Characteristics

Our results confirm the generally held belief that WWW is read-mostly environment and they are in accord with the analysis of server-based traces reporting daily update rates in the range 0.5% - 2% [4, 12]. It is possible that a larger fraction of documents is updated if one considers also dynamic CGI documents. However, since dynamic documents are not cacheable, such updates are irrelevant for the results presented here.

Performance Metrics and Yardsticks The *delay saving ratio* (DSR) defined in (4), Section 2 is the primary performance metric in our study. We also consider *hit ratio* as a secondary performance metric. The primary consistency metric is *staleness ratio* (SR) defined as a fraction of cache hits which return stale documents. We say that a document returned by the cache to client is stale if the trace record corresponding to the request has a later Last-Modified timestamp than the time when the document was brought to the cache.

The main objective of our experimental work is to answer two questions: What is the performance degradation due to consistency enforcement? and By how much does consistency enforcement reduce staleness of documents returned to clients? Therefore, we compare performance of LNC-R-W3-U against our previously published cache replacement algorithm LNC-R-W3 which does not enforce consistency (i.e. TTL is set to infinity) and a modified LRU using a simple cache consistency check. The modified LRU, which we call LRU-CC (Consistency Check), employs a consistency algorithm which sets TTL to (t_r - Last-Modified time) if the Expires timestamp is not available or (Expires - t_r) otherwise. LRU-CC corresponds to a typical caching proxy implementation [9, 15]. The performance of LNC-R-W3 was shown to be superior to other cache replacement algorithms in [17], we therefore do not repeat those experiments here. We found that the optimal setting of parameter K is between 2 and 3 and the optimal setting of parameter b is close to 1.3. We therefore set $K=2$ and $b=1.3$ in all experiments reported here.

4.2 Experimental Results

We found that although our new integrated algorithm LNC-R-W3-U incurs extra overhead for consistency maintenance, its performance is very close to that of LNC-R-W3 which does not make any effort to maintain consistency and superior to that of LRU-CC.

On average, the delay savings ratio of LNC-R-W3-U is only 1.0% below the DSR of LNC-R-W3. In the worst case, the DSR of LNC-R-W3-U is 2.5% below the DSR of LNC-R-W3 when the cache size is 10% of the total size of all documents. We found that LNC-R-W3-U consistently outperformed LRU-CC on all cache sizes. On average, LNC-R-W3-U provided 38.3% DSR improvement over LRU-CC. The improvement is maximal for the smallest cache size, when LNC-R-W3-U improves LRU-CC by 67.8%. The delay savings ratio comparison can be found in Fig. 3.

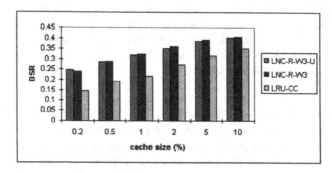

Fig. 3. Delay Saving Ratio

The performance comparison using our secondary metric, hit ratio, exhibits similar trends. On average, LNC-R-W3-U provided 43.4% improvement over LRU-CC and the maximal improvement reached 51.3%. The hit ratio of LNC-R-W3-U provides even closer to the hit ratio of LNC-R-W3; on average 0.4% and no more than 0.6% below the hit ratio of LNC-R-W3. The hit ratio comparison can be found in Fig. 4.

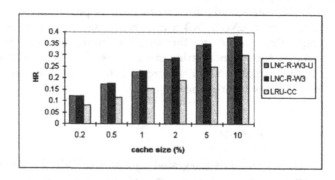

Fig. 4. Hit Ratio

Although LNC-R-W3-U provides performance close to LNC-R-W3 and better than that of LRU-CC, it significantly improves the consistency level of documents returned to clients. On the average, LNC-R-W3-U achieves a staleness ratio which is by factor of 3.2 better than the SR of LNC-R-W3, in the worst case it improves SR of LNC-R-W3 by factor of 1.9 when cache size is 0.5% of the total size of all documents. LNC-R-W3-U also improves the SR of LRU-CC by 10.2% in the worst case when cache size is 0.5%, and 47.8% on average. The staleness ratio comparison of all three algorithms can be found in Fig. 5.

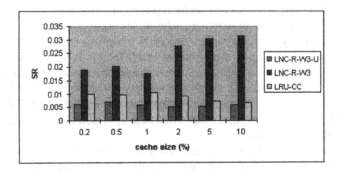

Fig. 5. Staleness Ratio

5 Related Work

Cache replacement algorithms have been extensively studied in the context of operating systems, databases [16, 19, 18] and also Web caching proxies [2, 3, 5, 8, 17, 20, 13]. The LNC-R-W3-U cache replacement algorithm is a direct extension of our previously published cache replacement algorithm LNC-R-W3 [17]. Both LNC-R-W3 and LNC-R-W3-U cache replacement algorithm distinguish themselves by their ability to consider also document size and network delays in cache replacement decisions. Furthermore, the LNC-R-W3-U cache replacement algorithm also considers validation rate of each document. Analytical motivation and mathematical proof behind our algorithms are shown in [18].

Cache consistency algorithms have been extensively studied in the context of distributed file systems and client/server database systems. Most of the algorithms guarantee strong consistency and require servers to maintain state about the data cached by clients. "Polling-every-time" approach [14] is another example of a strong consistency method. The Alex FTP cache is an exception in that it provides only weak consistency to the clients [6]. Its validation mechanism serves as a basis for most weak consistency algorithm used by many caching proxies [9, 15, 11, 12, 14] and also the LNC-R-W3-U cache consistency algorithm. The LNC-R-W3-U cache consistency algorithm estimates time-to-live intervals for cache documents using not only the most recent Last-Modified timestamp, but a sample of K most recent Last-Modified timestamps. It has been shown that more reliable estimates of reference rate to documents improve cache performance in presence of transient data access [16–18].

Finally, our analysis of update rates in Web client-based traces is consistent with the server-based results reported in [4, 12].

6 Conclusion

We present a design of an unified cache replacement and consistency algorithm LNC-R-W3-U. Unlike other existing cache replacement algorithm, the LNC-R-W3-U cache replacement algorithm explicitly considers the update rates estimated by cache consistency algorithm in order to select replacement victims. The LNC-R-W3-U cache consistency algorithm provides more reliable estimates of document's update rate using a sliding window of last K Last-Modified timestamps. We also show that similarly to our previously published LNC-R-W3, the LNC-R-W3-U cache replacement algorithm also approximates the optimal algorithm in a constrained model.

Using experiments based on client-level trace we show that although the LNC-R-W3-U cache replacement algorithm also considers update rate, its performance is comparable to the performance of LNC-R-W3 cache replacement algorithm and better than the performance of LRU cache replacement algorithm. At the same time, the LNC-R-W3-U cache replacement algorithm significantly reduces the number of stale documents returned to the clients.

We plan to conduct additional experiments to study the relationship between the staleness ratio and the update ratio, by using traces from different proxy servers. We also plan to finish integration of the LNC-R-W3-U library with the Apache proxy server code and make it publicly available.

References

1. The Apache Group, Apache HTTP Server, http://www.apache.org, 1998.
2. M. Abrams, C. Standridge, G. Abdulla, S. Williams, E. Fox, "Caching proxies: Limitations and potentials", *Proc. 4th WWW Conference*, 1995.
3. C. Aggrawal and P. Yu, "On Disk Caching of Web objects in Proxy Servers", *Proc. 6th International Conference on Information and Knowledge Management*, 1997.
4. A. Bestavros, "Speculative Data Dissemination and Service", *Proc. International Conference on Data Engineering*, 1996.
5. J. Bolot and P. Hoschka "Performance Engineering of the World Wide Web: Application to Dimensioning and Cache Design", *Proc. 5th Int. WWW Conference*.
6. V. Cate, "Alex- a global file system", *Proc. 1992 USENIX File System Workshop*, 1992.
7. World Wide Web Consortium(W3C), CERN HTTPD Server, http://www.w3.org/Daemon, 1995.
8. A. Chankhunthod, P. Danzig, C. Neerdaels, M. Schwartz, K. Worrell, "A hierarchical Internet object cache", *Proc. USENIX 1996 Annual Technical Conference*, http://excalibur.usc.edu/cache-html/cache.html.

9. A. Cormack, "Web Caching", http://www.nisc.ac.uk/education/-jisc/acn/caching.html, 1996.

10. C. Cunha, A. Bestavros, M. Crovella, "Characteristics of WWW Client-based Traces", *Technical Report TR-95-010*, Boston University, 1995.

11. A. Dingle and T. Partl, "Web Cache Coherence", *Proc. 5th WWW Conference*, 1996.

12. J. Gwertzman and M. Seltzer, "World-Wide Cache Consistency", *Proc. USENIX 1996 Annual Technical Conference*, 1996.

13. D. Karger, E. Lehman, T. Leighton, M. Levine, D. Lewin, R. Panigrahy, "Consistent hashing and random trees: Distributed caching protocols for relieving hot spots on the World Wide Web", *Proc. 29th ACM Sym. on Theory of Computing*, 1997.

14. C. Liu and P. Cao, "Maintaining Strong Cache Consistency in the World-Wide Web", *Proc. 17th International Conference on Distributed Computing Systems*, 1997.

15. Netscape, Netscape Proxy Server, http://www.netscape.com/, 1997.

16. E. O'Neil, P. O'Neil, G. Weikum, "The LRU-K page replacement algorithm for database disk buffering", *Proc. ACM SIGMOD International Conference on Management of Data*, 1993.

17. P. Scheuermann, J. Shim, R. Vingralek, "A Case for Delay-Conscious Caching of Web Documents", *Proc. 6th WWW Conference*, 1997.

18. P. Scheuermann, J. Shim, R. Vingralek, "WATCHMAN: A Data Warehouse Intelligent Cache Manager", *Proc. 22nd International Conference on Very Large Data Bases*, 1996.

19. D. Sleator and R. Tarjan, "Amortized Efficiency of List Update and Paging Rules", *Communication of ACM*, Vol.28, No.2, 1985.

20. R. Wooster and M. Abrams, "Proxy Caching That Estimates Page Load Delays", *Proc. 6th WWW Conference*, 1997.

Transactional Services for the Internet

David Billard

Computer Science Department, University of Geneva
David.Billard@cui.unige.ch,
WWW home page: http://cuiwww.unige.ch/~billard/index.html

Abstract. This paper investigates a new paradigm in transactional services, specially tailored for Internet purposes. This new paradigm considers transactions (called I-Transactions) as user's atomic actions spanned upon multiple databases present in the Internet. Whereas classical transactions are designed to cope with multiple users accessing a particular DBMS, or a federation of well-known DBMS, inversely, I-Transactions are related to a single user, *i.e.* they are not bounded to a particular DBMS, or a federation of DBMS. Therefore, I-Transactions are self-managed since they cannot be ruled by a common global transaction manager. They provide an atomic action upon a set of DBMS that possibly do not know each other (they are determined when a transaction is initiated) and which may not be simultaneously accessed again by another I-Transaction. They are tailored to be used in the Internet environment, which now does not support many kind of transactional facility, and are designed to be easily integrated in existing Internet applications. This paper proposes a description of the I-Transactions and the constraints related to their utilization, in particular from the security point of view. It also outlines the major differences among I-Transactions and the CORBA Transaction Service, TIP or the X/OPEN DTP. This paper considers two architectures for supporting I-Transactions: direct interactions among the participants or brokered interactions with the introduction of transaction brokers (agencies).

1   Introduction

The Internet is a network of networks created by scientists for scientists, but whose success recently exceeded the frontiers of academic, evolving from a university-oriented network to a business-oriented communication tool. Recent reports [14, 7, 25, 17] on the future of the Internet stress that the next evolution step will be the communication among business entities, communication including ordering and billing of services and products.

The Internet has not been designed for such utilization, and it lacks much features, ranging from security protections to accounting of its own resources. Nevertheless, and in spite of many insufficiencies, business develops itself in the Internet, resting on the World Wide Web architecture. One can now buy a novel through a virtual library or book a trip to a virtual travel agency with his Web browser. New services even allow Web users to create online their own electronic shopping center, e.g. Yaho!Store (http://store.yahoo.com/ad.html).

But this hatching of online services, and thus the emerging of thousands of databases, draw themselves new problems, not immediately perceivable. One of these problems is related to transactional services. Users have now the choice of multiple services, but have no possibility to include a combination of several services into one atomic action. One of the reasons for this impossibility is that all these services, *before* being asked to collaborate, do not know each other and thus cannot provide transaction facilities at a global level. As long as the users were individuals, the need of atomic and fault-resistant actions was not tremendous, but users are now companies which want reliable services over the Internet. One of the most demanding area for this kind of services is known as "The Virtual Enterprise".

This paper intends to present an efficient solution to this problem through the definition of I-Transactions (I stands for Internet), able to provide atomic and fault resistant services to users, even if this service is spanned over multiple and run-time determined sites.

For a better understanding of the I-Transactions utility, we propose the – very basic – example of Mister Badluck:

Example 1. Mr. BadLuck breaks his car engine: the components A and B of the engine block are wrecked. Two solutions are planed: 1) changing A (100$) and B (150$) or 2) changing the entire block (500$). Mr. Badluck chooses the first solution and finds in the Internet two web sites, S1 and S2, proposing respectively A and B. With the current Internet tools, M. Badluck buys A and B, S2 confirms the purchase but S1 cannot deliver A. Therefore, the only remaining solution for M. Badluck is to change the whole engine block (500$). Unfortunately, he also has to pay 150$ for the component B (useless) he has already purchased.

In order to avoid this problem, the obvious solution is to incorporate the purchases of A and B into a single transaction [2] of the form:

```
BeginOfTransaction (BOT)
Buy A on site S1
Buy B on site S2
Commit
EndOfTransaction (EOT)
```

But this transaction must meet several criterias in order to enforce the atomicity of the action and to cope with the Internet's pitfalls:

1. this transaction must be ACID, *i.e.* the properties of Atomicity, Consistency, Isolation and Durability must be enforced;
2. a participant of the transaction cannot deny its commitment (or its non-commitment);
3. a participant must really be who he claims to be;
4. the privacy of the transaction's actions must be ensured, since confidential informations are transmitted (credit card numbers, nature of the objects bought by the consumer, etc.);

5. this transaction is distributed and its commitment depends on an atomic commitment protocol;

6. the transactions must be self-managed, since there cannot exist a global transaction manager.

This paper aims at defining a model of I-Transaction that copes with the above criterias. In addition, the respective domain of competence between the I-Transaction and the local transaction managers are debated.

This paper is organized as follows. After the description (section 2) of some related works, we define (section 3) our model of transaction which we believe is suited for Internet use. The mandatory functions of a protocol and several cases of failure are studied in section 4. Furthermore, an architecture incorporating brokers (agencies), and destinated to overcome some basic problems, is presented in section 5. In the same section, we discuss some examples of applications taking advantage of I-Transactions, the Multipurpose Internet Shopping Basket (MIShoBa), and the reservation of global Top Level Domain Names in the Internet. Section 6 concludes this work and discusses some implementation aspects.

2 Related Works

2.1 Transaction Internet Protocol

To our knowledge, few research work has been done to put transactional services on the Web. The most important contribution is certainly the Transaction Internet Protocol (TIP) [15, 16], that consists essentially in a two-phase commit protocol for applications over the Internet. However, TIP requires that all the servers know each other, more in an optical of collaborative work than transaction processing, and finally the user has little latitude in choosing the servers and interacting with them.

Our view of an I-Transaction differs in many ways. The transaction managers of the sites involved in a single I-Transaction will never communicate with each other and the atomic commitment protocol is designed to ensure only the correctness of the user's actions. The correctness of the database state is left to the local transaction manager working with the DBMS. These choices are not ideological: they are guided by security, performance and scaleability considerations (see 3.2). However, TIP is a base upon which a protocol for I-Transactions can be built, for peer to peer communications.

2.2 Object Transaction Service - CORBA

The Common Object Request Broker Architecture (CORBA) [18, 19] defines the Object Transaction Service (OTS) [20], a component of the Object Management Architecture of the Object Management Group (OMG). The core of CORBA is the Object Request Broker (ORB) whose specification describes the object-oriented communication infrastructure for distributed applications.

In CORBA, everything is object, and every transaction manager that wants to cooperate with a CORBA-based transaction manager must comply with CORBA object-based interfaces and must rely on an ORB. We believed that in our view of I-Transaction, which is user-centered, there is no need of such a heavy structure to implement a transaction service over the Internet. The interoperability among transactions must be reduced to its simplest nature, otherwise the effort of compliance is too important with regards to the sought goal.

Furthermore, CORBA is not yet ready to interoperate at transaction level with other systems, even if in the latest revision of CORBA [19], the chapter 9 "Interoperability Overview" defines many interoperability protocols and in particular the Internet inter-ORB protocol (IIOP), a specialization of the General inter-ORB protocol (GIOP) tailored for TCP/IP connections. But if the interoperability at the ORB level is well defined, transaction interoperability is not mentioned. It therefore leads to problems for transaction interoperation, even if they form a single OTS domain over multiple ORB domains, e.g. a transaction identifier cannot be guaranteed to be unique [13].

Furthermore, OTS is running on top of one (or multiple) ORB, and this requirement is handicapping for legacy applications that must undertake an important effort to comply with.

2.3 Distributed Transaction Processing

The Distributed Transaction Processing (DTP) [27] is the X/OPEN standard for the distribution of transactions over several nodes. Transaction Managers can interoperate through the OSI Transaction Processing (OSI TP) that implements the transaction protocol of the OSI stack and the communication is realized thanks to Transaction Remote Procedure Call (TxRPC) [28]. Non-DCE applications must therefore be able to communicate through OSI TP and accept TxRPCs. Since the RPC paradigm is considered non-flexible when it is used in the Internet, the DTP approach seems not appropriated. In addition, even if DCE transactions are designed to interoperate easily (which is not the case with CORBA), their interoperation with other systems is conditioned to strong compliance, handicapping legacy applications.

2.4 Millicent

Millicent [11] is a protocol for electronic commerce over the internet, designed to support purchases costing less than a cent. Although the purpose of Millicent is not to provide a transactional service, its *structure*, based on brokers and scrip, implements a basic transaction consisting of a one-to-one purchase with fault tolerance. In Millicent, *brokers* are responsible for the management and *scrip* is the instance of digital cash a user actually buy to a broker. The structure (figure 1) is four-part: a customer (1) buys scrip to a broker (2) (say 10$ of digital money) and uses this scrip to purchase at a vendor (3) who asks the broker to turn the gathered scrips into real money. The fourth part is the Internet, linking the three other actors.

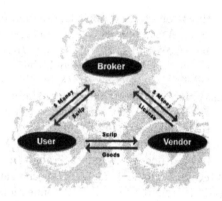

Fig. 1. Millicent's architecture.

Our advanced architecture for the transactions relies basically on the same components (see 5), eventhough the model can be used without brokers (or agencies as we call them). Therefore, an implementation of our model may be realized on top of such an architecture, which becomes common in electronic commerce applications.

2.5 Others

The NetBill system [23] outlined the importance of ACID properties for money- and goods-transfer, but these two kinds of atomicity are only studied between one customer and one vendor, with a bank acting as a caution. In [22], additional properties gathered under the acronym EDSIC (Economy, Divisibility, Scaleability, Interoperability and Conservation) are described, but they concern uniquely the electronic commerce and cannot be translated to other domains, exception made of Scaleability and Interoperability which are inherent properties of well designed distributed systems. [22] also investigates many other electronic commerce protocols (CAFE, CyberCash, DigiCash, NetBill,...) and compares each other thanks to the ACID and EDSIC properties. [6] is an in-depth evaluation of DigiCash and NetBill by confronting their respect of ACID properties.

The research done on federated databases [12] is not relevant in the context of the Internet because it supposes that all the databases are known and each transaction manager knows each other DBMS. This assumption cannot hold in the Internet that counts thousands of databases, and where the user chooses at run-time the databases he wants to access.

Other contributions focus on Web servers acting as Graphical User Interfaces to databases and from which transactions can be triggered (front-end servers).

2.6 Summary of Related Works

– Only [15] with the TIP seems to have perceived the importance of the nature of the Internet in a distributed transaction processing, but this work is only a first step that did not received all the attention it deserves. Furthermore, the security aspects that were ignored in the first versions are still treated only at communication level.

- Millicent [11] depicts the importance of a broker (agency) in the Internet environment. This intermediate structure is necessary for preserving the scaleability and security of the model.
- The transaction features present in NetBill [23] are important but limited to one-to-one exchanges.
- CORBA OTS [18, 20, 19] and X/OPEN DTP [27, 28] implement distributed transactions that are well suited for homogeneous networks, but which require heavy interfaces to interoperate. Nevertheless, the security aspects are well studied in both cases, eventhough they are still concentrated on the communication level (encryption / authentication).
- Federated databases are of little help since they assume that the databases are known to each other.

From the above statements, it is clear that I-Transactions must implement a very light interoperable protocol with the simplest mandatory functions; and considering the nature of the Internet, I-Transaction must implement security requirements.

3 I-Transaction Model

3.1 Definition

An I-Transaction (IT) is an atomic and fault-tolerant collection of orders destined to several heterogeneous and *a priori* not known databases, situated in the Internet and possibly accessed through a Web interface.

3.2 Properties

Standard ACID properties are not sufficient for IT running in the Internet, which is a very particular environment, far away from the closed and secured system for which ACID properties are stronger enough. Obviously, the Internet has become the nightmare of security managers, and without dedicated tools can be subject to attacks, either passive or active. [24] describes the following security threats (figure 2) for generic applications.

Interception means that an unauthorized user has access to a message contents; interruption is an attack on the availability of the system, modification is an attack on the message contents and fabrication is an attack on the authenticity of a message. Turned into our framework, these threats become.

- Interception of a message: a IT cannot help a message from being intercepted, but it must take precautions in order to prevent the message contents from being disclosed to an unauthorized party. Therefore IT must use, at least, an encryption service and provide the property of confidentiality.

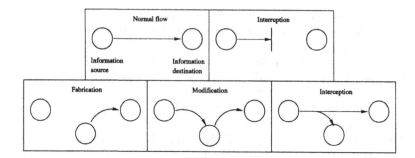

Fig. 2. Security threats.

- Interruption of the service: it means the brutal stop of a server activity, IT consider this interruption as a site failure and must be able to recover. Thereafter, it is related to the atomicity property.
- Modification and fabrication of a message: IT must use authentication algorithms to precisely identify the participants, in order to be sure that everybody is really who he claims to be. In addition, if a message is sent from A to B, neither A nor B should deny having received or sent the message, therefore a non-repudiation scheme must be enforced.

Considering the Internet as a valuable framework of execution, transactional services must be designed with basic security in mind, which cannot be treated with less than two properties: Privacy (Confidentiality) and Loyalty (Authentication and Non-repudiation). Therefore, IT are PLACID.

Privacy. This property is also known as Confidentiality. A IT may transmit confidential information that must not be disclosed to others (e.g. credit card number). The enforcement of this property leads to establish secure connections among the participants. Classic solutions use symmetric encryption with public and private keys. Practically speaking, implementation of secure dialogues can be handle by the Secure Socket Layer (SSL [9]) running on top of TCP/IP or by the Transport Layer Security (TLS [8]) Protocol.

In addition, this property has an impact on the Atomic Commitment Protocol (see below the properties of Atomicity and Durability) that must be implemented. This protocol is built to achieve an atomicity of outcome (abort or commit) when several sites are engaged. When the protocol has to face failures, the recovery procedure initiates a Termination phase, comming in several flavours, one of them being the "Cooperative Termination Protocol". In this cooperative protocol, the recovering site sends to all the participants of a transaction a "What is the outcome?" message. This protocol presumes that each site knows the identity of all the other sites. This *knowledge of the other sites* involved in a transaction cannot be granted without leaving a security breach. Therefore, the implementation of an ACP must be realized carefully, and without using the knowledge of the other sites participating to the transaction.

Loyalty. As sometimes in commercial exchanges, contests and disputes may appear among participants. In the presence of such litigations, IT must help by keeping a log of the messages exchanged. To be valid, these messages must be encrypted, authenticated and non-repudiable. Encryption prevents the message to be faked, authentication guarantees that the participants are really who they claim to be and non-repudiation prevents either sender or receiver from denying a transmitted message.

In addition, and similarly to Privacy, Loyalty has an impact on the ACP and the recovery procedures. If a user is bounded to two servers for its IT so authentication schemes have been set up between the user and each server individually, but not between the two servers. Therefore, in case of a server failure, the recovery procedure cannot ask the other server what is the outcome of the transaction because it cannot be sure to talk with the right server (no authentication protocol being established). This point advocates for a modification of standard ACP. Furthermore, the logging of confidential information like keys or certificates is still an open issue.

Atomicity. Atomicity is the all-or-nothing property. It ensures that a transaction commits all its effects, or none at all, even in the presence of failures (fault tolerance). For classic transactions, atomicity is realized by commit, rollback and recovery procedures. The rollback is used when a transaction is aborted and its purpose is to suppress the transaction's effects. The recovery is intended, after a site failure, to erase the effects that all the uncommitted transactions should have left in the persistent database and to restore all the effects of committed transactions (see Durability).

As IT uses the local transaction managers, these latter have to handle rollback and recovery for their own DBMS. A IT is confronted with faults only when it is notified of the failure of one of its participant, and as a consequence, it has to notify in turn all the other participants which handle locally the rollback. Therefore, this recovery is a local affair.

Since a IT is spanned over several nodes, atomicity is realized by an Atomic Commitment Protocol (ACP). The most famous ACP are the two-phase and the three-phase commit protocol [2].

Consequently, atomicity for IT is achieved by the atomicity of the local transactions and the application of an ACP.

Consistency. Consistency is often referred to as a transaction designer problem. Consistency is provided by the simplicity of the transaction's actions, since IT can only execute authorized actions, already registered for local transactions.

Isolation. Isolation for classic transactions is guaranteed by the implementation of a concurrency control protocol (CCP). Although CCP are essential for a correct execution of classic transactions, it cannot be a solution for IT since there exists none global control. Therefore, isolation among IT is only achieved thanks to the local transaction managers (LTM). And since locking is provided at LTM level, the problem of deadlock remains (figure 3).

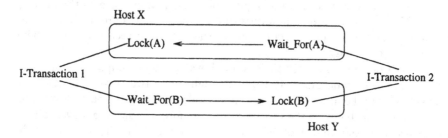

Fig. 3. Global deadlocks.

In the context of the Internet, considering the multitude of databases, we believe that few deadlocks will arise and that a basic time-out should be enough to ride this problem out. However, if the number of deadlocks among two hosts becomes important, other solutions (gathering of the two DBMS, setting of a global transaction manager, etc.) must be planned.

Durability. Durability means that, even in the presence of failures, committed effects cannot be dismissed. For classic transactional systems, durability is achieved by a recovery procedure, resting on a log, whose action is to restore committed effects lost in a site failure.

For IT, durability has another dimension that we can state as follows: even in the presence of a site failure, the user must know that his IT is committed and must have the ability to prove it, in case of dispute.

As a consequence, specific IT logs have to be kept at each participant. To comply with the Privacy and Loyalty requirements, these logs must store, one way or another, the encryption keys and the authentication certificates to be able to reconnect later, in a secure way. Furthermore, the log access must be secured to be append-only for the transaction manager and read / append for the recovery procedures [3]. In addition to the traditional recovery information, the log (or another structure) contains also security information that should be used by the recovery procedure to decypher the records.

4 Protocols

By essence, I-Transactions are distributed, since they are designed to access distant DBMS through the Internet. To comply with the atomicity property, the distribution leads necessarily to implement an atomic commitment protocol, respecting the Privacy and Loyalty properties.

The actions of a IT then fall into three categories:

1. orders destined to precommit, commit or abort distant transactions;
2. logging of the various records keeping track of the IT progress;
3. actions for recovering from failures.

In the following, the term user refers to the IT's owner and participant refers to a web site accessed. The first subsection describes a normal dialogue between a user and a participant whereas the second subsection precises how recovery procedure handles failures. The examples of dialogue given below have been designed with an electronic commerce application in mind.

4.1 Normal Dialogue

A normal dialogue is initiated when a user, browsing a web server, request an object through the classic web interface. If the participant (*i.e.* the web server) proposes IT services, he simply inserts the following tag inside the html page:

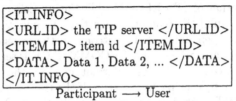

```
<IT_INFO>
<URL_ID> the TIP server </URL_ID>
<ITEM_ID> item id </ITEM_ID>
<DATA> Data 1, Data 2, ... </DATA>
</IT_INFO>
```
Participant ⟶ User

IT_INFO is the tag describing the contents of the IT. URL_ID is the URL to which further commands (commit, abort, etc.) have to be sent. This URL may refer to another port than the web server's one. ITEM_ID is the identifier of the item (a novel you want to buy), or action (an update of a database). DATA is all the other information the server provides to the client ("the expected delivery delay is 2 days", or "this item exists only in red", etc.). Other TAGs may be added, as the description of the commands to be send. At this point of time, nothing is reserved or even logged at the participant's site. The participant may even proposes the alternative of using IT or traditional forms.

When the user has collected as many objects from as many web servers he wants, he submits his transaction. A unique IT identifier is chosen at the user's site and a IT_PRECOMMIT message is sent to each participant. In order to respect the Privacy and Loyalty properties, a secure connection, encrypted, authenticated and non-repudiable, has to be first established.

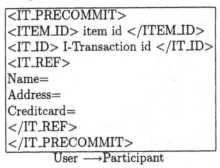

```
<IT_PRECOMMIT>
<ITEM_ID> item id </ITEM_ID>
<IT_ID> I-Transaction id </IT_ID>
<IT_REF>
Name=
Address=
Creditcard=
</IT_REF>
</IT_PRECOMMIT>
```
User ⟶Participant

IT_PRECOMMIT is the message asking the participants if they agree with the request. The choice of a unique IT_ID prevents confusion at the participant's site in case of simultaneous IT. The IT_REF field is the user's profile (e.g. for electronic commerce: name, address, phone, credit card number, etc.).

The entity receiving this message may be:

- the DBMS, compliant with the IT;
- a static IT server, downloaded from a ftp server, that will interact with the DBMS;
- or better a mobile IT server that the user has sent to the participant, embedded in the message.

It is not in the scope of this paper to investigate the use of mobile code, but we believed that it is the best suited paradigm for the Internet far ahead of RPC or Client/Server [26].

Upon the reception of IT_PRECOMMIT, the participant initiates a local transaction (LT) to fulfil the request. When the LT ends, the participant may have two behaviours, depending of the outcome. If the transaction is willing to commit (all the items are locked), IT_PRECOMMIT_OK is sent back to the user, with the field DATA containing latest information about the object ("a surprise will be added for free to your package", etc.). If the transaction cannot succeed, the IT_PRECOMMIT_NOK message is sent back, the DATA field containing the reason of the failure ("your credit card has expired", etc.).

```
<IT_PRECOMMIT_OK>
<IT_ID> I-Transaction id </IT_ID>
<DATA> Data 1, Data 2, ... </DATA>
</IT_PRECOMMIT_OK>
<IT_PRECOMMIT_NOK>
<IT_ID> I-Transaction id </IT_ID>
<DATA> Data 1, Data 2, ... </DATA>
</IT_PRECOMMIT_NOK>
```
Participant ⟶ User

Upon reception of at least one IT_PRECOMMIT_NOK, the user sends to each participant the message IT_ABORT with the IT identifier. Otherwise, if the user collects a IT_PRECOMMIT_OK from each participant, then it sends a IT_COMMIT message.

Upon reception of the IT_COMMIT, the participant commits the LT, otherwise it is aborted.

```
<IT_ABORT>
<IT_ID> I-Transaction id </IT_ID>
</IT_ABORT>
<IT_COMMIT>
<IT_ID> I-Transaction id </IT_ID>
</IT_COMMIT>
```
User ⟶ Participant

One can notice that the types of the messages can be considered as a subset of the messages used by the TIP protocol to implement a two-phase commit. Henceforth, an extension of TIP can be seriously envisioned to implement the protocol. Alternate ACP can be found in [1] and [21]. A framework of patterns for fault-tolerant computing (BAST), proposing several distributed protocol classes and design patterns can be found in [10]. In the optical of using mobile code for implementing the server at the participant site, BAST can be used to propose dynamically several alternate algorithms.

4.2 Fault Tolerance

In real life, and particularly in the Internet, things are rarely as neat as they should be, and a protocol has to survive failures. For instance, we suppose that communication failures will never arise, *i.e.* messages cannot get lost or duplicated and are error-free.

We consider each step of the dialogue and detail how the protocol will react when facing a failure (figure 4).

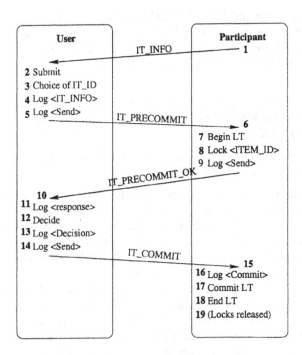

Fig. 4. Moments of faults.

The participant is noted P and the user U.

1 P fails after sending IT_INFO to U. When P recovers, nothing is recorded at P's site, so the recovery procedure has nothing to do. If

U fails before receiving the message, nothing is recorded and the user will have to re-send an HTTP request.

5 U fails after the logging of the IT_PRECOMMIT messages. When U recovers, some messages may have reach some participants. Therefore, U has to send to each participant IT_ABORT, and will ignore all IT_PRECOMMIT_OK or IT_PRECOMMIT_NOK he may receive later with the same IT identifier. If P already received IT_PRECOMMIT, he may have answered IT_PRECOMMIT_OK or _NOK and he is waiting for IT_ABORT or IT_PRECOMMIT.

6 P fails before receiving a IT_PRECOMMIT. Therefore, a time-out mechanism must be in place at U's site to detect the failure of P, and to send to each participant a IT_ABORT (equivalent to 5). When P recovers from the failure, he is not aware of the IT_PRECOMMIT, so he does nothing.

7 P fails after initiating the LT. When P recovers, the LT manager has to execute its recovery procedure to end the LT properly.

9 P fails after logging IT_PRECOMMIT_OK. The message may have reach U, and U may have decide to commit the IT. Therefore P has to ask U the outcome, and U answers either IT_COMMIT or IT_ABORT. If U is also down, P cannot know the outcome of the transaction (see 14).

10 U fails before receiving IT_PRECOMMIT_OK or IT_PRECOMMIT_NOK. Thereafter, when U wakes up, he sends IT_ABORT.

13 U fails after logging the outcome. When U recovers, whatever the outcome, he sends IT_ABORT.

14 U fails after logging the sending of the IT_COMMIT messages. When U recovers, some messages may have reach some participants and some may have not. This is the most ugly case the protocol has to face, since some participants may have commit their local transactions and some others may expect an answer in a reasonable delay. The protocol has to cope with two opposite requirements.
The first is the need for U to have a 100% guaranteed atomicity service. In this circumstance, P has to wait to receive from U the outcome of the transaction. In traditional ACP, P has the possibility to ask other participants if they do know the outcome, but it demands that U sends to each participant the list of all the other participants. Even if it may reduce the window of vulnerability this solution is not sufficient and blocking still may arise.
The second is to wait for a certain amount of time and if nothing has been received before the time elapsed to simply abort the transaction. Therefore, the unicity of the outcome is no more guaranteed since some participants may have commit whereas others may have abort.

15, 16, 17 are equivalent to 9.

18 and 19 are equivalent to 9.

This protocol is two-phase and can be used to face failures that may appear during the execution of IT. Nevertheless, other protocols may be implemented, provided that their interface with local TM is constituted with the commands *precommit*, *commit* and *abort*. These three commands constitute the minimal set of commands mandatory for interoperability of local transaction managers. Their interoperation consists only in the agreement of the IT outcome.

Unfortunately, this two-phase protocol is not well suited to implement IT, for reasons explained in the next section, and we must build a protocol on top of a new architecture, based on the notion of *agency*.

5 Agencies

5.1 Definition

We define an agency by its functionality. An agency is a middleware component which enables a secure and reliable cooperation among participants to a common task. In the transaction context, it takes the burden of the security and fault-tolerance management, and delivers the service of atomicity.

To make this definition clear, we propose an example from the electronic commerce field: the Multipurpose Internet Shopping Basket (MIShoBa) [4], currently under development at the University of Geneva.

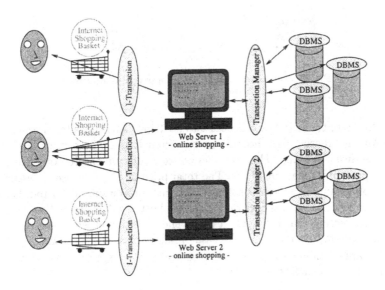

Fig. 5. Multipurpose Internet Shopping Basket overview.

The intention of the Multipurpose Internet Shopping Basket is to allow users to gather products of any kind from several vendors' sites into a single shopping basket. In figure 5, two web-servers (unknown to each other) provide on-line shopping facilities. The product databases are managed independently.

It is very important to comprehend that: (1) the two servers are required to work together for one I-Transaction initiated at the will of one user; (2) they will possibly never work together again later and (3) their collaboration will be hidden to each other. The collaboration is only meaningful for the user.

Once the user has finished to browse the Web, he reviews the items he gathered in his search and selects the products he actually wants to buy.

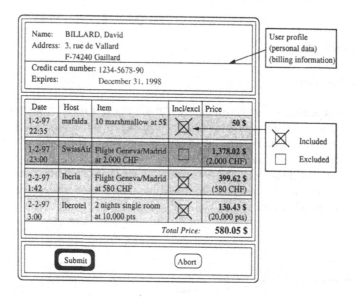

Fig. 6. Multipurpose Internet Shopping Basket screen.

In figure 6, the user has collected two air-trips Geneva-Madrid proposed by SwissAir and Iberia[1]. He chooses the trip from Iberia whose price is cheaper than the SwissAir's one. The user also books a room in the Iberotel hotel and buys a pack of 10 marshmallows. The total price of his purchases is estimated in US dollars and if the user is satisfied, he clicks on the submit button. For this particular application, the click on the submit button will generate the triggering of a I-Transaction that will contact each vendor's site and will reach an unique outcome: commit or abort, even in case of failure or security attack.

This application is confronted with several problems, related to security, reliability and scaleability.

---

[1] The fares are not reflecting the reality of the SwissAir or Iberia fares.

5.2 Security

As we stated earlier, the participants to the application must be authenticated and the messages exchanged must remain confidential and non-repudiable. To achieve these properties, the client must authenticate himself to the several vendors and the vendors must authenticate to the client. In addition, each pair (client, vendor$_i$) has to agree on a common encryption and non-repudiation mechanism. From the strict security point of view, it is a generic problem of identifying and authenticating a user, which is not fully resolved, especially in the Internet. But from the performance and reliability point of view, it is a very bad option, as well as for the juridic problems that may be generated as a consequence of a failure. The structure of the application can be depicted as in figure 7.

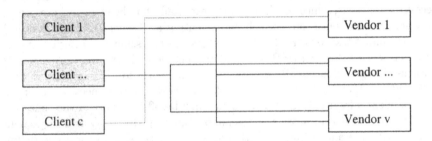

Fig. 7. Direct client to vendor architecture.

One can see that the client plays a coordinating role, which is not his purpose. The client should rely on a secure, reliable and legal entity whose function is to carry out the transaction for him (see figure 8). For the same reasons, the vendors themselves should rely on agencies.

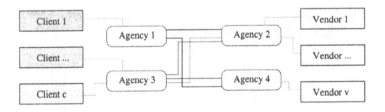

Fig. 8. Agencies Network Architecture.

From the client's point of view, the agency is its authenticated representative on the Internet. The agency takes orders from the client and performs actions (commands, payments) on the vendors' representatives. From the vendor's point of view, the agency is its salesman, taking commands, contacting stocks and receiving the payment.

Practically speaking, agencies should be legal entities, perfectly authenticated in an agency directory, to which a user or a vendor can subscribe. The subscribing process is left to the agency, knowing that the agency can be granted as responsible for some clients', or vendors', malevolence. For example, if the vendor (resp. the client) discovers that the client (resp. the vendor) is not really who he claims to be, then the agency should be responsible.

5.3 Reliability

Security attacks are not the only threats that agencies will face. Site or communication failures may arise in the Internet as well as in traditional environments. In our example, without agencies, clients and vendors must implement their own recovery protocols, which is a heavy duty, especially for the client, whose profile is a personal computer onto which implementing an efficient recovery protocol is more than hazardous. Futhermore, clients are accessing the Internet via an Internet Service Provider (ISP) with a dial-up modem. Therefore, the client's IP address changes (floating IP address) from connection to connection (e.g. *ppp-123.switch.ch*), and it becomes impossible for a server to reconnect to a client in case of client's failure. In addition, clients may be off-line most of the time.

Considering agencies, we can reasonably suppose that they will implement strong fault-tolerant techniques with ad-hoc hardware (e.g. mirror disks, redundant processors, etc.) and therefore provide to client and vendors a reliable service. The protocols used among agencies can be highly reliable protocols, with heavy interfaces (e.g. a three-phase commit), whereas the protocol agency-vendor can be a single protocol (e.g. two-phase commit) and the protocol client-agency can be a one-phase commit (submit of the query and reception of the outcome). The client-agency protocol can even be based on secured email (using PGP, Pretty Good Privacy), to overcome the problem of floating IP addresses.

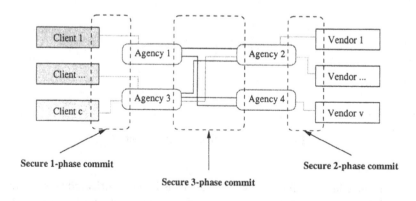

Fig. 9. Protocols in an Agencies Network.

5.4 Scaleability

The scaleability of Internet applications is definitely an important issue and a non-scalable application has little chance to survive excepted if it provides a monopoly service. Applications based on agencies are scalable, since new users can integrate the system which will handle them, provided that new agencies are created in proportion.

5.5 Benefit of Agencies

To sum up, in this example of electronic commerce, but one can easily extend the notion, the agencies:

– take the burden of the transaction management for clients and vendors;
– offer security features for sensible applications;
– act as a legal representative, either for the client and the server;
– are built upon a scalable architecture.

In addition, agencies in electronic commerce can offer the architectural support for micropayment mechanisms [5].

Agencies are also commonly found in the Internet, sometimes under disguized forms. For example, if we look at the management of global Top Level Domain (gTLD) Names in the Internet, a company (here the user) may want to reserve atomically the names "coco-colo.com", "coco-colo.web" and "coco-colo.store" (.web and .store are ones of the new gTLDs that may be added to the Internet). To reserve these three names, the user will send a request to a registrar, acting as our agency, and this registrar will try to reserve the names to the registries responsible for .com, .web and .store. If one registry answers that the name is already reserved, then the whole transaction might be aborted. At the time being, this process of reserving atomically several domain names is done manually.

6 Conclusion and Future Works

In this paper, we introduce a new model of transaction, called I-Transaction, tailored for Internet use. These I-Transactions are designed to provide atomicity for a set of actions triggered by a user upon different and a priori not known DBMS. Since these DBMS are not related to each other, they cannot offer a global management: the I-Transactions must be self-managed and implement they own atomicity and fault-tolerance.

In addition, the particularity of the Internet drives to implement security measures from the conception stage. A I-Transaction has to guarantee the PLACID properties, which is a superset of the ACID properties, integrating Privacy (the confidentiality of data) and Loyalty (the authentication of participants altogether with the non-repudiation of messages).

The scope of application for I-Transactions is really wide, even if in this paper we focus on electronic commerce, providing as an application example the Multipurpose Internet Shopping Basket, and the management of global Top Level

Domain (gTLD) Names in the Internet. Besides the use of I-Transactions by end-users, it is expected that application-to-application tasks will take advantage of I-Transactions, e.g. the Atomic File Transfer Protocol.

We present also in this paper an alternate architecture for I-Transactions, relying on the use of brokers (agencies), whose purpose is to take the burden of the transaction management for the client and the vendors; to offer security features for sensible applications; to act as a legal representative, either for the client and the server and who are built upon a – more – scalable architecture.

We have currently under consideration the implementation of I-Transaction, with agencies, for supporting electronic commerce and micropayment applications, the Atomic File Transfer Protocol and a prototype for the reservation of Internet domain names.

7 Acknowledgements

I gratefully acknowledge Irne Butor, for the first implementation of the Multi-purpose Internet Shopping Basket, my group at the University of Geneva for their comments1, and the anonymous referees who have help to improve the quality of this paper with their advises. Special thanks to Sonia and Corentin for their never falling support.

References

1. V. Atluri, E. Bertino, and S. Jajodia. Degrees of isolation, concurrency control protocols, and commit protocols. *Database Security VIII: Status and Prospects (J. Biskup et al. ed.)*, pages 259–274, 1994. North-Holland.
2. P. A. Bernstein, V. Hadzilacos, and N. Goodman. *Concurrency Control and Recovery in Databases Systems.* Addison-Wesley, 1987.
3. D. Billard. Transactional services for the internet. Technical Report 117, University of Geneva, December 1997.
4. D. Billard. Multipurpose Internet Shopping Basket. In *9th International Conference on Database and Expert Systems Applications (DEXA), workshop on Business Process Reengineering and Supporting Technologies for Electronic Commerce*, August 1998. Vienna, Austria.
5. D. Billard. Transactions and electronic commerce for the internet. Technical Report 118, University of Geneva, February 1998.
6. L. J. Camp, M. Sirbu, and J. D. Tygar. Token and notational money in electronic commerce. In *Usenix Workshop on Electronic Commerce*, July 1995. http://www.ksg.harvard.edu/people/jcamp/usenix/usenix.html.
7. European Commission. *Business Transformation through Technology.* EC Information Society Project Office, 1998. http://www.ispo.cec.be/ecommerce/-tbpbook.html.
8. T. Dierks and C. Allen. *Transport Layer Security Protocol.* Internet Draft, November 1997. http://www.ietf.org/internet-drafts/draft-ietf-tls-protocol-05.txt.
9. A. Freier, P. Karlton, and P. Kocher. *The SSL protocol version 3.0*, November 1996.

10. B. Garbinato and R. Guerraoui. Using the strategy design pattern to compose reliable distributed protocols. In *3rd USENIX Conference on O-O Technologies and Systems (COOTS'97)*, June 1997. Portland (Oregon).

11. S. Glassman, M. Manasse, M. Abadi, P. Gauthier, and P. Sobalvarro. The millicent protocol for inexpensive electronic commerce. In *4th International World Wide Web Conference*, December 1995. Boston, USA, http://www.cs.berkeley.edu/ gauthier/millicent/millicent.html.

12. D. K. Hsiao, E. J. Neuhold, and R. Sacks-Davis. Interoperable database systems. In *IFIP WG 2.6 Database Semantics Conference on Interoperable Database Systems (DS-5), IFIP Transactions, ISBN 0 444 89879 4*, November 1992. Lorne, Victoria, Australia.

13. T. Kunkelmann, H. Vogler, and S. Thomas. Interoperability of distributed transaction processing systems. *Lecture Notes on Computer Science, Proceedings of TreDS'96 International Workshop, Aachen, Germany*, 1161:177–190, October 1996.

14. F. Lorentz. *Electronic commerce, A new factor for consumers, companies, citizens and governement*. French Ministry of Economy, Finance and Industry, 1998. http://www.telecom.gouv.fr/francais/activ/techno/florentzsom.htm.

15. J. Lyon, K. Evans, and J. Klein. *Transaction Internet Protocol*. Request for Comments 2371, July 1998. http://www.ietf.org/ids.by.wg/tip.html.

16. J. Lyon, K. Evans, and J. Klein. *Transaction Internet Protocol Demonstration*, July 1998. http://oss.tandem.com:2490/tip/.

17. OECD/EC. Access and pricing for information infrastructure services: Communication tariffication, regulation and the internet. In *OECD/EC Workshop*, 1996. Dublin, Ireland. http://www.oecd.org/dsti/iccp/dublin.html.

18. OMG. The common object request broker: Architecture and specifications, 1996. http://www.omg.org/corba/c2indx.htm.

19. OMG. The common object request broker: Architecture and specifications, 1997. http://www.omg.org/corba/corbiiop.htm.

20. OMG. Corbaservices: Common object service specification, 1997. http://www.omg.org/corba/csindx.htm.

21. I. Ray, E. Bertino, S. Jajodia, and L. Mancini. An advanced commit protocol for mls distributed database systems. In *3rd ACM Conf. on Computer and Communications Security*, pages 119–128, March 1996. New Delhi, India.

22. A. Schöter and R. Willmer. Digital money online, a review of some existing technologies. Technical report, Intertrader Ltd., February 1997. http://www.intertrader.com/library/DigitalMoneyOnline/dmo/dmo.htm.

23. M. Sirbu and J. D. Tygar. Netbill: An internet commerce system optimized for network delivered services. In *IEEE CompCom*, pages 20–25, March 1995. St Francisco, USA.

24. W. Stallings. *Network and Internetwork Security, Principles and Practice*. Prentice Hall International Edition, 1995. ISBN 0-13-180050-7.

25. B. Stiller, G. Frankhauser, B. Plattner, and N. Weiler. *Pre-study on Customer Care, Accounting, Charging, Billing, and Pricing*, February 1998. ftp://ftp.tik.ee.ethz.ch/pub/people/stiller/pre-study/all.ps.gz.

26. C. F. Tschudin. *On the Structuring of Computer Communications*. PhD thesis, University of Geneva, 1993.

27. XOPEN. *X/OPEN Guide : Distributed Transaction Processing: Reference Model, Version 2*. X/OPEN company ltd, 1993.

28. XOPEN. *X/OPEN CAE Specification: Distributed Transaction Processing: The TxRPC Specification*. X/OPEN company ltd, 1995.

On the Unification of Persistent Programming and the World-Wide Web

Richard Connor, Keith Sibson and Paolo Manghi

Department of Computing Science,
University of Glasgow,
Glasgow G12 8QQ
{richard, sibsonk, manghi}@dcs.gla.ac.uk

Abstract. In its infancy, the World-Wide Web consisted of a web of largely static hypertext documents. As time progresses it is evolving into a domain which supports almost arbitrary networked computations. Central to its successful operation is the agreement of the HTML and http standards, which provide inter-node communication via the medium of streamed files. Our hypothesis is that, as application sophistication increases, this file-based interface will present the same limitations to programmers as the use of traditional file and database system interfaces within programming languages. Persistent programming systems were designed to overcome these problems in traditional domains; our investigation is to reapply the resulting research to the new domain of the Web. The result of this should be the ability to pass typed data layered on top of the existing standards, in a manner that is fully integrated with them. A typed object protocol integrated with existing standards would allow the Web to be used to host a global persistent address space, thus making it a potential data repository for a generation of database programming languages.

1. Overview

There are two fundamentally different approaches to the integration of databases and the World-Wide Web. The first is the "embedded database" approach, where well-behaved and regular segments of data available from the Web are implemented using various forms of database technology. These interfaces may be as simple as accepting embedded SQL queries, or may be more subtle so that the purpose of the database is only to provide efficient and regular storage. In this case the existence of the database metastructure can not be detected from its interface on the Web.

The alternative approach is to view the entire Web as a database. At the current state of the art, the data collection that is the Web has only one thing in common with a traditional database - it is large. To talk of the Web as a single vast database is at best premature: databases have other attributes, which are in fact more significant than their size, such as an enforced semantic model and guarantees about the quality and consistency of the data contained in them. The Web has no such guarantees, and never can in any general sense.

Nonetheless, this is the approach taken in this paper. We seek to improve the potential for the Web to be viewed as a single data collection, significant subsets of which can be treated as global databases. The approach is one of a database programming language where the Web namespace of URLs is overloaded as a naming scheme for typed data which can be manipulated by a strongly and largely statically typed programming language. This language can therefore act as a query language over those parts of the Web whose data is well-behaved, as well as providing a system in which the production of such data can be made easier for a programmer.

The approach proposed is to extend the semantics of a database programming language (more accurately, a higher-order persistent programming language) to include the Web within its semantic domain. One of the most notable features of such languages is that they include passive data and program fragments, in the form of functions and procedures, in the same persistent data domain [AM95]. Therefore the notion of Web data within this context includes higher-order executable code. The investigation described is an attempt to integrate such a system with the existing state of the Web; in particular, there is no suggestion of attempting to replace the Web, by which term we include its host of evolving and emerging standards, with new technology.

2. Introduction

The world-wide web is starting to see an increase in the sophistication of its component documents and applications. Although the origin of the Web was relatively humble browsable text documents, the use of dynamic applications using the same interfaces is becoming commonplace. A number of different models have been developed to support this within the original protocols, including client-side computation via scripts and applets, and server-side computation via CGI and API plugins.

Although these mechanisms allow arbitrary computations to be described within a networked application, the medium by which data is transferred among them is the text file, as defined by the http protocol. This is scarcely a limitation for the majority of current applications, as the common model of computation is based on a client-server interaction whereby the end result is to produce an HTML document to be viewed by a browser. It is envisaged however that, as sophistication of use increases, the requirement for application components to pass more complex data among themselves will increase, and in this context the text file will become a limitation.

The scenario of applications sharing typed data via the medium of text files is exactly that which prompted research into persistent programming systems, and the main intention of the work described here is to reapply that research in the domain of the Web. This paper describes some initial ideas, currently under investigation in the

Hippo project at the University of Glasgow [Hip98], which allow the layering of a typed object protocol on top of the HTML and http standards.

One further motivation, of a more pragmatic nature, is that the successful unification of a persistent programming language with the Web will inevitably have the secondary effect of creating an open persistent system. One of the most interesting fundamental properties of the Web is the autonomy of its users, and any system which attempted to control this would not therefore meet the selected challenge. A major fundamental drawback of orthogonally persistent systems is that they are closed-world, this aspect making them seem unacceptable for much commercial use. Integrating a persistent system with the Web requires the management of an essential set of compromises between a pure model of orthogonal persistence and something that can be engineered within the shared semantic space of the Web. Thus success in the investigation will also address the more general problem of openness in persistent systems; however, it should be admitted, a fundamental incompatibility is not always the best starting point for an investigation!

It must finally be stressed that this investigation is not an attempt to reinvent the industrial standards of CORBA and DCOM. While these successfully allow the modeling of objects with internet interfaces, the main advantages of orthogonal persistence stem from the seamless semantic model of data that is shared across program invocations within a single language. The CORBA and DCOM models have quite a different agenda, in that they provide language-independent interfaces, allowing the objects provided to be implemented by and incorporated into programs in arbitrary languages. The use of CORBA or DCOM objects requires translation from an interface definition written in an Interface Description Language (IDL) into the particular language being used. A major consequence of this is that the descriptive power of the IDL is necessarily compromised to maximise the set of languages that can use the technology, as it must provide something akin to a common subset of their type systems. An IDL can therefore provide at best a way of describing structured scalar types, and references to other interfaces in the same standard. In particular, an IDL could never hope to support types representing values such as function closures or abstract data types. Thus, although there is some overlap, our investigation is into a quite different paradigm of typed internet data.

3. Orthogonal persistence

3.1. Persistence for data-intensive applications

The concept of orthogonal persistence was identified by Atkinson [Atk78] whilst working on systems where general purpose programming was required over data stored in databases and file systems. The key observation is that data stored in these domains is available externally only in a flat file format, which causes a serious mismatch when it must be translated into a programming language type system. An independent internal investigation by IBM revealed that in some application areas up to 30% of source code was involved purely in translation between the two domains.

Furthermore this code attracts high management costs, as it must be changed in detail depending upon the external environment in which it is executed.

Considerable research has been devoted to the investigation of persistence and its application to the integration of database systems and programming languages [ABC+83, AM95]. A number of persistent systems have been developed including PS-algol [PS88], Napier88 [MBC+89], Galileo [ACO85], TI Persistent Memory System [Tha86] and Trellis/Owl [SCW85]. Most of the object-oriented database products now commercially available provide some form of persistent language interface, and most recently Sun Microsystems and others are involved in a number of experiments in adding the concepts of persistence to Java [AJDS97, GN98]. Whilst many of the systems listed may not be perfect examples of an academic definition of persistence, they clearly borrow the essential concepts, albeit in a commercially viable setting.

The benefits of orthogonal persistence have been described extensively in the literature [AM95], and can be summarised as

- improving programming productivity from simpler semantics;
- removing ad hoc arrangements for data translation and long term data storage; and
- providing protection mechanisms over the whole environment.

Figure 1 gives a simplified pictorial view of the traditional data-sharing scenario. In this diagram, the rectangles represent program invocations, the circles inside them being the executing code and the graphs representing the data manipulated by these invocations.

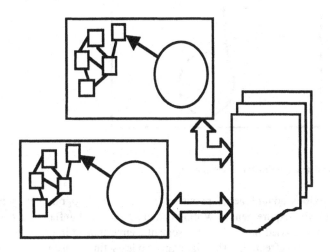

Fig. 1. Traditional file-sharing model of long-lived data

For data to be shared between invocations, either concurrently or after an elapsed time, graphs of complex objects must be explicitly flattened into some format supported by the file system. These objects must then be recreated in the domain of the other invocation, which executes in its own closed semantic domain. In simple terms this increases the burden on the application programmer; however in a sophisticated application domain there are greater problems also, such as the creation of copies of the data and the inability to share data represented by abstract data types. Whilst these problems can be overcome through coding in any computationally complete system, the key observation is that the complexity introduced by the traditional domain is unnecessary, in that the code which solves these problems is superfluous to the description of the problem the programmer is addressing.

Figure 2 shows the same scenario with a persistent application domain. The rectangle in this figure represents the persistent application environment which, unlike traditional program language environments, encompasses all the data within the domain of that programming system. The apparent simplification is clear; the file system and translation arrows have disappeared, as has the (semantically superfluous) copy of the graph of objects. In a nutshell, this has been achieved by extending the boundary of the programming system semantics beyond that of shared and long-term data.

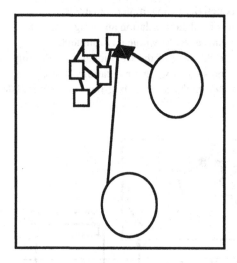

Fig. 2. The persistent application environment

The most obvious advantage of persistence is that the programmer is no longer burdened with the requirement of writing code to flatten and unflatten data structures which have to be passed into a different semantic environment in order for their long-term storage to be effected. The flattening code is time-consuming to write and sensitive to maintain, as it typically relies upon the semantics of an external system which is subject to change.

Although this was one of the initial motivations of the work, this is now viewed as relatively insignificant compared to the later advantages found through more advanced research. Such code is relatively straightforward to write, and many modern programming systems provide some support for the process; for instance the "pickle" operator in Modula-3 [CDG+89] and the "persistence" support in Metrowerks

Codewarrior [MW98]. Persistence starts to show its true power in contexts where it is difficult or impossible to write such code, such as high-level languages where values significant to the semantics of a program are not necessarily denotable. Prime examples of these constructs are first-class closures and abstract data types, and the reader is referred to the literature to find examples of the power of persistence in such contexts [POS8, POS7, Con90].

3.2. Persistence and the Web

The observation here is that, as applications which require to process data from around the Web become more sophisticated, they will start to encounter the same class of problems as those identified at the start of persistence research. Communicating processes around the Web can address each other directly, rather than using the intermediary of a file system[1]; however all current Web protocols are based on the transfer of files around the network. This gives almost the same scenario as sharing through file systems, except that the logical namespace ranges over a different set of values. The scenario is as pictured in Figure 3; the Web processes may be able to name each other, but are still required to perform the translation code and, perhaps more importantly, to keep semantically incongruous copies of the data associated with each invocation.

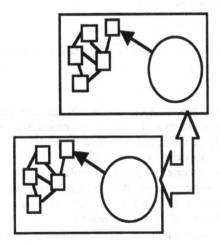

Fig. 3. Sharing data among Web processes

The topic of investigation is therefore whether the same solution, that of extending the boundary of data handled in the semantic domain of a programming language to

---

[1] This is ignoring the fact that the naming service of the Web is essentially derived from file system conventions. In this description we assume that URLs name resources orthogonally to their type, and may be used for example to name data channels between processes.

include that of all process invocations, is viable in the context of the Web. At the start of persistence research it was clear that this approach was semantically preferable, but not that such systems were feasible to engineer and use. In the context of the Web, even the desired semantics of such an arrangement are less straightforward.

The good news is that, if a useful semantic model exists, then much of the research committed to persistent systems should be applicable to the new domain. Many of the engineering problems that have been successfully solved in closed persistent systems have clear parallels in the Web environment, and the implementation problems following a clear model might not be so great. The rest of this paper categorises the classes of problem which occur in the semantic integration, and outlines some areas in which possible solutions may be found.

4. A model for persistence and the Web

In its most general manifestation, orthogonal persistence is a property of a programming language whereby the treatment of data is entirely orthogonal to its lifetime. One model of this is to replace traditional file system access primitives by two language meta-constructs, *intern* and *extern*. Given a value x, of type t, and a global external namespace ranged over by n, then

```
extern( n, x )
```

causes a conceptual link to the value x to be placed in the global namespace, such that the call

```
intern( n, t )
```

results in the same value, formerly denoted by x. *intern* will fail dynamically if the identifier n does not denote a binding of type t in the external namespace. The crucial property of this model is that the semantics of the value is unaffected, even when concepts such as identity and mutability are in the semantic model.

The observation that the *intern* and *extern* calls can take place in different program invocations gives rise to the sharing of typed data among programs in different contexts. This single, shared namespace which allows any program invocation to access the same data roots is the key to orthogonal persistence.

It should also be noted that the notation of *intern* and *extern*, although used consistently since the inception of persistence research, is not necessarily helpful as it gives the intuition of a namespace external to the programming system domain. In reality these meta-functions give a mechanism whereby the data that hangs from the namespace is internal to the semantics of the programming system as a whole: thus the namespace is not in any sense external, but in fact shared internally by all program invocations.

We have chosen the intern/extern model as a starting point because it is the simplest model which, by its addition to an arbitrary programming language, provides orthogonal persistence. In this sense it is a core model, rather than a useful model for programming persistent applications, where more support is generally considered desirable. However we assert that if this model can be extended to an understandable semantics in the domain of Web data, then other more programmer-friendly models can also follow.

Our aim is then to apply this model of persistence in the domain of the internet, and more specifically the Web. Three main conflicts have been identified:

- the Web and the persistence model each have their own namespaces, which must therefore be unified
- the Web and any programming language each have their own preconceptions about the representation and structure of data, which must again be unified
- the Web has an (implicit) data model whose semantics necessarily allow the description of remote, unreliable, and autonomous data; desirable programming systems include notions such as static typing and referential integrity, which appear to be fundamentally at odds with this.

Each of this is now examined in turn.

4.1. Unification of the namespaces

The simplest way to achieve unification with the global persistent namespace assumed by the intern/extern model involves compromising it by the use of two different namespaces, that of a local file system and that of URLs. *extern* is used with the local file system namespace, and there are two forms of *intern*, one using the local file system namespace and one using the URL namespace.

In this way, the namespaces used by the proposed system are in fact identical to those used by the writers and readers of standard HTML documents in the domain of a web server. These are written into locations (filenames) resolved in the context of the local file system, and read as either local filenames or URLs, depending on the context and purpose of the reader. The author of an HTML document needs to understand both namespaces to allow the placement of anything other than simple relative resource names within the HTML code.

The use of these namespaces to share data between program invocations requires knowledge of the implicit mapping between them. For example, the local filename

```
/users/staff/richard/public_html/fred.html
```

and the URL

```
http://www.dcs.gla.ac.uk/~richard/fred.html
```

might map to the same physical file, but this is not normally specified by any formal arrangement. This mapping must for the moment remain beyond the semantics of the persistent system, and the programmer's knowledge of it must be assumed. Once again, the situation is identical with the human user's view of the namespaces.

Having simply established the namespaces, their use for the storage and retrieval of persistent data looks simple. To give a concrete example, the following code creates a new object of class *person* and stores it in an external namespace within the domain of an *http* server:

```
fred = new person( "Frederick", 31 )

extern(    "/users/staff/richard/public_html/fred.html",
           fred )
```

This object may subsequently be retrieved by a remote application executing the following code, and the identifier *thisFred* is typed locally as *person*.

```
thisFred =
internURL(
           "http://www.dcs.gla.ac.uk/richard/fred.html",
           person )
```

If the data is not accessible, or has some other type, the *internURL* operation fails and the binding is not made.

Readers unfamiliar with orthogonal persistence may at this point become suspicious about the simplicity of this code, and make guesses about the semantics of these statements. It is important to note that the definition of orthogonal persistence requires that the values associated with the bindings *fred* and *thisFred* in the example are semantically indistinguishable; preserving this is a serious implementation problem, but one that is now known to be tractable. Note also that another definitional feature of orthogonal persistence is that values of any type in the semantic domain are allowed the full range of persistence. Although the type *person* might be relatively straightforward to handle, the operations *intern* and *extern* are available on values of any type, including for example functions, closures and abstract data types.

However our task currently is to provide a clean semantic model for persistence and the Web. Although such a model is clearly of no use if it is not possible to implement, we do not discuss issues of implementation further in this context.

One unfortunate effect of the two-namespace model is to lose the nice property of context-free name resolution within the persistent system, as the resolution of local filenames depends upon the physical location in which the application is executing. One of the major perceived advantages of closed-world persistent systems is that the semantics of an application is entirely independent of its physical context, depending only on how the persistent store is populated.

This model relies upon a single global namespace, which is believed by many to be impossible to engineer, and some compromise is necessary in a system which extends beyond a local context. It is perhaps ironic that the URL model provides precisely this, but in reality this is only viable because of the update restrictions that exist with it. An alternative approach, for example using the URL namespace as a parameter to *extern*, could provide context-free name resolution, but the significant behaviour of the application would nonetheless necessarily depend upon protection issues based on the context of execution. It is pleasing at least that the intern namespace is a single global model, a feature which has so far evaded the engineers of closed persistent systems.

One final point that must be stressed is that it is only the concept of namespace that has been discussed in this section. With many Web and file system protocols, URL naming directly corresponds to the presence of physical files which contain the data being referenced; this is not necessarily the case in the system we are describing. The names describe only entry points into a general graph of persistent data, and not necessarily the physical location of a file in which the data is stored. Ultimately, of course, resource names are interpreted according to the whim of the http server that happens to be listening at the specified socket; however, to keep within the initial brief, it would be helpful to assume a standard server arrangement.

4.2. Representing persistent values

To give the most useful unification of persistence with the Web it is a requirement that documents created to represent persistent values are not only transmitted via the standard protocols, but can also make sense outside the context of the persistent system. It is a major feature of the internet, and undoubtedly one of the reasons for its success, that documents are in open standard formats and may be interpreted by a choice of viewers. We therefore avoid the choice of inventing a new document standard which would require all users of persistent data to adopt our technology.

That choice leaves the further question of how best to use existing and emerging standards to represent persistent values. There are currently a plethora of new standards emerging which allow better specification of Web resources than simple HTML. For example the W3C [W3C] standard XML, in conjunction with a DTD and XLL, could be used to describe a way of laying out text files to capture the semantics of values in any particular type system. Such an approach would seem unexciting, however; although in principle such resources would be re-usable by other systems, they would effectively be closed outside the persistent environment as a very high degree of interpretation would be required to allow their semantics to emerge. Claiming that a system using such protocols would be open would be similar to claiming any other system is open if viewed at the level of its base implementation.

The Resource Description Framework [RDF] allows the association of meta-data, loosely comparable to programming language types, with Web resources. Even if a high-level type system could be modeled, however, the granularity of the abstraction would appear to be too coarse-grained for use in a persistent Web system. The fundamental cost of remote resource fetching is generally believed to be in the connection cost, rather than bandwidth limitation, and it would appear that the fine-grained value model of persistent programming would not map well to every persistent value being represented as a separate resource. The model also suffers from the same problem of interpretation identified with the XML approach.

Another emerging standard of particular interest is that of semi-structured data. This data format emerged, amongst other uses, as a data interchange format, and some recent research has concentrated on the derivation of structure and semantics from this common level description [NAM98, NUW+97]. It may turn out to be possible to store persistent data in a semi-structured arrangement automatically derived from the static language typing, in such a way that its type-safe re-introduction can be automated [CS98c]. The beauty of this approach is that the semi-structured data is effectively self-describing, and its interpretation does not depend upon understanding a meta-level description. Therefore it could be used by any other application system capable of understanding semi-structured data. If this approach is tractable, it may also be possible to safely import semi-structured data with a different derivation into a typed persistent computation. However there are some fundamental research issues to be solved before this approach can be deemed tractable.

For the moment, it was decided to take a purely pragmatic approach simply to test the concept in an open and highly available manner. Entry points to persistent data are represented as HTML files, in a way that can be usefully interpreted by Web browsers as well as by a persistent program. This is achieved by creating HTML documents that contain persistent data formatted in a human-readable manner, according to their type, via a simple set of rules. This allows programs to communicate with each other directly using typed data, and also allows this data to be understood by a human using a standard browser. It also provides the simplest of mechanisms for an applications builder to place the results of programs on the Web.

The necessary non-human-readable content, such as the canonical type representations required for run-time structural checking, are placed immediately before the data in HTML comment fields. This information can then be used when a persistent binding is specified using an *intern* statement, and the HTML code which represents the data can be properly interpreted according to its type. This arrangement also allows other strategies to be used in cases where the efficiency of the parsing might be an issue, for example a comment field might contain a compressed format of the same data, or information on how to fetch it from a different physical location.

The rules required to translate from typed values to human-readable versions are relatively straightforward to describe for most types. The reverse mapping is less so, but given that this can be guided by the embedded type representation it presents no real technical problems. Types such as closures and abstract types present more of a challenge; however previous research on hyper-programming [KCC+92] can be used to solve many of the problems very neatly, by providing a model of closure that bears a textual representation. The issues of protection in abstract data types should also be noted, although it seems unlikely that there is a perfect solution. This is maybe one of the fundamental type system compromises that will have to be made.

Figure 4 gives an example of the HTML generated by the execution of the following program fragment:

```
fred = new person( "fred", 31 )
extern( "/users/staff/richard/public_html/fred.html",
        fred )
```

```
<HTML>
<HEAD>

...

</HEAD>
<BODY>
<!--HIPPO TYPE ANNOTATION
t0=str(age*name#int*string)

-->
<TABLE BORDER="2">
<TR><TD COLSPAN=2>Structure of type Person</TD></TR>
<TR><TD>name</TD><TD>age</TD></TR>
<TR><TD>Fred</TD><TD>23</TD></TR>
</TABLE></BODY>
</HTML>
```

Fig. 4. Example HTML generation

An important point to notice is that such files need be generated only at the execution of a call to *extern*. The semantics of these calls is to generate only entry points into arbitrary graphs of data, rather than having the effect of storing a flattened closure as in a non-persistent system; what is outlined above, therefore, is not a data storage paradigm, but only a way of representing entry points. Data storage may be handled in a relatively traditional manner by a persistent object storage mechanism, provided that the illusion is somehow preserved of the same data being accessed either from a local persistent system, from a remote persistent system, or from a Web browser. Furthermore, accesses in the last two categories should generate the same text streams through the http protocol.

The problems left to handle are those of object identity (including the correct semantics of mutable objects), and the representation of references to other objects.

Object identity can not be equated with URL equality, the latter including aliases that are in general undetectable. Instead, however, unique identities can be manufactured by the persistent run-time system, as is common in any case, and stored along with type information as an invisible field. On intern, the identity information can be handled by the persistent store layer of a run-time system to avoid duplication. The fact that the identity is not observable to HTML browsers is actually desirable, as it fits with that apparent semantic model. Preserving correct update semantics poses a further problem, which will be dealt with in the next section as the proposed solution is based upon a typing mechanism. Given this can be handled, however, this approach gives a level of flexibility in that semantically identical values can safely have multiple representations, in more than one text file.

There is an easy conceptual solution to the problem of representing references in the dual format. It is necessary for them to be represented as URLs in a textual view of the data, to allow human browsing of the graph of objects accessible from the persistent entry point. Given this, all that is required is to generate a new text file to represent each reachable persistent object, generate a unique local filename for it, and plug a corresponding URL into the textual description of the referring object. The disadvantage of this approach, as mentioned before, is that transmitting each persistent object with a separate http request seems to be an inappropriate level of granularity. A solution to this exists however in the use of HTML anchors, which allow arbitrary numbers of objects to be transmitted in a single stream. Rather than pre-calculate these multi-object files, it is possible to embed unresolved references as CGI calls based on the identity of the referred object, allowing them to be dynamically generated. Given that we can solve the problem of the same semantic values appearing in multiple text files, this mechanism can be used strategically in conjunction with established techniques such as object clustering to send an appropriate set of values through each connection.

4.3. A type system for Web-based persistence

Even given that standard HTML documents can be used to represent typed data, there are still two problems with persistent applications which operate over such data. These are due to fundamental mismatches between the semantics of programming languages and the normal model of Web usage:

- referential integrity, normally guaranteed within a programming system, can not be expected in general in this domain
- many programming models include update, with locations contained within arbitrary data structures; however, most data provided on the web is read-only, and not allowed to be updated in an arbitrary manner by users other than its provider

We conclude with brief descriptions of type system mechanisms we have introduced to combat these problems.

4.3.1. Typing for referential integrity

A great deal of research in persistent programming systems has concentrated on the subject of dynamic binding, often referred to as flexible, incremental binding. The binding of code to persistent data, captured above through the *intern* operation, requires a check both on the existence and the type of the data referred to. The consensus model to emerge is that the existence of the data does not require to be individually checked, and can be folded into the same language mechanism as the type check. This is safe, as a failed type check prevents any further execution on the value referred to, although not general, as the programmer can not distinguish between the two classes of failure. However experience with persistent programming has not shown any convincing requirement to do this. In the new domain of the internet our initial assumption is that any dynamic unavailability of data is best exposed to the programmer of a persistent application as a dynamic type error. It should be noted that the fundamental differences in the context may turn out to invalidate this assumption.

The problem is easily solved by resorting to a type system where the each use of an object is dynamically checked. This was the approach taken in the first persistent programming language, PS-algol [ABC+83]. However further work on persistent languages showed that a much better solution could be achieved, with the addition of explicit dynamic typing constructs to an otherwise statically checked system [MBC+89, Con90].

The semantics of *internURL* includes a dynamic check on the availability and type of the data, and this provides a failure point in the case where the data is unavailable or of the wrong type. The problem is that after such a check has succeeded, the data is integrated with the ongoing typed computation in a context where further dynamic checks are not normally desirable. The only way to ensure the soundness of the type system is to make a locally cached copy of any data integrated in this manner.[2]

It is impossible in general to cache the transitive closure of data fetched from a particular entry point in the persistent graph, as this could itself form a global web of data. We have therefore designed a type system which distinguishes between data which is known to be available and that which may be dynamically unavailable. It is important to note that this does not by itself solve the problems of closure and referential integrity, but is proposed merely as a platform on which to conduct experiments with the relationship. Any final solution must include some element of compromise between purity of semantics and a pragmatic approach to the downloading of data files, so at the moment we strive only to have at least some definition of data movement within the programming language domain.

The type constructor *refR* (remote reference) is added to an otherwise standard type system to denote the type of data which is not guaranteed to be available. *refR(t)* is, in general, a supertype of t, and a dynamic coercion is required to use the denotation as type t. The semantics of this type are similar to that of that of the type *any* in Napier88 [MBC+89] and *dynamic* in [Car85, ACP+95], except that an indication of the value's expected type is included with its static denotation. The typing of a denotation as *refr(t)* gives no guarantee whatsoever about the type of the value referred to, and in this sense contains no static type information whatever. However a value of such a type has the specialisation operation to t defined over it, and before type-specific computation can take place the type must undergo an explicit dynamic check. If the check succeeds then the value is cached at that time and can be subsequently relied upon during the computation.

Although the typing *ref(t)* does not carry a guarantee, it is however the case that where the link to the data is dynamically available, and where the data has not been interfered with by any other autonomous system, then the dynamic specialisation will succeed. In this sense the t can be regarded as a static hint to the real type of the data, and the programmer may have some useful model about the probability of success.

---

[2] For the purposes of this description we ignore the issues of cache coherency, although this does present a major problem. Our current thinking is to handle this at a different level from the programming model which we describe here. The prevention of remote update, as described later, greatly alleviates the general problem.

The reference type mechanism allows the programmer fine-grain yet implicit control over the point at which data is fetched. For example

```
thisFred = internURL(
            "http://www.dcs.gla.ac.uk/richard/fred.html",
            refR( person ) )
```

causes an association to be made between the identifier *thisFred* and the URL, but does not cause the data to be fetched and cached, whereas this statement

```
thisFred =internURL(
            "http://www.dcs.gla.ac.uk/richard/fred.html",
            person )
```

causes the data to be fetched also. In a less trivial example,

```
internURL(
            n,
            structure( x : int; y : refR( person ) ) )
```

allows the programmer to specify the fetch of the top-level structure, but not necessarily its closure. The subtyping relationship between *person* and *refR(person)* allows the type check to succeed only when the record originally placed at that binding contained a person or any subtype of person. If the closure is fetched for pragmatic reasons, such as the object clustering referred to earlier, any later dynamic checks can be elided.

Although this construct gives the potential for applications which perform arbitrary dynamic typing, and which may therefore fail at any point with a type error, it is nonetheless possible to adopt a coding style where all dynamic checks are factored out at the start of a application. This can give all the desirable properties of static typing whilst retaining the required flexibility of type-safe remote binding.

It is our final hope, at this point completely untested, that such a typing strategy might be integrated with remote object batching strategy, as hinted at above, in a way which is able to allow robust distributed applications with clear semantics.

4.3.2.   Typing for remote update

Update causes a final problem in the context of a persistent language operating over data available from the internet. There is one easy solution, which is to claim that traditional query languages are essentially declarative, and any such language used to query the internet should be a declarative subset of the general persistent system. While this solves the problem of programs specifying updates to remote data that they do not own, we prefer if possible to handle the problem without losing the ability to update data that is owned locally.

There are two problems with this model in the context as described so far. The first is that multiple file representations of objects that contain mutable locations may potentially lead to inconsistent views of a set of data. The second is that unprotected remote update is not generally acceptable in the context of the internet, and some protection is required to prevent this from being specified within computations.

A location type is used to control the problem of generalised network update. The Hippo language has an explicit type constructor, *loc*(*t*), which must be used to denote a mutable location. Furthermore, the system contains a subtyping rule that states for any type *t*, *loc*(*t*) is a subtype of that type. This is a fairly standard subtyping arrangement where mutability is explicitly typed (see for example [Car89]).

A corollory of such typing is that, for any type *t* which contains location types, there exists another type *s* which does not contain location types, and of which *t* is a subtype. A denotation typed as *s* has the operational ability to dereference any locations contained in any value typed at *t*; however, the same value typed as *s* does not allow any update operation to its locations. We refer to *s* as the immutable supertype of *t*.

When remote data is typed at an *intern* command, the dynamic test for success is that the statically asserted type is an immutable supertype of the type associated with the physical data. This gives that static knowledge that it is impossible to specify a well-typed computation that causes an update to occur to a value which is not locally resident.

This mechanism does not solve the generalised problem of cache coherency over the programming system, although it may make it considerably more tractable. In particular a fundamental attribute of the subtyped location model is that values which are not typed as locations may nonetheless change by side-effect, and this is the required semantics in this case. Two possibilities are under investigation, details of which are beyond the scope of this paper; one is to build a re-fetch model into the *refR* type scheme, and the other is to impose a causal consistency model over the networked persistent processes. The latter of these, whilst obviously more complex, may turn out to fit neatly with other aspects of persistent Web computation that are not discussed here [CS98b].

5. Conclusions and future work

This paper gives only an introduction to the key concepts used in the Hippo language in terms of its intention to integrate an orthogonally persistent programming system with the World-Wide Web. The overall task is greater than those problems and outline solutions presented here, and further information about the project is available from the Web site[3] and other recent publications [CS98a, CS98b]. It should be stressed that this is a position paper from an early stage of the project, and whilst the ideas contained in this paper are believed to be robust, they are not immune to change.

The methodology underlying the project is strongly directed towards implementing robust programming systems that can be used to program Web-based applications, to therefore achieve maximum feedback as to useful design. To this purpose programming systems are available to researchers who might be interested in writing applications in the domain; please contact the authors for details.

---

[3] http://www.hippo.org.uk/

6. Acknowledgements

Richard Connor is supported by an EPSRC Advanced Research Fellowship B/94/AF/1921, and Keith Sibson by an EPSRC studentship. Some of the work described is based on earlier work supported by EPSRC grant GR/K79222. Paolo Manghi holds a Marie Curie TMR award.

We would also particularly and sincerely like to thank an anonymous referee who made many helpful comments on unclear areas and unspoken assumptions in the original text.

7. References

[ABC+83] Atkinson, M.P., Bailey, P.J., Chisholm, K.J., Cockshott, W.P. & Morrison, R. "An Approach to Persistent Programming". Computer Journal 26, 4 (1983) pp 360-365.

[ACO85] Albano, A., Cardelli, L. & Orsini, R. "Galileo: a Strongly Typed, Interactive Conceptual Language" ACM Transactions on Database Systems 10, 2 (1985) pp 230-260.

[ACP+91] Martín Abadi, Luca Cardelli, Benjamin C. Pierce, and Gordon D. Plotkin. "Dynamic typing in a statically-typed language" ACM Transactions on Programming Languages and Systems, 13(2):237-268, April 1991

[ACP+95] Martín Abadi, Luca Cardelli, Benjamin C. Pierce, and Didier Rémy "Dynamic typing in polymorphic languages" Journal of Functional Programming, 5(1):111-130, January 1995

[AJDS97] M.P. Atkinson, M. Jordan, L. Daynès and S. Spence "Design Issues for Persistent Java: a Type-Safe, Object-Oriented, Orthogonally Persistent System" *in Persistent Object Systems - Principles and Practice*, Connor and Nettles (Eds), Morgan Kaufmann, 1997 pp 33-47.

[AM95] M.P Atkinson and R Morrison *Orthogonally Persistent Object Systems* VLDB Journal 4, 3 pp 319 - 401

[Atk78] Atkinson, M.P. "Programming Languages and Databases". In Proc. 4th IEEE International Conference on Very Large Databases (1978) pp 408-419.

[Car85] Cardelli, L. "Amber". AT&T Bell Labs, Murray Hill Technical Report AT7T (1985).

[Car89] L. Cardelli "Typeful Programming" DEC SRC Technical Report No. 45 (May 1989)

[CDG+89] Luca Cardelli, James Donahue, Lucille Glassman, Mick Jordan, Bill Kalsow, and Greg Nelson. Modula-3 report (revised). Research Report 52, Digital Equipment Corporation Systems Research Center, 1989.

[Con90] Richard Connor "Types and Polymorphism in Persistent Programming Systems" PhD Thesis, University of St Andrews, 1990.

[CS98a] Richard Connor and Keith Sibson "Paradigms for Global Computation - an Overview of the Hippo Project" Proc. Workshop on Internet Programming Languages, in conjunction with the IEEE Computer Society International Conference on Computer Languages 1998 (to appear).

[CS98b] Richard Connor and Keith Sibson "HCL - the Hippo Core Langauge"Proc. Workshop on Internet Programming Languages, in conjunction with the IEEE

Computer Society International Conference on Computer Languages 1998 (to appear).

[CS98c]   Richard Connor and Fabio Simeoni "SSSub – a subtyping system for abstracting over semi-structured data." Submitted for publication.

[GN98]   Garthwaite A. and Nettles S. "Transactions for Java" in Proc. 1998 International Conference of Programming Lanuages, May 1998 pp 16-27.

[Hip98]   The Hippo Project Homepage, http://www.hippo.org.uk/

[KCC+92]   Kirby G.N.C., Connor R.C.H., Cutts Q.I., Dearle A., Farkas A. & Morrison R. "Persistent Hyper-Programs" Proc. 5th International Workshop on Persistent Object Systems, San Miniato, Italy, September 1992, in **Persistent Object Systems, San Miniato 1992**, Springer-Verlag, pp 86 - 106.

[MBC+89]   Morrison, R., Brown, A.L., Connor, R.C.H. & Dearle, A. "The Napier88 Reference Manual". University of St Andrews Technical Report PPRR-77-89 (1989).

[MW98]   Metrowerks Codewarrior, http://www.metrowerks.com/

[NAM98]   Nestorov S., Abiteboul S. and Motwani R Extracting Schema from Semistructured Data Proc SIGMOD'98, SIGMOD Record 27, 2, June 1998 pp 295 - 306

[NUW+97]   Nestorov S., Ullman J., Wiener J and Chawathe S. Representative Objects: Concise Representations of Semistructured, Hierarchical Data Proc ICDE, Birmingham, UK 1997, pp 79 - 90

[POS7]   *Persistent Object Systems, Tarascon 1994* Atkinson M., Maier D. and Benzaken V. (Eds), Springer-Verlag Workshops in Computer Science, 1995.

[POS8]   *Persistent Object Systems - Principles and Practice*, Connor R. and Nettles S. (Eds), Morgan Kaufmann, 1997

[PS88]   "PS-algol Reference Manual, 4th edition". Universities of Glasgow and St Andrews Technical Report PPRR-12-88 (1988).

[RDF]   http://www.w3c.org/RDF/

[SCW85]   Schaffert, C., Cooper, T. & Wilpot, C. "Trellis Object-Based Environment Language Reference Manual". DEC Technical Report 372 (1985).

[Tha86]   Thatte, S.M. "Persistent Memory: A Storage Architecture for Object Oriented Database Systems". In Proc. ACM/IEEE International Workshop on Object-Oriented Database Systems, Pacific Grove, California (1986) pp 148-159.

[W3C]   http://www.w3c.org/

Interactive Query and Search in Semistructured Databases*

Roy Goldman, Jennifer Widom

Stanford University
{royg,widom}@cs.stanford.edu
www-db.stanford.edu

Abstract. Semistructured graph-based databases have been proposed as well-suited stores for World-Wide Web data. Yet so far, languages for querying such data are too complex for casual Web users. Further, proposed query approaches do not take advantage of the interactive nature of typical Web sessions—users are proficient at iteratively refining their Web explorations. In this paper we propose a new model for interactively querying and searching semistructured databases. Users can begin with a simple keyword search, dynamically browse the structure of the result, and then submit further refining queries. Enabling this model exposes new requirements of a semistructured database management system that are not apparent under traditional database uses. We demonstrate the importance of efficient keyword search, structural summaries of query results, and support for inverse pointers. We also describe some preliminary solutions to these technical issues.

1 Introduction

Querying the Web has understandably gathered much attention from both research and industry. For searching the entire Web, search engines are a well-proven, successful technology [Dig97,Ink96]. Search engines assume little about the semantics of a document, which works well for the conglomeration of disparate data sources that make up the Web. But for searching within a single Web site, a search engine may be too blunt a tool. Large Web sites, with thousands of pages, are attracting millions of users. The ESPN Sports site (espn.com), for example, has over 90,000 pages [Sta96] and several million page views a day [Sta97]. As large as some sites may be, they are fundamentally different from the Web as a whole since a single site usually has a controlled point of administration. Thus, it becomes possible to consistently assign and expose the site's semantic data relationships and thereby enable more expressive searches.

Consider any of the large commercial news Web sites, such as CNN (cnn.com), ABC News (abcnews.com), etc. Currently, users have very limited querying ability over the large amounts of data at these sites. A user can browse the hard-coded menu system, examine a hand-made subject index, or use a keyword-based

---

* This work was supported by the Air Force Rome Laboratories and DARPA under Contracts F30602-95-C-0119 and F30602-96-1-031.

search engine. When looking for specific data, traversing the menus may be far too time consuming, and of course a hand-made subject index will be of limited scope. Finally, while a keyword search engine may help locate relevant data, it doesn't take advantage of the conceptual data relationships known and maintained at the site. For example, at any such Web site today there is no convenient way to find:

- All photos of Bill Clinton in 1997
- All articles about snow written during the summer
- All basketball teams that won last night by more than 10 points

Such queries become possible if most or all of the site's data is stored in a database system. Recently, researchers have proposed *semistructured* data models, databases, and languages for modeling, storing, and querying World-Wide Web data [AQM+97,BDHS96,BDS95,FFLS97,MAG+97]. Such proposals argue that a graph-based semistructured database, without the requirement of an explicit schema, is better suited than traditional database systems for storing the varied, dynamic data of the Web. So far, however, there has been little discussion of who will query such data and what typical queries will look like. Given the domain, we believe that a large and important group of clients will be casual Web users, who will want to pose interesting queries over a site's data.

How would a typical Web user pose such queries? Asking casual users to type a query in any database language is unrealistic. It is possible to handle certain queries by having users fill in hard-coded forms, but this approach by nature limits query flexibility. Our previous work on *DataGuides* [GW97] has proposed an interactive query tool that presents a dynamic structural summary of semistructured data and allows users to specify queries "by example." (*Pesto* [CHMW96] and *QBE* [Zlo77], designed for object-relational and relational databases, respectively, enable users to specify queries in a similar manner.) A DataGuide summarizes all paths through a database, starting from its root. While such dynamic summaries are an important basic technology for several reasons [GW97], presenting the user with a complete summary of paths may still force him to explore much unnecessary database structure.

In this paper, targeting casual users, our strategy is to model and exploit two key techniques that Web users are intimately familiar with:

1. specifying a simple query to begin a search, usually with keywords
2. further exploring and refining the results

For the first technique, we want to support very simple queries that help "focus" the user on relevant data. The many search engines on the Web have shown that keyword search is an easy and effective technique for beginning a search. To enable the second technique, we want to expose and summarize the structure of the database "surrounding" any query result. To do this, we dynamically build and present a DataGuide that summarizes paths not from the database root, but instead from the objects returned in the query result. A user can then repeat

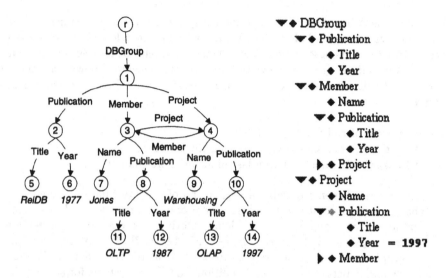

Fig. 1. A sample OEM database and its Java DataGuide

the process by submitting a query from this "focused" DataGuide or specifying additional keywords, ultimately locating the desired results.

Our discussions are in the context of the *Lore* project [MAG+97], which uses the *OEM* graph-based data model [PGMW95] and the *Lorel* query language [AQM+97]. Our results are applicable to other similar graph-based data models, as well as the emerging XML standard for defining the semantic structure of Web documents [Con97].

In the rest of the paper, we first provide background and context in Section 2. In Section 3, we present a simple motivating example to illustrate why new functionality is needed in a semistructured database system to support interactive query and search. Our session model is described in Section 4, followed by three sections covering the new required technology:

- Keyword search (Section 5): Efficient data structures and indexing techniques are needed for quickly finding objects that match keyword search criteria. While we may borrow heavily from well-proven information retrieval (IR) technology, the new context of a graph database is sufficiently different from a simple set of documents to warrant investigation.
- DataGuide enhancements (Section 6): Computing a DataGuide over each query result can be very expensive, so we have developed new algorithms for computing and presenting DataGuides piecewise, computing more on demand.
- Inverse pointers (Section 7): To fully expose the structural context of a query result, it is crucial to exploit inverse pointers when creating the DataGuide for the result, browsing the data, and submitting refining queries. While support for inverse pointers may seem straightforward, the major

proposed models for semistructured data are based on directed graphs, and inverse pointers have not been considered in the proposed query languages [AQM+97,BDHS96,FFLS97].

2 Background

To set the stage for the rest of the paper, we briefly describe the OEM data model, introduce the Lorel query language, and summarize DataGuides. In OEM, each object contains an object identifier (oid) and a value. A value may be atomic or complex. Atomic values may be integers, reals, strings, images, or any other indivisible data. A complex OEM value is a collection of OEM subobjects, each linked to the parent via a descriptive textual label. An OEM database can be thought of as a rooted, directed graph. The left side of Figure 1 is a tiny fictional portion of an OEM database describing a research group, rooted at object *r*.

The Lorel query language, derived from OQL [Cat94], evaluates queries based on *path expressions* describing traversals through the database. Special edges coming from the root are designated as *names*, which serve as entry points into the database. In Figure 1, DBGroup is the only name. As a very simple example, the Lorel query "Select DBGroup.Member.Publication.Title" returns a set containing object 11, with value "OLTP." More specifically, when a query returns a result, a new named Answer object is created in the database, and all objects in the result are made children of the Answer.[1] The Answer edge is available as a name for successive queries.

A DataGuide is a dynamic structural summary of an OEM database. It is an OEM object *G* that summarizes the OEM database (object) *D*, such that every distinct label path from the root of *D* appears exactly once as a path from the root of *G*. Further, every path from the root of *G* corresponds to a path that exists in *D*. We have carefully chosen Figure 1 to be a DataGuide of itself (ignoring atomic values). For any given sequence of labels, there is only one corresponding path in the database. (In a real database, there may be many Member objects under DBGroup, several Publication objects per Project, etc.) Through a Web-accessible Java interface, a DataGuide is presented as a hierarchical structure, and a user can interactively explore it. The right side of Figure 1 shows the Java DataGuide for our sample database. Clicking on an arrow expands or collapses complex objects. We have expanded most of the links, but because of the cycle we have not expanded the deepest Project or Member arrows.

Users can also specify queries directly from the Java DataGuide with two simple steps: 1) selecting paths for the query result, and 2) adding filtering conditions. Each diamond in the DataGuide corresponds to a label path through

---

[1] Identifying labels are assigned to the edges connecting the Answer object to each query result object, based on the last edge traversed to reach the result object during query evaluation. In this example, the label is Title. Also, Lorel queries may create more complicated object structures as query results, but for simplicity we do not consider such queries in this paper; our work can easily be generalized.

the database. By clicking on a diamond, a user can specify a condition for the path or select the path for the query result. Filtering conditions are rendered next to the label, and the diamonds for selected paths are highlighted. The Java DataGuide in Figure 1 shows the query to select all project publications from 1997. The DataGuide generates Lorel queries, which are sent to the Lore server to be evaluated. In our Web user interface, we format the query results hierarchically in HTML for easy browsing.

3 Motivating Example

In this section we trace a motivating example, using the sample database presented in Figure 1. Suppose a user wishes to find all publications from 1997, a seemingly simple query. (In the previous section, our sample query only found publications of projects.) It is possible to write a Lorel query to find this result, but a casual user will not want to enter a textual Lorel query. This example also illustrates some limitations of using the DataGuide to locate information. Even in this simple case, there are numerous paths to all of the publications; in a larger database the situation may be much worse. In short, while the DataGuide does a good job of summarizing paths from the root, a user may be interested in certain data independent of the particular topology of a database.

In this situation, a typical Web user would be comfortable entering keywords: "Publication," "1997," or both. Suppose for now the user types "Publication" to get started. (We will address the case where the user types "1997" momentarily, and we discuss the issue of multiple keywords in Section 5.) If the system generates a collection of all Publication objects, the answer is {2, 8, 10}, identified by the name Answer. While this initial result has helped focus our search, we really only wanted the Publications in 1997. One approach would be to browse all of the objects in the result, but again in a larger database this may be difficult. Rather, we dynamically generate a DataGuide over the answer, as shown in Figure 2. Notice now that even though Title and Year objects were reachable along numerous paths in the original DataGuide, they are consolidated in Figure 2. As shown in the Java DataGuide, the user can mark Publication for selection and enter a filtering condition for Year to retrieve all 1997 publications. Getting the same result in the original DataGuide would have required three selection/filtering condition pairs, one for each possible path to a Publication.

The above scenario motivates the need for efficient keyword search and efficient DataGuide creation over query results. Next, we show how these features essentially force a system to support inverse pointers as well. Suppose the user had typed "1997" rather than "Publication." This time, the answer in our sample database is the singleton set {14}, and the DataGuide over the result is empty since the result is just an atomic object. This example illustrates that what the user needs to see in general is the area "surrounding" the result objects, not just their subobject structure as encapsulated by the DataGuide. Given a set of objects, we can consider inverse pointers to present the "surrounding area" to the user; for example, we can give context to a specific year object by showing that it

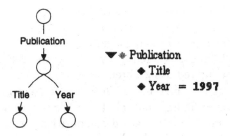

Fig. 2. DataGuide constructed over result of finding all publications

is the child of a publication object. By exploring both child and parent pointers of objects in a query result, we can create a more descriptive DataGuide.

4   Query and Search Session Model

We define a Lore *session* over an initial database D_0, with root r and initial Data-Guide $G_0(r)$, as a sequence of *queries* $q_1, q_2, ... q_n$. A query can be a "by example" DataGuide query, a list of keywords, or, for advanced users, an arbitrary Lorel query. The objects returned by each query q_i are accessible via a complex object a_i with name *Answer$_i$*. After each query, we generate and present a DataGuide $G_i(a_i)$ over the result, and users can also browse the objects in each query result. Perhaps counterintuitive to the notion of narrowing a search, we do not restrict the database after each query. In fact, the database D will grow monotonically after each query q_i. After q_i, $D_i = D_{i-1} \cup a_i$. Essentially, each DataGuide helps focus the user's next query without restricting the available data. In the following three sections, we discuss three technologies that enable efficient realization of this model of interaction.

5   Keyword Search

In the IR arena, a keyword search typically returns a ranked list of documents containing the specified keywords. In a semistructured database, pertinent information is found both in atomic values and in labels on edges. Thus, it makes sense to identify both atomic objects matching the specified word(s) and objects with matching incoming labels. For example, if a user enters "Publication," we would like to return all objects pointed to by a "Publication" edge, along with all atomic objects with the word "Publication" in their data. This approach is similar in spirit to the way keyword searches are handled by Yahoo! (yahoo.com). There, search results contain both the *category* and *site* matches for the specified keywords.

While a keyword search over values and labels is expressible as a query in Lorel (and also in *UnQl* [BDHS96]), the issue of how to efficiently execute this particular type of query has not been addressed. In Lore, we have built two inverted-list indexes to handle this type of query. The first index maps words to atomic objects containing those words, with some limited IR capabilities such as *and*, *or*, *near*, etc. The second index maps words to edges with matching labels. Our keyword search indexes currently range over the entire database, though query results can be filtered using Lorel.

An interesting issue is how to handle multiple keywords. It is limiting to restrict our searches to finding multiple keywords within a single OEM object or label, since our model encourages decomposition into many small objects. Hence, we would like to efficiently identify objects and/or edges that contain the specified keywords and are also near each other in terms of link distance. Further, we must decide how to group or rank the results of a keyword search, an essential aspect of any search engine that may return large answer sets. These issues are discussed in detail in [GSVGM98]: we formalize the notion of link distance and ranking, and we introduce specialized indexes to speed up distance computations.

6   DataGuide Enhancements

As described in the motivating example, we wish to build DataGuides over query results. For this section, let us ignore the issue of inverse pointers. As shown in [GW97], computing a DataGuide can be expensive: the worst case running time is exponential in the size of the database, and for a large database even linear running time would be too slow for an interactive session. We thus introduce two techniques to improve the running time.

First, we can exploit certain auxiliary data structures that are built to provide incremental DataGuide maintenance [GW97]. These structures guarantee that we never need to recompute a "sub-DataGuide" that has previously been constructed. In Figure 1, suppose a user searches for all "Projects," a query that would return the singleton set {4}. In this case, the DataGuide over {4} is the same as the sub-DataGuide reachable along DBGroup.Project in the original DataGuide. We can dynamically determine this fact with a single hash table lookup, and no additional computation is needed.

Second, we observe that an interactive user will rarely need to explore the entire DataGuide. Our experience shows that even in the initial DataGuide, users rarely explore more than a few levels. Most likely, after a reasonable "focusing" query, users will want to browse the structure of objects near the objects in the query result. Hence, we have modified the original depth-first DataGuide construction algorithm to instead work breadth-first, and we have changed the algorithm to build the DataGuide "lazily," i.e., a piece at a time. From the user's perspective, the difference is transparent except with respect to speed. When a user clicks on an arrow for a region that hasn't yet been computed, behind the scenes we send a request to Lore to generate and return more of the DataGuide. Our maintenance structures make it easy to interrupt DataGuide computation and continue later with no redundant work.

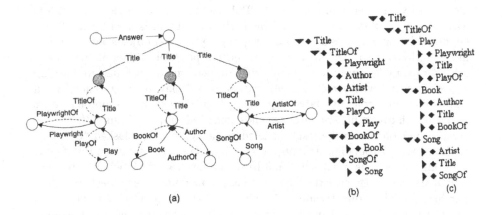

Fig. 3. An OEM query result and two potential DataGuides

7 Inverse Pointers

Directed graphs are a popular choice for modeling semistructured data, and the proposed query languages are closely tied to this model. While powerful regular expressions have been proposed for traversing forward links, essentially no language support has been given to the problem of directly traversing inverse pointers. As our motivating example demonstrates, a parent may be just as important as a child for locating relevant data.

Adding inverse pointers affects many levels of a semistructured database system, including object storage, creation of DataGuides (or any other summarizing technique), query language design, and query execution. Physically, inverse pointers may be clustered with each object's data or stored in a separate index. Logically, we try to make access to inverse pointers as seamless as possible: for an object O with an incoming label "X" from another object P, we conceptually make P a child of O via the label "XOf." With this approach, inverse edges can be treated for the most part as additional forward edges. Next, we focus on how exposing inverse pointers affects DataGuides, graph query languages, and query execution. (Note that even if inverse pointers are not added to the model or query language, they can still be very useful for "bottom-up" query processing, as described in [MW97].)

DataGuide Creation We wish to extend DataGuides to summarize a database in all directions, rather than only by following forward links. If the "Of" links described above are simply added to the database graph, then we need not even modify our DataGuide algorithms. Unfortunately, this approach can yield some unintuitive results. In OEM and most graph-based database models, objects are identified by their incoming labels. A "Publication," for example, is an object with an incoming Publication edge. This basic assumption is used by the Data-Guide, which summarizes a database by grouping together objects with identical incoming labels. An "Of" link, however, does a poor job of identifying an object. For example, given an object O with an incoming TitleOf link, we have no way of knowing whether O is a publication, book, play, or song. Therefore, a DataGuide may group unrelated objects together. For example, suppose a user's initial search over a library database finds some Title objects. Figure 3(a) shows three atomic objects in the result (shaded in the figure), with dashed "Of" links to show their surrounding structure. Figure 3(b) shows the standard DataGuide over this Answer. The problems with 3(b) should be clear: the labels shown under TitleOf are confusing, since the algorithm has grouped unrelated objects together. Further, the labels directly under TitleOf do not clearly indicate that our result includes titles of books, plays, and songs. To address the problem, we have modified the DataGuide algorithm slightly to further decompose all objects reachable along an "Of" link based on the non-"Of" links to those objects. Figure 3(c) shows the more intuitive result, which we refer to as a *Panoramic DataGuide*. Of course, since OEM databases can have arbitrary labels and topologies, we have no guarantees that a Panoramic DataGuide will be the ideal summary; still, in practice it seems appropriate for many OEM databases. Note that adding inverse pointers to DataGuide creation adds many more edges and objects than in the original DataGuide, making our new support for "lazy" DataGuides (Seciton 6) even more important.

Query Language & Execution Just as users can specify queries "by example" with the original DataGuide, we would like to allow users to specify queries with Panoramic DataGuides as well. Suppose in Figure 3(c) a user selects Author to find the authors of all books having titles in the initial result. In Lorel, which currently does not support direct access to inverse pointers, the generated query is:

```
Select A
From Answer.Title T1, #.Book B, B.Title T2, B.Author A
Where T1 = T2
```

This query essentially performs a join between the titles in our answer and all book titles in the entire database, returning the authors of each such book. The # is a "wildcard" representing any path, and because of this wildcard a naive execution strategy could be very expensive. Efficient execution based on forward pointers alone depends on having an index that quickly returns all Book objects in the database, and we do support such an index in Lore. If we store inverse pointers in the system, we might be able to train the optimizer to exploit them for such queries [MW97]; rather than finding all Book objects and performing the join, the system could simply follow inverse and then forward pointers from each Title in the initial result. However, it could be difficult to recognize and optimize these cases. Another approach is to allow inverse links to be specified directly in path expressions in the language.

As an alternative to storing inverse pointers, the query processor could "remember" the (forward) path traversed to evaluate a query. The user could then explore this path to see some of the result's context. Lore can in fact provide such a *matched path* for each query result. However, when an execution strategy does not involve navigating paths from the root, generating a matched path from the root would drastically increase query execution time. Further, a matched path still does not allow a user to arbitrarily explore the database after a query result.

8 Implementation Status

Our interactive query and search model, along with the necessary supporting features discussed in this paper, are under development within the Lore project. We keep our online Lore demo up-to-date, reflecting new designs as they are completed. Please visit www-db.stanford.edu/lore.

References

[AQM+97]   S. Abiteboul, D. Quass, J. McHugh, J. Widom, and J. Wiener. The Lorel query language for semistructured data. *International Journal on Digital Libraries*, 1(1):68–88, April 1997.

[BDHS96]   P. Buneman, S. Davidson, G. Hillebrand, and D. Suciu. A query language and optimization techniques for unstructured data. In *Proceedings of the ACM SIGMOD International Conference on Management of Data*, pages 505–516, Montreal, Canada, June 1996.

[BDS95]   P. Buneman, S. Davidson, and D. Suciu. Programming constructs for unstructured data. In *Proceedings of the 1995 International Workshop on Database Programming Languages (DBPL)*, 1995.

[Cat94]   R.G.G. Cattell. *The Object Database Standard: ODMG-93*. Morgan Kaufmann, San Francisco, California, 1994.

[CHMW96]   M. Carey, L. Haas, V. Maganty, and J. Williams. Pesto: An integrated query/browser for object databases. In *Proceedings of the Twenty-Second International Conference on Very Large Data Bases*, pages 203–214, Bombay, India, August 1996.

[Con97]   World Wide Web Consortium. Extensible markup language (XML). http://www.w3.org/TR/WD-xml-lang-970331.html, December 1997. Proposed recommendation.

[Dig97]   Digital Equipment Corp. About AltaVista: our technology. http:// altavista.digital.com/av/content/ about_our_technology.htm, 1997.

[FFLS97]   M. Fernandez, D. Florescu, A. Levy, and D. Suciu. A query language for a Web-site management system. *SIGMOD Record*, 26(3):4–11, September 1997.

[GSVGM98]   R. Goldman, N. Shivakumar, S. Venkatasubramanian, and H. Garcia-Molina. Proximity search in databases. In *Proceedings of the Twenty-Fourth International Conference on Very Large Data Bases*, New York, New York, 1998.

[GW97]   R. Goldman and J. Widom. DataGuides: Enabling query formulation and optimization in semistructured databases. In *Proceedings of the Twenty-Third International Conference on Very Large Data Bases*, pages 436–445, Athens, Greece, August 1997.

[Ink96]   Inktomi Corp.   The technology behind HotBot.   http:// www.inktomi.com/Tech/CoupClustWhitePap.html, 1996. White paper.

[MAG⁺97]   J. McHugh, S. Abiteboul, R. Goldman, D. Quass, and J. Widom. Lore: A database management system for semistructured data. *SIGMOD Record*, 26(3):54–66, September 1997.

[MW97]   J. McHugh and J. Widom. Query optimization for semistructured data. Technical report, Database Group, Stanford University, November 1997. Available at URL http://www-db.stanford.edu/pub/papers/qo.ps.

[PGMW95]   Y. Papakonstantinou, H. Garcia-Molina, and J. Widom. Object exchange across heterogeneous information sources. In *Proceedings of the Eleventh International Conference on Data Engineering*, pages 251–260, Taipei, Taiwan, March 1995.

[Sta96]   Starwave Corp.   About ESPN.   http://www.starwave.com/starwave/ about.espn.html, 1996.

[Sta97]   Starwave Corp.   ESPN SportsZone surpasses 2 billion page views. http://www.starwave.com/ starwave/releases.sz.billion.html, December 1997. Press release.

[Zlo77]   M. Zloof. Query by example. *IBM Systems Journal*, 16(4):324–343, 1977.

Bringing Database Functionality to the WWW

David Konopnicki and Oded Shmueli

Computer Science Department
Technion, Haifa, 32000, Israel
{konop,oshmu}@cs.technion.ac.il

Abstract. Database Management Systems excel at managing large quantities of data, primarily enterprise data. The WWW is a huge heterogeneous distributed database. To support advanced, robust and reliable applications, such as efficient and powerful querying, groupware and electronic commerce, database functionalities need be added to the WWW.

A major difficulty is that database techniques were traditionally targeted at a single enterprise environment, providing a centralized control over data and meta-data, statistics for query processing and the ability to utilize monolithic mechanisms for concurrency control, replication and recovery.

Previously, we have defined and implemented a query language (W3QL) and a query system for the WWW (W3QS). We dealt with some of the typical problems posed by data management on the WWW: the diversity of data types, the active components (online forms) and the difficulty in defining an adequate data model.

In this work we introduce new mechanisms and concepts in order to add database functionalities to the WWW. Namely, a useful abstract model and a blue print of a query language for the WWW, new research directions concerning WWW query processing and the concept of "data stability".

1 Introduction

Database Management Systems excel at managing large quantities of data, primarily enterprise data. The WWW is a huge heterogeneous distributed database. To support advanced, robust and reliable applications, such as efficient and powerful querying, groupware and electronic commerce, database functionalities need be added to the WWW.

A major difficulty is that database techniques were traditionally targeted at a single enterprise environment, providing a centralized control over data and meta-data, statistics for query processing and the ability to utilize monolithic mechanisms for concurrency control, replication and recovery.

We divide the timeline of the WWW data organization development into three phases:

1. At its beginning, WWW data was almost totally semantically opaque for automatic analysis. This was due to the lack of schema and semantic tagging. In this framework, we have defined and implemented a query language (W3QL) and a query system for the WWW (W3QS) [21]. We dealt with some of the typical problems posed by data management on the WWW: the diversity of data types, the active components (online forms) and the difficulty in defining an adequate data model.

   Since the WWW is semantics free, the query language relies on the user to specify the syntactic properties of the data he/she is interested in, such as its placement within pages or its hypertext structure.

2. Currently, the WWW moves into a new era. XML [7] and several metadata standards promise a semantically richer WWW. Systems that generate WWW sites automatically (e.g. Araneus [5] or Strudel [13]) will allow the development of sites that comply with a database-like schema. The mechanisms and concepts introduced in this article are useful in this framework. In particular, the idea of embedding any WWW data type into semantically rich objects, and a data model in which the WWW organization is captured at several levels of abstraction, including sites and intra-page objects.

   At this phase, a query language can utilize the semantic tags found in WWW pages. However, due to the lack of standardization (one can define arbitrary tags) some semantics must still be encoded in the query.

3. In the future, the WWW will be organized using universal dictionaries of terms and notions, called ontologies [12]. In this framework, the challenge will be the integration of services, i.e. being able to automatically mix and match distributed services in order to provide more complex services.

This work mainly addresses issues within phase 2 above. We introduce new mechanisms and concepts that add database functionalities to the WWW. Namely, a useful abstract model and a blue print of a query language for the WWW (based on the object-oriented paradigm), new research directions concerning WWW query processing and the concept of "data stability".

Due to space limitation, we only reference relevant related works. Query languages for hypertext appear in [10, 6, 28], and for text files in [1, 4], WWW query languages that use graphs or regular expressions are described in [22, 27]. WebLog [23] is a query language based on Datalog. Kogan et. al. [20] introduce semantic intra-page objects and a language for querying them. Theoretical models of the WWW have been introduced in [2, 24]. Mendelzon et. al. [24] consider the issue of querying the WWW as it changes over time. Languages for automatic creation of WWW sites are introduced in [5] and [13].

This article is organized as follows. In Section 2, we describe a new abstract data model of the WWW based on the object-oriented paradigm and hierarchical graphs and we present the requirements for a standard WWW query language. In Section 3, we introduce our approach to WWW query optimization. Section 4 introduces the concept of data stability in WWW queries. Section 5 presents conclusions.

2 An Abstract Data Model

2.1 Data Types

Traditional database systems deal with a relatively small set of types such as integer, float and string. These types may be used to construct new types such as classes in object-oriented databases or abstract data types in object-relational databases. However, the set of types in use, together with the operators and the functions used to manage them, are known to the DBMS. This is not the case in the WWW. The WWW accessible data items are objects whose types are described using the MIME [18] standard. New types are continuously being introduced and a WWW query processor may encounter new types during query processing. Browsers use extension mechanisms such as Netscape's Plug-Ins [29], Microsoft's ActiveX controls [26] or Java [19] to handle new data types. This avalanche of types presents a problem for query languages which handle WWW data, that need be able to state *content conditions* (i.e. conditions on the content of the accessible data items). Therefore, most existing systems [27, 33, 3] are restricted to HTML files.

W3QL has a more general approach (influenced by the Harvest system [17]). W3QL treats content conditions as *execution directives*, i.e. as specifying external programs to be executed. Content conditions are defined by specifying programs that perform file content analysis. For example, a standard W3QS program, called **PERLCOND**, is used to evaluate Boolean expressions, which are similar to SQL's where-clause conditions, on HTML, LATEX and Postscript files. Using **PERLCOND**, a user can select WWW nodes that satisfy certain conditions. For example, the condition **node.format eq "Latex" && node.author eq "A. Einstein"** selects LATEX files whose author is "A. Einstein". The node-content query language may be considered as an *extension* of W3QL for specific file formats. The user may construct and use such extensions for new data formats.

The W3QL approach raises several technical problems:

- **Generality:** W3QL allows the integration of analysis program extensions to the query language. However, if, for example, one analysis program is capable of extracting the title tag from a HTML file, while another analysis program extracts titles of PDF files, there is no way to express a condition comparing these two titles. In general, W3QL does not provide a way to integrate the results of analysis done by different programs and use them in *the same* condition language.
- **Uniformity of conditions:** Allowing analysis programs to define their node-content query sub-language leads to inconsistencies. One program may choose to define "**file.title**" and another "**file.TITLE**". As new formats appear, the user will have to learn new extension languages and keep in mind the differences between them.
- **Analysis Program Installation:** In W3QS, condition programs must be installed as part of the system to enable invocation at query execution time. If a user defines a new data type and an analysis program for this type,

these cannot be automatically used by W3QS. Rather, they must be first installed by the W3QS administrator. Furthermore, if an unknown data type is encountered during query processing, the query processor will not be able to analyze it.

In general, a content condition language for the WWW should be *general*, *uniform* and *dynamic*. We introduce a mechanism that solves these problems, based on the MIME standard, the object-oriented paradigm and Java.

The WWW accessible data items are objects, whose type is conveyed using the MIME standard. Currently, these objects define only one method, "View", used by browsers for presentation. For a condition language, these objects should provide additional methods such as "Title", "Author" and "Length". Therefore, we associate each data type with an *analyzer*, i.e. a program that can analyze the files (of this type) and provide methods that can be used by the condition language. To assure uniformity, we utilize the *type/subtype* structure of MIME. In the MIME structure, the data types are organized in a tree of depth two. For example, subtypes of type text are text/html, text/plain etc.

Analyzers will be defined as (object-oriented) classes. Abstract classes will be defined for the data types and subtypes. Analyzers of a certain data subtype inherit their method prototypes from the abstract class defined for their type. For example, the abstract class for text will define common method prototypes for the text objects: Author(), Title() etc. Classes for subtypes of text, for example text/html, will add specific methods for the HTML format, for example Anchors(). Analyzers for HTML must implement these methods and may supply additional methods. The implementation of analyzers in Java will allow using a common, and safe, platform for condition languages. Furthermore, Java will allow a query processor to load and execute analyzer methods when a new type is encountered during query processing.

This approach seems promising and raises several theoretical and practical problems concerning query optimization. For example:

- In relational databases, query optimization involves a stage of evaluating the *selectivity* of conditions. In this stage, statistics are used to estimate the fraction of data items that satisfy a condition. Is it possible to extend these techniques to predict the selectivity of conditions involving analyzers?
- Is it possible to distribute the execution of analyzers over several sites? For example, if server s contains a huge postscript file, it is more efficient to ask s to run a postscript analyzer on the file and send the results of the analysis to the query processor (by using, for example, servlets [32]), rather than download the file (to the query processor site) and run the analyzer locally.
- Since analyzers for a specific data type form a core set of standard services, this set can be used by the query processor. There is a problem with analyzers that offer non-standard services. These new services must be somehow identified by the query processor.

To solve these problems, an analyzer class must be associated with a meta-class which provides information about it. For example, consider the analyzer for HTML files:

- The method **contain(s)** (that checks if a file contains the string **s**), may be associated with the "meta-method" **containSelectivity(s)**, that approximates the selectivity of the condition by checking the number of HTML documents containing **s** in AltaVista's Index.
- The **titleCost()** method, associated with the **title()** method, informs the query optimizer that (1) its cost is independent of the file length (since the title is always found in the HTML header) (2) it is better to execute it on the server side (if possible).
- A description of additional non-standard services.

It should be clear that the use of analyzers does not preclude semantics tagging "a la" XML. In fact, it should be easy to write analyzers for XML tagged files. Conversely, XML tags may be used to convey the services provided by analyzer classes.

Analyzer could use any distributed object standard, for example DCOM [25], Java [19] or CORBA [30]. However, Java has an advantage due to its ability to run code securely over different sites, enabling to distribute the development and execution of analyzers.

2.2 A Hierarchical Graph Model

We have formally defined a graph model of the WWW against which W3QL queries are posed [21]. This model captures the following characteristics of WWW data:

- **The information content:** The data model includes the information content and some meta-information data.
- **The hypertext structure:** In hypertext environments, the organization of documents conveys information. The data model reflects the graph structure of the hypertext in order to allow for the search of structural hypertext information.
- **The service providers:** A very powerful way to access WWW information is through service providers, by using HTML forms. The user should be able to automatically access the various services. Therefore, the data model includes HTML forms and the responses, sent by servers, to filled out forms.

The granularity of the model is WWW accessible files. However, during the development of W3QL, we have identified the need for a more detailed model in order to capture, in the query language, other facets of WWW accessible data. Having WWW pages as first-class citizens of the model is not enough. A query language must be able to deal with other constructs in a straightforward way:

- **Intra-page Information:** Most of the WWW accessible data is stored in *semi-structured files* i.e. pages containing formatting information such as \title{} in LaTeX or <TITLE></TITLE> in HTML. Since the syntax of such files complies, generally, with a grammar, their content may also be viewed as a graph, i.e. the parse tree.

With the development of the XML standard [7], that allows the use of SGML [34] on the WWW and the definition of semantic tagging, the analysis of intra-page information will become crucial. Therefore, a model of the WWW must explicitly capture the intra-page information and its structure so that these aspects may be queried.

- **Hypertext Structure:** As in W3QL, the model should capture WWW Pages and their hypertext organization (including forms).

- **Sites:** The term *WWW site* is used to refer to a set of pages belonging, in some way, to a common authority. Since this concept is very important in people's conceptualization of the organization of the WWW, a model of the WWW should capture the organization of pages into sites. Sites may, in turn, be organized in groups (*clusters*), for example, the cluster consisting of the set of some Israeli universities sites.

The resulting model is no longer a graph but a hierarchical structure as schematically depicted in Fig 1.

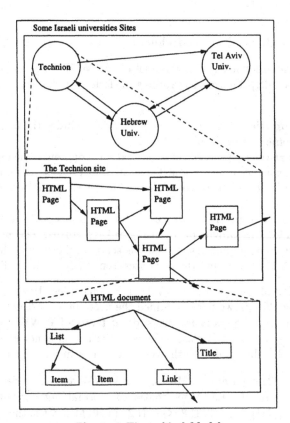

Fig. 1. A Hierarchical Model

Note that, while intra-page tags and WWW pages can be defined in an unequivocal way, sites and clusters are fuzzy notions. In particular, sites can be defined:

- Explicitly in the query. For example:
  - By a subquery, e.g. *define the IBM site as the set of all the pages accessible from the IBM home page up to depth 5.*
  - By a predicate, e.g. *define the IBM site as the set of all the pages whose URL contains the string* www.ibm.
  - Explicitly (by site managers), e.g. *define the IBM site as the set of all the pages referred to in the file* http://www.ibm.com/plan.html.
- Implicitly dictated in the query language semantics, by using some heuristics, e.g. *use the World-Wide Web yellow pages to find the home page of IBM, then collect all the pages accessible from the home page that are situated on the same server.*
- By some combination of explicit and implicit techniques.

The intra-page information may be analyzed differently depending on the analyzer used. Therefore, the hierarchical model is *not* fixed but is dynamically defined by (1) the analyzers used for the data types, (2) the definitions of sites and clusters. Therefore, we introduce a model consisting of two layers:

- The *basic level* layer is defined as for W3QL. This layer captures the aspects of the physical organization of the WWW. The main data types in this layer are WWW nodes and links.
- The *refined level* layer. This level refines the basic-level layer as a hierarchical graph of objects. The main data types in this layer are WWW sites, nodes and intra-page objects.

Since sites and intra-page objects do not *physically* exist in the WWW but are logically defined by the user (in the query) to provide the abstraction over which the query is formulated, the model is called the *virtual object hierarchical graph model*.

Note that systems that build well-organized sites, for example Araneus [5], could add to the site a description of the refined level organization (using ADM in the Araneus case) and free the user from the task of defining it in the query.

Most existing WWW query languages do not define such a hierarchical structure and therefore are limited to the granularity of a WWW page or to a fixed set of HTML constructs. Answering a hierarchical query, in which a query variable may correspond to a whole site, involves different algorithms than the traditional path regular expressions matching and subgraph isomorphism identification. Interesting issues to address are:

- Query containment and equivalence.
- Estimation of subqueries size (for query optimization).
- Query rewriting for optimization.
- Using of previous query results to optimize new queries.
- Query results organization and presentation.

The idea of a hierarchical graph data model was first introduced in the Hy+ [9] graph visualization system. The query language used in Hy+ is Graphlog [11]. However, our approach has several original components:

- In Hy+, the graphs and the hierarchy are fixed. In our model, they are dynamic and are defined by the query.
- Hy+ relies on several database back-end servers (supporting LDL, Coral etc.) for query optimization and evaluation, whereas we are interested in developing special algorithms tailored for the WWW.

An example of intra-page objects may be found in the OHTML model [20] in which a semi-structured object model (based on OEM [31]) is superimposed on top of HTML. This allows the definition of objects specifying the semantics of the data within WWW pages.

2.3   Towards a New WWW Query Language

We plan to extend W3QL in the following directions:

- Queries on the hierarchical WWW model. A query will have two main parts:
  - *Constraints*, used to define the virtual object hierarchical graph instance, and,
  - *Conditions*, used to select sets of objects from the instance.

  The query language will uniformly treat intra-page data items, WWW pages and WWW sites. While most of the existing query languages define *points-to* as the only relationship between data items, we will add a *sub-structure* relationship.
- Content conditions based on the concepts of objects and analyzers.
- Support for the various meta-data techniques. In databases, the semantics of the data is captured not only in the schema but also in extra documentation, local organization and local culture. In a global data facility such as the WWW, this is not the case. The problem of semantic tagging and meta-data on the WWW has been studied from the WWW's very beginning. Three different approaches have emerged:
  - **The meta-data approach** in which standard attributes (defined by committees) are used to characterize data sources [8].
  - **The semantic tagging approach** in which semantic tags are added to HTML based on two new standards XML [7] and RDF [35].
  - **The Ontology approach** in which the data semantics is defined using AI techniques [12].

  These approaches are complementary: meta-data tags are used to catalog files, semantic tagging is used to add structure and semantics to files' contents, and ontologies are used for automatic reasoning, information integration and translation.

  We do not intend to introduce new semantic tagging mechanisms, but we shall take into account the fact that a query system must support existing and emerging standards. Therefore, objects will support (i.e. evaluate) conditions based on the meta-data attributes defined in [8], for example TITLE, CREATOR, and semantic tagging will be accessible using intra-page analysis.

3 Query Optimization for Exploration Queries

Exploration queries are WWW queries, directed at a single site or multiple sites such that limited, or no, meta-information is available at the site level. Currently, most of the WWW fits this description. In order to study the optimization of exploration queries, we study the optimization of *graph queries*. *Graph queries* is a simple graph based query language. In this language, both the query and its target are graphs. The algorithms' definitions take into account two important facts about the WWW: (1) The dominant cost is that of communication, (2) The data graph is usually unknown prior to query evaluation. The consequences of these facts are that: (1) the query processor should minimize the communication needed to answer a query and (2) the query processor does not have complete knowledge of the topology of the data graph prior to query evaluation. Therefore, query evaluation involves a process of data graph *discovery*.

3.1 The Basic Approach

Consider first the basic problem of searching for a hypertext structure in an unknown set of WWW pages. We are given a query graph $G = (V, E)$ (corresponding to the hypertext structure searched for) and a data graph $G' = (V', E')$ (corresponding to the WWW). A partial mapping from V to $2^{V'}$, called the *starting point function* (SPF), is used to represent constraints on how the query graph must be mapped to the data graph. The query graph nodes on which the SPF is defined are called the *starting points* of the query graph. The solution of the graph query is the set of all mappings g that map G to some isomorphic subgraph of G' and agree with the starting point function, i.e. for a starting point v, $g(v) \in SPF(v)$. It should be clear that, since an exhaustive search of the WWW is impractical, not all graph queries solutions have *practically computable* solutions. We define the *practically computable graph queries* to be the queries in which, for every node v, the query graph contains a path from some starting point to v. We represent the query solution as a relation. For example, if $G = (V = \{1, 2, 3\}, E = \{(1, 2), (1, 3)\})$, $G' = (V' = \{a, b, c\}, E' = \{(a, b), (a, c)\})$ and the SPF is $f = \{1 \mapsto \{a\}\}$, the query solution is $S(1, 2, 3) = \{(a, b, c), (a, c, b), (a, b, b), (a, c, c)\}$.

Since our algorithms are tailored for the WWW, we encode the data graph as a set of tables, one for each data graph node. The single column table for node u, designated by $Target_u$, contains a tuple (v) for each edge (u, v) in E'. Such a table models a hypertext page and its hypertext links, and is called a *data graph table*. The query solution is built by operating on the data graph tables.

We have defined a general class of algorithms, called *progressive algorithms*, that solve graph queries by finding solutions for subgraphs of the query graph and which incrementally build a solution for the entire query graph. The central concept underlying progressive algorithms is the *capture* of query graph nodes. Let v be a node of the query graph. There are edges from v to the set of nodes $T(v)$. If we know that the solution for v, i.e. the nodes onto which v is mapped in the query solution, is contained in a given set, say *Sol*, we can use the tables

$Target_{v'}$ where $v' \in Sol$, to find a superset of the solution set for each node in $T(v)$. This superset is the same for all such nodes in $T(v)$: $\bigcup_{v' \in Sol} Target_{v'}$. This operation is called *capturing* v.

Capturing a node v leads to the creation of a table, called the *query graph table for* v, containing a superset of the query solutions for v and the nodes it points to. Joining the query graph tables for all the nodes of the query graph (and taking into account the SPF) leads to the solution of the query. Practically, there is no need to keep the query graph tables generated at each step but only the result of the join of the query graph tables of nodes that are captured thus far. This table is called the *temporary result table*.

Since the SPF defines a superset of the solution set for the starting points and, for every graph node v, there is a path from some starting point to v, a progressive algorithm can capture all the nodes of the query graph, one by one, beginning with the starting points.

3.2   Combinatorial Explosion

Although we are mostly concerned with reducing the communication cost, we should address some local processing problems we may encounter. The query processing techniques described above lead to a combinatorial explosion problem. Consider a node $n0$ in the query graph whose out-degree is 4 which points to $n1$, $n2$, $n3$ and $n4$. Suppose $n0$ is mapped by the SPF onto 10 data graph nodes, each of them with out-degree 100. The capture of $n0$ leads to the creation of a table that contains all the combinations of mapping the query graph nodes $n1$, $n2$, $n3$ and $n4$ to the data graph nodes, namely a table containing 10^9 tuples. Clearly, it is very difficult to deal with tables of such size. Fortunately, in most cases, it is possible to reduce the size of the created tables by using simple heuristic techniques.

- Query solutions are obtained by joining all the query graph tables. Therefore, when generating a new query graph table, it is necessary to insert a value a into column ni only if a appears in all the columns labeled ni in the query graph tables already generated (or if $a \in SPF(ni)$ when ni is a starting point). If the query graph is "sufficiently connected" the number of tuples in the query graph tables tends to be small.
- Let ni be a column in the query graph table we are about to generate. If ni appears in an already generated query graph table, we say that ni is *constrained*. Generally, at each step of the algorithm, several query graph nodes are candidates for capture. We can reduce the size of the query graph table generated by choosing to capture the query graph node that points to as few unconstrained nodes as possible.
- Generating a query graph table for a node v necessitates the calculation of the cartesian product of the solutions for all the query graph nodes to which v points. It is possible to implicitly encode the cartesian product in the query graph table (using "generalized tuples" in which a column value may consist of a set of nodes). The (tuple-based) cartesian product will be, partially or

totally, expanded only if necessary, e.g. when there is a join constraint on two nodes to which v points.

– Usually users do not just search for hypertext structures, but they also impose some content conditions on the WWW pages they search for. These conditions allow applying a selection condition on the WWW pages considered, and therefore lead to inserting less tuples in the query graph tables.

Similar to joins in relational databases, query graphs that are not sufficiently constrained may lead to very large intermediate results. However, for practical cases, it seems possible to keep the generated intermediate tables at manageable sizes.

3.3 Optimizing the Capture Ordering

Query graph nodes may be captured in different orders. The goal of query optimization is to find a capture order that minimizes the number of data graph tables consulted in order to build the solution. Since data graph tables correspond to hypertext pages, the query optimization process attempts to minimize the number of pages that are requested from the network. We have defined several algorithms for determining a capturing order. For example, if, at some point in the execution, the query processor has the choice between capturing different nodes, it may use the following rule of thumb: *Capture the node such that most of the nodes which point to it are already captured.* Since such a node must satisfy more constraints, the number of solutions for it tends to be small. This is an example for *rule based optimization.*

Cost-based optimization algorithms estimate the cost of capturing a query graph node by examining the topology of the query graph or by gathering statistical information on the topological structure on the WWW pages discovered.

3.4 Adding Predicates

Users do not usually search just for hypertext structures but they also impose content conditions on the WWW pages they search for. In order to model such queries we consider edge and node labeled data graphs. The query graph is augmented with a set of *condition hyperedges.* For example, a condition hyperedge involving three query graph nodes may state that two corresponding WWW pages must contain the title of the third one. The optimization of graph queries augmented with predicates can be done in two stages:

1. Estimating the selectivity of the condition hyperedges.
2. Using this estimation in finding a capture order.

Selectivity estimation is difficult because of the lack of statistical information. However, as we remarked earlier, it is possible to use information gathered by traditional search engine indices (e.g. AltaVista) or previous searches.

The optimization algorithms for graph queries have natural extensions when predicates are added to the queries. For example, the rule-based algorithm described above may be modified as follows. Given a candidate node for capture

v, let a be the number of captured nodes pointing to v. Let $c_1, ..., c_n$ be the condition hyperedges of the query graph that are induced by the captured nodes plus a and let $s_1, .., s_n$ be the corresponding selectivities. The *constraint factor* of v is defined as $\alpha a + \beta F(s_1, ..., s_n)$ where F computes the combined selectivity of the conditions, α and β are weighting factors. We capture the node with the largest constraint factor.

We have built a graph database simulator and began using it for testing several query optimization algorithms. Further work on this subject includes:

- Defining and testing parallel algorithms.
- Analyzing the effect of projections, i.e. nodes in the final required answer.
- Analyzing caching algorithms.
- Finding appropriate query algorithms for the language extended with regular expressions.
- Finding appropriate query algorithms for the language extended with hierarchical graphs.
- Define and study the behavior of adaptive algorithms, i.e. algorithms that improve their initial assumptions as they navigate the WWW, refine their knowledge, and dynamically redefine the execution plan.
- Taking into account the local processing cost.

4 Data Stability

Concurrency control mechanisms in database systems make concurrent accesses to data items satisfy some "desirable" properties, mainly Atomicity, Consistency, Isolation and Durability (ACID)[16]. Considering the WWW as a distributed database, one may wonder if similar properties may be defined and enforced within the WWW context.

Currently, the implemented WWW query languages do not make any consistency guarantees and the query languages semantics is usually defined for a "static" WWW (for a detailed examination of this issue, see [24]).

4.1 Existing Support in WWW Standards

Our ability to control the time-varying aspects of the WWW depends on the standard WWW protocols. Most concurrency control mechanisms in database systems are based on *locks*, *timestamps* or *versioning*. The state of affairs is as follows:

- HTTP provides time-related information, for data being sent, that may allow the implementation of timestamp based mechanisms [14].
- A new standard (in preparation, [15]) will allow the implementation of locks and versioning.

Therefore, in the near future, some tools needed to construct a data concurrency framework will become available. However, database techniques may not be applicable in their traditional forms. We address this issue in the next subsection.

4.2 Degrees of Data Stability

In the WWW, change rates for different objects may be very different. Such rates may vary from once a year (a home page) to every minute (meteorological satellite maps). We are interested in (1) characterizing the time-related behavior of WWW objects and (2) providing the user of our query language with tools to define the *degree of data stability* required for his queries. For example, a user searching for some information in a "stable" site may not need to ensure that the site has not changed during query processing. However, a user searching a site that changes often, may request the query processor to ensure that the query results are still valid when they are returned, or that the query results correspond to a "consistent" state of the server pages (no pages have been added or removed during query execution). Therefore,

– We intend to define degrees of data stability for our queries. For example:
  • Degree-A: No data stability.
  • Degree-B: The data being returned by a query is guaranteed to correspond to a "consistent" state of the WWW, possibly outdated because pages may have been *added* to the accessed sites or because consulted pages may have *changed*.
  • Degree-C: The data being returned by a query is guaranteed to correspond to a "consistent" state of the WWW, possibly outdated because pages may have been *added* to the accessed sites.
  • Degree-D: The data being returned by a query is guaranteed to correspond to the state of the WWW when the user receives it and up to some later point in time T.
– We intend to explore mechanisms to ensure these degrees of data stability. An interesting issue is, given an outdated query solution, how can the query processor minimize the work needed to build an up-to-date solution.

5 Conclusions

We propose to add database functionalities to the WWW. That is:

– Define a new abstract data model for the WWW. The data model will consist of two layers:
  • A basic layer which describes the physical organization of the WWW.
  • A refined layer which refines the basic layer in terms of a virtual hierarchical object graph. The main data types in this layer will be sites, nodes and intra-page objects.
  The low level layer depends solely on the WWW data while the refined layer is defined by the user and analysis tools.
– Extend the capabilities of the W3QL language in the following directions:
  • Queries on the model are based on *constraints* that specify the organization of the data in a hierarchical object graph, and *conditions*, which are used to select sets of objects in the graph.

- Content conditions based on analyzers.
- Support for the various meta-data implementation techniques.
- Further study of query optimization in the context of the WWW.
- Define data stability properties and study protocols to enforce them.

These improvements will facilitate the development of advanced applications such as effective querying, groupware and electronic commerce.

References

1. Abiteboul, S., Cluet, S., Milo, T., Querying and Updating the File. In *Proc. VLDB*, 1993.
2. Abiteboul, S., Vianu, V., Queries and Computation on the Web. In *Proc. ICDT*, 1997.
3. AltaVista. Http://altavista.digital.com/.
4. Atzeni, P., Mecca, G., Cut and Paste. In *ACM PODS Conf.*, 1997.
5. Atzeni, P., Mecca, G., Merialdo, P., To Weave the Web. In *Proc. VLDB*, 97.
6. Beeri, C., Kornatzky, Y., A Logical Query Language for Hypertext Systems. In *Proceeding of the European Conference on Hypertext*, 1990.
7. Bray, T., Paoli, J., Sperberg-McQueen, C. M., Extensible Markup Language (XML), W3C working draft, http://www.w3.org/TR/WD-xml-970807.
8. Cathrow, W., Metadata: An Overview, http://www.nla.gov.au/nla/staffpaper-/cathro3.html.
9. Consens, M. P., Mendelzon, A., Hy+: A Hygraph-based Query and Visualization System. In *ACM SIGMOD Conf.*, 1993.
10. Consens, M. P., Mendelzon, A. O., Expressing Structural Hypertext Queries in Graphlog. In *Hypertext'89*, 1989.
11. Consens, M. P., Mendelzon, A. O., GraphLog: a Visual Formalism for Real Life Recursion. In *ACM PODS Conf.*, 1990.
12. Farquhar, A., Fikes, R., Pratt, W., Rice, J., Collaborative Ontology Construction for Information Integration. Tech. rep., Computer Science, Stanford, 1995.
13. Fernandez, M., Florescu, D., Kang, J., Levy, A., Suciu, D., System Demonstration - Strudel: A Web-site Management System. In *ACM SIGMOD Conf.*, 1997.
14. Fielding, R., Gettys, J., Mogul, J., Frystyk, H., Berners-Lee, T., RFC 2068: Hypertext Transfer Protocol HTTP/1.1. January 1997, http://www.ietf.org.
15. Goland, Y. Y., Whitehead, E. J., Faizi, A., Carter, S. R., Jensen, D., Extensions for Distributed Authoring and Versioning on the World-Wide Web, Internet Draft, draft-ietf-webdav-protocol-04, http://www.ietf.org.
16. Gray, J., Reuter, A., *Transaction Processing: Concepts and Techniques*. Morgan Kaufmann, 1993.
17. Harvest - Effective Use of Internet Information. http://harvest.transarc.com.
18. IETF, Multipurpose Internet Mail Extension, defined in RFC 822, 2045, 2046, 2047, 2048, 2049.
19. The Java Language Home Page. http://java.sun.com.
20. Kogan, Y., Michaeli, D., Sagiv, Y., Shmueli, O., Utilizing the Multiple Facets of WWW Content. In *Proc. NGITS*, 1997.
21. Konopnicki, D., Shmueli, O., Information Gathering in the World-Wide Web: The W3QL Query Language and the W3QS system. *ACM TODS, to appear, http://-www.cs.technion.ac.il/~konop/w3qs.html*.

22. Konopnicki, D., Shmueli, O., W3QS: A Query System for the World-Wide Web. In *Proc. VLDB*, 1995.

23. Lakshmanan, L. V. S., Sadri, F., Subramania, I. N., A Declarative Language for Querying and Restructuring the WEB. In *Sixth International Workshop on Research Issues in Data Engineering*, 1996.

24. Mendelzon, A. O., Milo, T., Formal Models of Web Queries. In *ACM PODS Conf.*, May 1997.

25. COM Home. http://www.microsoft.com/infocom.

26. Microsoft ActiveX Controls. http://www.microsoft.com/com/activex.htm.

27. Mihaila, G. A., Mendelzon, A. O., Milo, T., Querying the World-Wide Web. In *Proc. PDIS*, 1996.

28. Minohara, T., Wanatabe, R., Queries on Structure in Hypertext. In *Proc. FODO*, 1993.

29. Netscape Plug-In Guide. http://developer.netscape.com/library/documentation-/communicator/plugin/index.htm.

30. Orfali, R., Harkey, D., Edwards, J., *The Essential Distributed Objects Survival Guide*. John Wiley & Sons, 1996.

31. Papakonstantinou, Y., Garcia-Molina, H., Widom, J., Object exchange across heterogeneous information sources. In *Proc. ICDE*, 1995.

32. Servlets. Http://jserv.javasoft.com/products/java-server/servlets.

33. Spertus, E., Stein, L. A., A SQL interface to the World-Wide Web, unpublished.

34. Van Herwijnen, E., *Practical SGML*. Kluwer Academic Pub, 1994.

35. W3C, Resource Description Framework (RDF) Model and Syntax, W3C Working Draft, http://www.w3.org/TR/WD-rdf-syntax.

Fixpoint Calculus for Querying Semistructured Data

N. Bidoit and M. Ykhlef

LaBRI (U.M.R. 5800 du CNRS) Université Bordeaux I
351, Cours de la Libération, F-33405 Talence
email : {Nicole.Bidoit, Mourad.Ykhlef}@labri.u-bordeaux.fr

Abstract. The paper proposes two query languages for semistructured data G-Fixpoint and G-While whose expressive power is comparable to Fixpoint and While respectively. These languages are multi-sorted like logic languages integrating fixpoint path expressions.

1 Introduction

Defining query languages for semistructured data has received a lot of attention during the last few years [2, 7] [11, 10] [20, 3, 8] [14, 15] [16, 4, 17, 12] [13, 21, 5, 9]. The target applications are biological data management, structured documents, heterogeneous data integration, etc. Semistructured data, that is data whose structure is not constrained by a schema, are usually represented in a graph-like manner. The data graph models vary slightly from one approach to an other: graphs may be restricted to trees, data may be associated to edges only, or to edges and terminal vertices, etc. In our framework, we make the choice to represent semistructured data by general multi-graphs called db-graphs whose vertices and edges both carry data. This choice seems to fit in a more natural way applications such as the Web.

Most of the languages proposed so far have been designed as extensions of SQL with, among others, the advantage to provide a userfriendly syntax and commercial flavor. The major focus of the paper is on defining a graph query language in a multi-sorted calculus like style.

This graph query language is closed, meaning that the answer to a query over a db-graph is a db-graph (in the same spirit as the answer of a query over a relational database is a relation). Let us consider the Web db-graph of Figure 3 and the query asking for DB group's projects. The answer will be the sub-graph(s) rooted at the node labeled by projects. Obviously, from a practical point of view, for some application, it may be more convenient to give as equivalent answers the nodes labeled by projects.

In the relational model, a query extracts a relation from the database based on properties of tuples in the database. In our framework, a graph query extracts sub-graphs from the db-graph based on properties of paths. The two major properties that we use to retrieve sub-graphs are: reachability of the root of a sub-graph via a specified path; existence of some paths in the sub-graph.

Thus the core of our language is a path calculus providing a form of navigational querying. The path calculus investigated here is based on path expressions as most other languages do. Its main feature is that path expressions are extended with a fixpoint operator in order to increase its expressive power. The fixpoint operator introduced here has two effects: it allows one to use some form of iteration; it gives the ability to define n-ary properties over paths. The first point is standard. Unsurprisingly, although the Kleene closure is not part of our path expression constructors, we are able to simulate it using the fixpoint operator. The second point concerns the fact that standard path expressions define monadic properties over paths. In some cases, for instance in order to collect pairs of paths having same length, it is useful to have the ability to express n-ary properties over paths. The fixpoint operator allows us to translate the transitive closure of a binary relation represented by a specific db-graph. This is done without the need to introduce new edges in the db-graph. The main results of the paper investigate the expressive power of the fixpoint path calculus. In the one hand, we show that, while hiding the computation of simple paths, any query in Path-Fixpoint can be expressed by a query in Fixpoint [1] over a relational database. The same kind of result holds for the non inflationary version of the fixpoint path calculus Path-While versus While [1]. On the other hand, any query in Fixpoint (resp. in While) over a relational database can be expressed by a query in Path-Fixpoint (resp. in Path-While) by converting the relational database into a db-graph. Thus we claim that our graph query languages G-Fixpoint and G-While based respectively on the fixpoint path query sublanguages Path-Fixpoint and Path-While subsume all known existing semistructured data query languages. However, it is important to know that these languages lack one of the expected features for query languages: the complexity of answering a Path-fixpoint (resp. a Path-While) query may not be polynomial because of simple path computation. Conditions in the spirit of range-restriction [16] have to be studied in order to specify reasonably computable graph queries.

Related Work: The language GraphLog [11, 10] specifies queries using path regular expression. It is shown equivalent to FO+TC or to stratified linear Datalog.

The language UnQL [8] includes the kleene closure which is not sufficient to express the transitive closure of a binary relation represented by a graph. The expressive power of UnQL is strictly included in NLOGSPACE.

Lorel [3] and POQL [9] as UnQL can not compute the transitive closure of a binary relation.

WebLog [15] is a language defined in the spirit of Datalog and recursive Datalog like rules play the role of path regular expressions used in other languages. WebLog is not powerful enough to express transitive closure. The same holds for W3QS [14] and WebSQL [16]. The language STRUQL [12] allows one to express the transitive closure of a binary relation although this requires the creation of edges. STRUQL is equivalent to FO+TC. The hypertext language Gram [6] is strictly less expressive than the class of FO queries when the Kleene closure is not included and express some form of transitive closure when it is added.

Outline of the paper: The next section presents the data model. Section 3 develops the presentation of the path calculus and its fixpoint (Path-Fixpoint) and while (Path-While) extensions. In section 4, the graph query language G-Fixpoint (resp. G-While) induced by the path query language Path-Fixpoint (resp. Path-While) are presented. Section 5 investigates the expressive power of the path query languages Path-Fixpoint and Path-While.

2   Data model

Definition 1. [db-graph] *Let $\mathcal{V}$ be an infinite set of values. A db-graph $G = (N, E, \lambda_N, \lambda_E, org, dest)$ over $\mathcal{V}$ is a directed labeled multi-graph where:*

1. *N is a finite set of vertex identifiers and E is a finite set of edge identifiers,*
2. *org (resp. dest) is a mapping from E into N which gives the origin (resp. destination) of edges,*
3. *λ_N is a partial labeling mapping from N into $\mathcal{V}$,*
4. *λ_E is a partial labeling mapping from E into $\mathcal{V}$ such that:*
   $$(\forall e_1 \in E)(\forall e_2 \in E) \ (e_1 \neq e_2 \wedge org(e_1) = org(e_2) \wedge dest(e_1) = dest(e_2))$$
   $$\Rightarrow \lambda_E(e_1) \neq \lambda_E(e_2).$$

Condition 4 says that pairs of vertices having same origin and same destination should have different labels. Although the definition allows multiple labeled edges linking two vertices (as long as the labels are distinct), we make the restriction that only one unlabeled edge may link two vertices.

An edge e is totally defined by its origin, its destination and its label ($org(e)$, $dest(e)$, $\lambda_E(e)$). A path is given by a list of edges $\langle e_1, e_2, \ldots, e_k \rangle$ such that $dest(e_i) = org(e_{i+1})$ for i=1..k-1. The empty path ε is an empty list of edges. A path is simple w.r.t edges if all its edges are distinct. The mappings org and $dest$ defined on edges are extended to path in the usual manner.

Definition 2. [Rooted and maximal subgraph] *A vertex r of a graph G is a source for G if there exists a path from r to any other vertex of G. A rooted graph is a graph with at least one source [1]. If G' is a graph rooted at r and is a subgraph of G, the graph G' is said maximal if each vertex of G reachable from r is also reachable from r in G', each edge e of G such that $org(e)$ is reachable from r is an edge of G'.*

A maximal subgraph rooted at r is totally characterized by (one of) its source. Given a db-graph G, it will be convenient in the sequel to consider the set of all maximal rooted subgraphs of G. This set is denoted Ext(G). For instance, considering again the Web example, each of the maximal rooted subgraphs corresponds to the part of the Web which can be explored in a "forward manner" via the links starting from a specific Web page.

---

[1] The path $\langle (n_1, n_2, l_1), (n_2, n_1, l_2) \rangle$ is a graph with two sources n_1 and n_2.

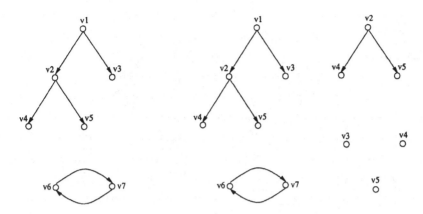

Fig. 1. An example db-graph.   Fig. 2. Db-graph extension.

Example 1. The Figure 1 gives a simple example of a db-graph G. For the sake of simplicity vertex and edge labels are not mentioned. The set $\text{Ext}(G)$ contains six subgraphs which are depicted in Figure 2.

The notion of equality over graphs adopted here is that of bisimulation [19].

Definition 3. [Bisimulation] *Two rooted graphs* $G_1 = (N_1, E_1, \lambda_{N_1}, \lambda_{E_1}, org_1,$
$dest_1)$ *and* $G_2 = (N_2, E_2, \lambda_{N_2}, \lambda_{E_2}, org_2, dest_2)$ *are bisimilar, denoted* $G_1 \sim G_2$,
if there is a binary relation $\simeq \subseteq N_1 \times N_2$ *such that:*

1. $r_1 \simeq r_2$ *where* r_1 *(resp.* r_2*) is a source of* G_1 *(resp.* G_2*).*
2. $(\forall n \in N_1)(\forall n' \in N_2) \ (n \simeq n' \Rightarrow \lambda_{N_1}(n) = \lambda_{N_2}(n'))$.
3. $(\forall n \in N_1)(\forall n' \in N_2)$
   $((\exists(n, m, l) \in E_1) \ n \simeq n') \Rightarrow ((\exists(n', m', l) \in E_2) \ m \simeq m')$ *and*
   $((\exists(n', m', l) \in E_2) \ n \simeq n') \Rightarrow ((\exists(n, m, l) \in E_1) \ m \simeq m')$.

Example 2. Figure 3 represents a small portion of the Web as an example of a db-graph. The vertices (resp. the edges) represent HTML documents (resp. links between documents). Vertex identifiers are http addresses of documents. The vertex identified by `http://www.labri.u-bordeaux.fr` characterizes a maximal rooted subgraph and represents the LaBRI server. The vertex identified by `http://www-db.stanford.edu` has two outgoing edges resp. labeled by `members` and `projects` which point to subgraphs containing information about the members of the DB group at Stanford and resp. its projects.

3   Path calculus

In the remainder of the paper, in order to simplify the presentation, the term **path** always refers a path which is **simple w.r.t edges**.
As outlined in the introduction, the graph query language defined here intends

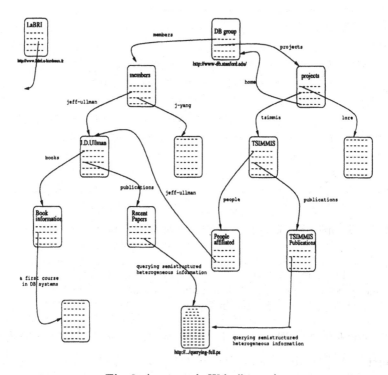

Fig. 3. An example Web db-graph.

to retrieve some subgraphs of the database, as a matter of fact maximal rooted subgraphs (or equivalently their sources). The retrieval process is essentially supported by specifying paths and roughly speaking, the subgraphs returned are either those rooted at the destination or at the source of these paths. Thus it obviously turns out that the first task is to define a path query language. The core of our path query language is rather classical and based on path expressions. However our language is made more powerful by introducing fixpoint on path formulas which, intuitively, allows one to use some form of iteration and also to define intentional n-ary predicates over paths. Thus fixpoint path expressions introduce much richer "contexts" than simple path expression for querying db-graphs.

The language used to define path expressions and formulas is very similar to a multi-sorted first order language. Because in our data model, data are associated to vertices, our path expressions are slightly different from those of Lorel [20, 3] or UnQL [8]. They may contain data variables as abstractions of the content of vertices.

In the following, we assume that the set of values $\mathcal{V}$ is fixed and that four sorts of variable sets are given: a set of graph (resp. path, label, and data) variables.

Graph and path variables are denoted $X, Y, Z, \ldots$. Label (resp. data) variables are denoted $x, y, z, \ldots$ (resp. $\alpha, \beta, \gamma, \ldots$). A **graph term** is either a rooted graph or a graph variable. A **path term** is either a path or a path variable. A **label** (resp. a **data**) **term** is either a label in $\mathcal{V}$ (resp. a value in $\mathcal{V}$) or a label (resp. data) variable.

Although introduced above, graph variables and terms are not needed in this section.

Definition 4. [**Path expression**] *A path expression over $\mathcal{V}$ is defined recursively by:*

1. *An (elementary) path expression is either a path variable or a label term. An elementary path expression is a pre-free and post-free path expression.*
2. *If s is a pre-free (resp. post-free) path expression and t is a data term then $t \lhd s$ (resp. $s \rhd t$) is a path expression such that:*
   if s is post-free then $t \lhd s$ is pre-bound and post-free otherwise it is pre-bound and post-bound and if s is pre-free then $s \rhd t$ is pre-free and post-bound otherwise it is pre-bound and post-bound.
3. *If s_1 (resp. s_2) is a post-free (resp. pre-free) path expression then $s_1.s_2$ is a path expression such that:*
   if s_1 is pre-free then $s_1.s_2$ is pre-free otherwise it is pre-bound and if s_2 is post-free then $s_1.s_2$ is post-free otherwise it is post-bound.

Example 3. The path expression `members.y.publications` intends to represent all paths of length three whose first (resp. last) edge is labeled by `members` (resp. `publications`). It is pre-free and post-free.
The path expression "`DB group`"$\lhd X \rhd$"`Ullman`" intends to capture all paths whose origin (resp. destination) is equal to the data "`DB group`" (resp. "`Ullman`"). It is pre-bound because the origin is constrained (here by a value) and post-bound because the destination is also constrained.

Note that we do not include path expressions of the form s^* where $*$ denotes the Kleene closure as it is usually done in most path query languages. We will see later on that these expressions are special cases of fixpoint path expressions. Note also that we do not make use of a special symbol $\#$ usually called "joker" and intended to abstract any label. The paths captured in a db-graph G by a path expression are now defined formally. The definition makes use of the notion of active domain.

Definition 5. [**Active domain**] *The active domain of a db-graph G denoted $adom(G)$ is the triple $(\mathcal{P}_G, \mathcal{L}_G, \mathcal{D}_G)$ such that $\mathcal{P}_G$ (resp. $\mathcal{L}_G, \mathcal{D}_G$) is the set of all paths (resp. labels and data) in G, including the empty path ϵ.*

A valuation of a variable x over the active domain $adom(G)$ assigns to x a value in either $\mathcal{P}_G$, or $\mathcal{L}_G$, or $\mathcal{D}_G$ depending on the sort of x (path, label or data). The notion of a valuation is extended to a set of variables in the usual manner.

Definition 6. [Spelling] *Let* $G = (N, E, \lambda_N, \lambda_E, org, dest)$ *be a db-graph. Let* s *be a path expression whose set of variables is* $Var(s)$. *Let* ν *be a valuation of* $Var(s)$ *over* $adom(G)$. *The set of paths spelled in* G *by* s *under the valuation* ν, *denoted* $Spell_G(\nu(s))$ *is defined by:*

1. s *is* X *and* $Spell_G(\nu(s)) = \{\nu(X)\}$,
2. s *is* t *and* $Spell_G(\nu(s)) = \{\langle e \rangle \mid e \in E \text{ and } \lambda_E(e) = \nu(t)\}$,
3. s *is* $t \triangleleft s_1$ *and* $Spell_G(\nu(s)) = \{p \mid p \in Spell_G(\nu(s_1)) \text{ and } \lambda_N(org(p)) = \nu(t)\}$,
4. s *is* $s_1 \triangleright t$ *and* $Spell_G(\nu(s)) = \{p \mid p \in Spell_G(\nu(s_1)) \text{ and } \lambda_N(dest(p)) = \nu(t)\}$,
5. s *is* $s_1.s_2$ *and*
$$Spell_G(\nu(s)) = \{p_1.p_2 \mid p_1 \in Spell_G(\nu(s_1)) \text{ and } p_2 \in Spell_G(\nu(s_2))$$
$$\text{and } dest(p_1) = org(p_2) \text{ and } p_1.p_2 \text{ is simple } \}\ ^2.$$

Example 4. Let G be the path $\langle (n_1, n_2, l_2), (n_2, n_1, l_1), (n_1, n_3, l_2) \rangle$ and let s be the path expression $l_1.l_2$. The set of paths $Spell_G(\nu(s))$ is

$$\{\langle (n_2, n_1, l_1), (n_1, n_2, l_2) \rangle, \langle (n_2, n_1, l_1), (n_1, n_3, l_2) \rangle\}.$$

Path queries are specified by path formulas.

Definition 7. [Atomic path formula] *An atomic path formula is an expression having one of the following forms:*

1. *a path expression,*
2. $t_1 = t_2$ *where* t_1 *and* t_2 *are terms of the same sort among path, label, data;* $=$ *is the (polymorphic) equality predicate symbol,*
3. $t \in s$ *where* t *is a path term, s is a path expression and $\in$ is a set membership predicate symbol.*

Note here that paths are compared using equality. Intuitively, the formula $t \in s$ intends to check whether t is one of the paths spelled by the path expression s.

Definition 8. [Path formula] *A path formula is an expression having one of the following forms:*

1. *an atomic path formula,*
2. $(\phi \wedge \psi)$ *(resp.* $(\phi \vee \psi)$*),* $\neg\phi$*,* $(\exists x)\ \phi$*, and* $(\forall x)\ \phi$
where ϕ and ψ are path formulas and x is a variable (of any of the sort path, label, data).

The notion of "free" and "bound" occurrences of variables is defined in the usual manner. In the remainder, we will assume that path formulas are normalized in the sense that no distinct pair of quantifiers bind the same variable and no variable occurs both free and bound. Variable substitution may be used to normalize a path formula [1]. The set of variables having at least one free occurrence in the path formula φ is denoted by $Free(\varphi)$.

---

[2] Note that we use the same symbol to denote the concatenation over path expressions and the concatenation of paths. Recall also that $\epsilon.p = p.\epsilon = p$ for any path p where ϵ is the empty path.

Example 5. Intuitively, the path formula

"DB group"◁X▷"Ullman" ∧ ¬(∃U)(∃V) X∈U.projects.V

related to the Web database, will be true for a path valuation p of X such that p connects the "DB group"'s page to the "Ullman"'s page and p does not contain any edge labeled by projects.

Path queries (simple ones) are now defined in a straightforward manner.

Definition 9. [Path Query] *A path query is an expression of the form*

$$\{(X_1,\ldots,X_n) \mid \varphi\}$$

where φ is a path formula, $Free(\varphi)=\{X_1,\ldots,X_n\}$ and for $i=1..n$, X_i is a path variable.

Note that in general, a path query will return **tuples** of paths.

Example 6. **[Navigation and Content search]** The following path query, evaluated on the Web database, will return all paths linking the "DB group"'s page and the "Ullman"'s'page.

{(X) | "DB group"◁X▷"Ullman"}

Example 7. **[Common edge]** The path query below is a yes/no query and will return "yes" if the db-graph queried contains two distinct paths having at least a common edge.

{ | (∃X)(∃Y)(∃Z)(∃U)(∃V)(∃y) (X.Y.Z ∧ U.Y.V ∧ Y∈y
            ∧ (¬(X = U) ∨ ¬(Z = V)))}

The next definitions formally define the answer of a path query. The notion of active domain needs to be extended before.

Definition 10. [Active domain of a path formula] *The active domain of a path formula φ denoted $adom(\varphi)$ is the triple $(\mathcal{P}_\varphi, \mathcal{L}_\varphi, \mathcal{D}_\varphi)$ where $\mathcal{P}_\varphi$ is the set of all ground path terms in φ, $\mathcal{L}_\varphi$ is the set of all ground label terms in φ and all labels of the paths in $\mathcal{P}_\varphi$, and $\mathcal{D}_\varphi$ is the set of all ground data terms in φ and all vertex data of the paths in $\mathcal{P}_\varphi$.*

When G and φ are clearly identified from the context, *adom* denotes $(\mathcal{P}_G \cup \mathcal{P}_\varphi, \mathcal{L}_G \cup \mathcal{L}_\varphi, \mathcal{D}_G \cup \mathcal{D}_\varphi)$. A valuation of a variable x over the active domain *adom* assigns to x a value in either $\mathcal{P}_G \cup \mathcal{P}_\varphi$, $\mathcal{L}_G \cup \mathcal{L}_\varphi$, or $\mathcal{D}_G \cup \mathcal{D}_\varphi$ depending on the sort of x (path, label or data).

Definition 11. [Path formula satisfaction] *Let φ be a path formula and ν be a valuation of $Free(\varphi)$ over adom. The db-graph G satisfies the formula φ under the valuation ν, denoted $G \models \varphi[\nu]$, if*

1. φ is a path expression and $Spell_G(\varphi[\nu]) \neq \emptyset$.
2. φ is $t_1 = t_2$ and $\nu(t_1) = \nu(t_2)$ if t_1 and t_2 are both path/label/data terms.
3. φ is $t \in s$ and $\nu(t) \in Spell_G(\nu(s))$.
4. φ is $(\phi \wedge \psi)$ and $G \models \phi[\nu]$ and $G \models \psi[\nu]$.
5. φ is $(\phi \vee \psi)$ and $G \models \phi[\nu]$ or $G \models \psi[\nu]$.
6. φ is $\neg\phi$ and $G \not\models \varphi[\nu]$ (i.e. $G \models \varphi[\nu]$ does not hold).
7. φ is $(\exists x)\,\phi$ and
   if x is a path (resp. label or data) variable then there exists a value a in $\mathcal{P}_G \cup \mathcal{P}_\varphi$ (resp. in $\mathcal{L}_G \cup \mathcal{L}_\varphi$ or in $\mathcal{D}_G \cup \mathcal{D}_\varphi$) such that $G \models \phi[\nu \cup \{x/a\}]$.
8. φ is $(\forall x)\,\phi$ and
   if x is a path (resp. label or data) variable then for each value a in $\mathcal{P}_G \cup \mathcal{P}_\varphi$ (resp. in $\mathcal{L}_G \cup \mathcal{L}_\varphi$ or in $\mathcal{D}_G \cup \mathcal{D}_\varphi$), $G \models \phi[\nu \cup \{x/a\}]$.

Note that if φ is the path expression X then there exists at least a valuation of X, namely $\nu(X) = \epsilon$, such that $Spell_G(\varphi[\nu]) \neq \emptyset$. To extract non empty paths through a path expression X, one needs to explicitly express it by $X \wedge \neg(X = \epsilon)$. As this situation may occur frequently, it could be convenient to introduce an abbreviation for such a formula like X^+. This point is not developed further here.

Definition 12. [**Path query answering**] *The image of a db-graph G under the path query q specified by $\{(X_1, \ldots, X_n) \mid \varphi\}$ is*

$$q(G) = \{(\nu(X_1), \ldots, \nu(X_n)) \mid \nu \text{ valuation of } \mathrm{Free}(\varphi) \text{ over } adom \text{ and } G \models \varphi[\nu]\}.$$

The size of the active domain (which include all **simple paths**) of a db-graph is exponential in the input. This entails that evaluation of path queries with universal quantifiers, for instance, will lead to an exponential cost. This is not reasonable for database querying and restrictions on bindings and quantifications should be added in order to solve this problem. We do not proceed to this study here although ideas from [16] can be borrowed.

Our path query language is quite similar to the relational calculus although relation predicate symbols do not occur. However, the reader would have noticed that path expressions define unary relations and path formulas define intentional n-ary relations over paths. Just as in the case of the relational calculus, we now provide an inflationary extension of path queries with recursion by introducing a fixpoint operator construct allowing the iteration of path formulas evaluation up to a fixpoint. The difficulty to define such fixpoint operator resides in the absence of relation predicate symbols. It turns out that a rather simple notation convention solves this difficulty.

Definition 13. [**Path fixpoint operator**] *Let $\varphi(s_{X_1}, \ldots, s_{X_n}, X_1, \ldots, X_n)$ be a path formula with $2 \times n$ free path variables namely $s_{X_1}, \ldots, s_{X_n}$ called distinguished free path variables and $X_1, \ldots, X_n$.*
$\mu^+_{s_{X_1}, \ldots, s_{X_n}}(\varphi)$ *is called a fixpoint path expression of arity n and given a db-graph G, it denotes the n-ary relation that is the limit of the inflationary sequence $\{\mathcal{S}_k\}_{k \geq 0}$ defined by:*

1. $S_0 = \{(\varepsilon, \ldots, \varepsilon)\}$ [3]
2. $S_{k+1} = S_k \cup \varphi(S_k)$ *where*
   $\varphi(S_k)$ *denotes the union of the evaluation of the path queries* $\{(X_1, \ldots, X_n) \mid \varphi[\nu_k]\}$ [4] *where* ν_k *is any valuation of the distinguished variables* $s_{X_1}, \ldots, s_{X_n}$ *induced by* S_k.
   A valuation ν_k *is induced by* S_k *if there exists a tuple* $(v_1, \ldots, v_n)$ *in* S_k *such that* $\nu_k(s_{X_i}) = v_i$ *for* $i = 1..n$.

As usual, the n-ary fixpoint path expression $\mu^+_{s_{X_1}, \ldots, s_{X_n}}(\varphi)$ can be used to build a more complex path formula. For instance, now $\mu^+_{s_{X_1}, \ldots, s_{X_n}}(\varphi)(t_1, \ldots, t_n)$ where each t_i is a path term, can be considered as an atomic path formula. Nesting fixpoint operators does not raise any problem. The extension of the path calculus with the fixpoint construct μ^+ is called **Path-Fixpoint**.

In a straightforward way, a partial non inflationary extension of our path calculus can be provided. It suffices to define a fixpoint operator μ as in the above definition except for item 2. replaced by $S_{k+1} = \varphi(S_k)$. This extension is called **Path-While**.

Note that because of the initialization of the relation S_0 the inflationist fixpoint of a path expression is never empty as it contains at least a tuple of empty paths. It may be convenient to get rid of this tuple in the limit of the sequence $\{S_k\}_{k \geq 0}$. This could be achieved for instance by defining S_1 as $\varphi(S_0)$.

Example 8. The following three queries show how the Kleene closure can be expressed through a fixpoint path expression. All three queries are of the form $\{(X) \mid \mu^+_{s_X}(\varphi)(X)\}$ and differ by the specification of φ.

1. φ is $(\exists x)(\exists y)\ X \in s_X.x.y$
2. φ is $X \in s_X.a.b$
3. φ is $(\exists x)(\exists y)\ (X \in x.y \vee (X \in s_X.x.y \wedge (\exists Y)\ s_X \in Y.x.y))$

The first query returns paths of even length. This query can be expressed in most known languages using the Kleene closure of the path expression $(\#.\#)$ where $\#$ is the so-called *joker* symbol. The second query is equivalent to the Kleene closure $(a.b)^*$. The third query is a generalization of the Kleene closure $(a.b)^*$ where a and b are not constants.

Example 9. Below, the first (resp. second) query returns pairs of paths with identical sequence of edges (resp. vertices). Both queries are of the form $\{(X,Y) \mid \mu^+_{s_X, s_Y}(\varphi)(X,Y)\}$ and differ by the specification of φ.

1. φ is $(\exists x)\ (X \in s_X.x \wedge Y \in s_Y.x)$
2. φ is $(\exists x)(\exists y)(\exists \alpha)(\exists \beta)\ ((X \in \alpha \vartriangleleft x \vartriangleright \beta \wedge Y \in \alpha \vartriangleleft y \vartriangleright \beta) \vee (X \in s_X.x \vartriangleright \beta \wedge Y \in s_Y.y \vartriangleright \beta))$

---

[3] $(\varepsilon, \ldots, \varepsilon)$ is the tuple of empty paths of arity n.
[4] We have taken some liberty with the writing of path queries here in order to simplify the presentation.

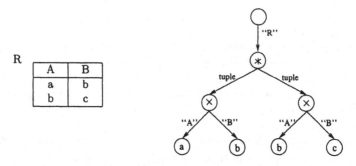

Fig. 4. Representation of a relational database by a db-graph.

Example 10. [**Equal length path**]   The query $\{(X,Y) \mid \mu^+_{s_X,s_Y}(\mathbf{SL})(X,Y) \}$ where the path formula **SL** is defined below is rather interesting: it extracts pairs of paths having same length. The formula **SL** is:

$$(\exists x)(\exists y) \ (X \in s_X.x \ \wedge \ Y \in s_Y.y)$$

Note that this query does not make use of any predefined counting predicate. This query illustrates how combining binary intentionally defined "predicate" with iteration increases the expressive power of path languages. This query cannot be expressed neither in Lorel, nor in UnQL. POQL can express it only by using the interpreted function length over paths. This query is rather important for sequence data. One can express a query that extracts all paths generated for example by the language $\{a^n b^n \mid n \in \mathbb{N}\}$ by using the fixpoint of the formula **SL**.

Example 11. [**Transitive closure**]   The query $\{(X,Y) \mid \mu^+_{s_X,s_Y}(\mathbf{TC})(X,Y)\}$ where the path formula **TC** is defined below, computes (besides the pair of empty paths) pairs of paths whose respective pairs of destination is the transitive closure of a binary relation R represented in a naive way by a db-graph (see Figure 4). It proves that our path query language is powerful enough to express the transitive closure without requiring the creation of new edges as it is done in [12]. The formula **TC** is:

$$(\exists U_1) \ (U_1 \in \text{``R''}.\text{tuple} \ \wedge \ X \in U_1.\text{``A''} \ \wedge \ Y \in U_1.\text{``B''})$$
$$\vee \ (\exists Z)(\exists U_2)(\exists \alpha) \ (U_2 \in \text{``R''}.\text{tuple} \ \wedge \ X \in U_2.\text{``A''} \ \wedge \ Z \in U_2.\text{``B''}$$
$$\wedge \ Z \triangleright \alpha \ \wedge \ S_X \triangleright \alpha \ \wedge \ Y = S_Y)$$

Example 12. [**Same generation**] Let us consider the theoretical computer science genealogy of http://sigact.acm.org/genealogy/ Web page (see figure 5) that gives for each researcher some information such as his/her name, his/her adviser and his/her students. The path query $\{(X,Y) \mid \mu^+_{s_X,s_Y}(\mathbf{SG})(X,Y)\}$ where the path formula **SG** is defined below, computes pairs of researchers that have some common ancestor which is at the same number of generations away from

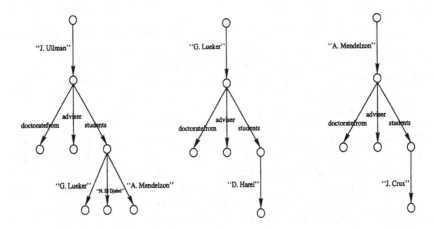

Fig. 5. A TCS genealogy.

each (some sort of cousins). The formula **SG** is:

```
(∃u) (X.doctoratefrom ∧ X∈u ∧ Y=X)
∨ (∃Xa)(∃Ya)(∃x)(∃y)(∃u₁)(∃v₁)(∃u₂)(∃v₂)
  ((Xa.students.X ∧ Xa∈u₁ ∧ X∈v₁)
  ∧ (Ya.students.Y ∧ Ya∈u₂ ∧ Y∈v₂)
  ∧ (Xa∈x ∧ Sₓ ∈x ∧ Ya∈y ∧ Sᵧ ∈y))
```

4   Graph calculus

Now that a path query language (Path-Fixpoint or Path-While) is available allowing us to specify some kind of navigation in a db-graph, it remains to explain how path sub-queries will be combined with graph constructs (and which graph constructs) in order to retrieve subgraphs (or their sources). Intuitively, a subgraph may be retrieved in two different ways: its source is the destination of some path specified by a path expression or its source is the origin of some path specified by a path expression. In fact, we also introduce a third way to select a (maximal) subgraph which checks if it is a path. This implies introducing an equality predicate symbol whose first operand is a graph variable and second operand is a path term[5]. This predicate is denoted = for sake of simplicity.

Definition 14. [Atomic graph formula] *An atomic graph formula is an expression of one of the following forms:*

---

[5] In a first version of the language, this predicate was not needed because path variables and graph variables were merged. However, this unique sort of variables (for paths and graphs) entailed a rather cumbersome definition of the graph calculus which is now avoided at the price of this special predicate.

1. *a Path-Fixpoint (or a Path-While) formula,*
2. *$t : s$ where t is a graph term (i.e. a graph variable or a rooted graph) and s is a path expression,*
3. *$s[t]$ where s is a path expression and t is a graph term,*
4. *$t_1 \sim t_2$ where t_1 and t_2 are both graph terms where $\sim$ is the bisimulation predicate symbol.*
5. *$X = t$ where X is a graph variable and t is a path term.*

Roughly speaking, $t : s$ tells that s spells at least one path p of the graph t and that the origin of p is the source of t; the intention of $s[t]$ is to check that the graph t has a source which is the destination of a path spelt by s.

A **graph formula** is defined in the usual way by introducing logical connectors and quantifications. We assume that graph formulas are normalized just as path formulas in order to avoid having both free and bound occurrences of the same variable. The notion of active domain of a db-graph G is extended in a straightforward manner.

Definition 15. [**Active domain**] *The active domain of a db-graph G denoted $adom(G)$ is the quadruple $(\mathcal{G}_G, \mathcal{P}_G, \mathcal{L}_G, \mathcal{D}_G)$ where $(\mathcal{P}_G, \mathcal{L}_G, \mathcal{D}_G)$ is exactly defined as in Definition 5 and $\mathcal{G}_G$ is the set $Ext(G)$ of maximal rooted subgraphs of G defined in section 2.*

The notion of active domain of a graph formula φ extends in a simple way the notion of active domain of a path formula. When G and φ are clearly identified from the context, *adom* denotes the union of the active domains of G and φ. graph(*adom*) (resp. path(adom), label(adom) and data(adom)) denotes the first (resp. second, third and fourth) component of *adom*. The notion of a valuation is extended in a straightforward manner.

The definition of satisfaction of a graph formula is restricted to atomic graph formula. The general case does not present any difficulty and is omitted here.

Definition 16. [**Graph formula satisfaction**] *Let φ be a graph formula and let ν be a valuation of $Free(\varphi)$. The db-graph G satisfies φ under the valuation ν over adom, denoted $G \models \varphi[\nu]$, if*

1. *φ is a Path-Fixpoint (or Path-While) formula and $G \models \varphi[\nu]$.*
2. *φ is an entry $t : s$ and there exists a path p in $Spell_{\nu(t)}(\nu(s))$ such that $org(p)$ is (one of) the source of $\nu(t)$.*
3. *φ is a selector $s[t]$ and there exists a path p in $Spell_G(\nu(s))$ such that $dest(p)$ is (one of) the source of the graph $\nu(t)$.*
4. *φ is $t_1 \sim t_2$ and $\nu(t_1) \sim \nu(t_2)$.*
5. *φ is $X = t$ and the maximal subgraph $\nu(X) = \nu(t)$.*

This section concludes by defining graph queries and their evaluation.

Definition 17. [**Graph query**] *A graph query is an expression of the form*

$$\{X \mid \varphi\}$$

where $Free(\varphi) = \{X\}$.

In the definition above, we have restricted the free variable X of φ to be a graph variable because our aim is to return maximal subgraphs as answers to a graph query. The intuition behind is that a graph query is essentially expressed by specifying paths in the graph leading to some vertices of interest and the results of the query are the maximal graph rooted at these vertices i.e. all the information that can be reached from these vertices. Considering the Web example, this definition of an answer is not as unpractical as it may seem: the maximal subgraphs (the answers) can be synthesized by (one of) their source and represent all the information reachable from these sources. For simplicity, we have restricted φ to have a single free variable. The generalization to more than one free variable can be done easily.

Definition 18. [Graph query answering] *The image of a db-graph G under a graph query q is defined by*

$$q(G) = \{\nu(X) \mid \nu \text{ is a valuation of } Free(\varphi) \text{ and } G \models \varphi[\nu]\}$$

Thus considering a given graph G as its extension $\text{Ext}(G)$ i.e. the set of all its maximal rooted subgraphs, a query defines a mapping from $\text{Ext}(G)$ into $\text{Ext}(G)$. The answer of a query may well be mapped to a db-graph, the "smallest" db-graph whose extension contains $q(G)$. We have made the choice to develop a formal presentation of the language but it is clear that it may be useful for the purpose of specific applications to customize the outputs of answers. An obvious alternative would be to produce as an answer the set of the sources of the graphs in $q(G)$ instead of $q(G)$ itself.

The graph query language G-Fixpoint (based on Path-Fixpoint) is now illustrated through several examples.

Example 13. The following queries are examples of graph queries followed by a brief description of what each query does.

1. [**Identity query**] $\{X \mid (\exists U)\ (U=\epsilon \wedge U[X])\}$
2. $\{X \mid \text{tsimmis.publications}[X]\}$
3. $\{X \mid (\exists U)(\exists V)\ \text{"DB group"}\triangleleft U.\text{members}.V.\text{books}[X]\}$
4. $\{X \mid (\forall y)\ ((\exists U)\ (\text{members}.y.U.\text{publications}[X]$
   $\Rightarrow (\exists V)\ \text{tsimmis}.V.\text{people}.y))\}$
5. $\{X \mid \text{"R"}.\text{tuple}[X]\}$
6. $\{X \mid (\exists U)(\exists V)\ (U[X] \wedge V[X] \wedge \neg(U=V) \wedge \neg(U=\epsilon) \wedge \neg(V=\epsilon))\}$
7. [**Cycles**] $\{X \mid (\exists U)\ (X:U \wedge U[X] \wedge \neg(U=\epsilon))\ \}$
8. $\{(X,Y) \mid (\exists U)(\exists V)\ (\mu^+_{s_X,s_Y}(\textbf{TC})(U,V) \wedge U[X] \wedge V[Y]$
   $\wedge \neg(U=\epsilon) \wedge \neg(V=\epsilon))\}$

The second query retrieves all publications of tsimmis. The third graph query retrieves the books of the Stanford database group members. The fourth query returns publications whose authors are all members of the Tsimmis project. The fifth query returns all tuples of a binary relation R (see Figure 4). The sixth query returns all maximal subgraph reached by two non identical paths. The eighth query illustrates how our language can be generalized to generate tuples of graphs as answers. This query returns the transitive closure of the binary relation R by selecting the extremities of pairs of paths returned by the fixpoint path query (Example 11) of course discarding the pair of empty paths.

5 Expressive power

In this section, we investigate the expressive power of Path-Fixpoint and Path-While. The two results presented here are complementary and provide an equivalence between Path-Fixpoint over db-graphs (resp. Path-While) and Fixpoint over relational instances (resp. While). However this equivalence hides the computation of simple paths (discussion about simple path computation can be found in [18]). In other words, db-graphs are translated into relational instances whose domain is primarily edge identifiers. In order to simulate (simple) paths, concatenation is provided through a pre-defined predicate *concat*.

The first result maps the semistructured data framework on a specific relational structure and shows that Path-Fixpoint (resp. Path-While) queries can be translated into Fixpoint (resp. While) queries over instances over this schema. The second result goes the other way around: relational instances are mapped on db-graphs and it is showed that Fixpoint (resp. While) queries over relational instances can be expressed by Path-Fixpoint (resp. Path-While) queries over the corresponding db-graphs.

Theorem 1. *There exists a translation T mapping db-graphs onto relational instances over a fixed schema $\mathcal{R}$ and mapping Path-Fixpoint (resp. Path-While) queries onto Fixpoint (resp. While) queries such that:*

if q_{path} is a Path-Fixpoint (resp. Path-While) query and G is a db-graph then

$$T(q_{path}(G)) = (T(q_{path}))(T(G)).$$

Proof. The transformation T is outlined below. Db-graphs are translated into relational instances using a fixed relational schema composed of four relation schemas: the unary relation *edge* ($edge(X)$ meaning that X is an edge[6]); the binary relations *dataorig*, *datadest* ($dataorig(X, x)$, resp. $datadest(X, x)$, meaning that the data contents of the origin, resp. the destination, of the edge X is x); the binary relation *label* ($label(X, x)$ meaning that the label of the edge X is x). The transformation of a specific db-graph into an instance over this relational schema is straightforward and omitted here.

For the purpose of translating path expressions and path formulas, we introduce a build-in predicate *concat*, the literal $concat(Z, X, Y)$ meaning that the path Z is simple and is the result of the concatenation of the simple paths X and Y.

---

[6] In fact, to be correct, we should have coded the edges of the graph using a ternary relation associating the origin node identity, the destination node identity and the edge identity.

A first order formula denoted $exp\text{-}s(Z)$ is associated to each path expression s. Intuitively, the formula $exp\text{-}s(Z)$ means that Z is a path which is spelt by the path expression s. The variable Z should be a "new" variable (not occurring in s).

Note that, in the proof, for sake of simplicity, we do not detail all restrictions that should naturally be taken while "choosing" variable names. Moreover, we abusively use the same notation for a path/label/data variable X in a path formula and its "translation" in a relational calculus formula.
The formula $exp\text{-}s(Z)$ is defined inductively as follows :

1. if s is X then $exp\text{-}s(Z)$ is $concat(X, Z, \epsilon)$ where ϵ is the empty path,
2. if s is t then $exp\text{-}s(Z)$ is $edge(Z) \wedge label(Z, t)$,
3. if s is $t \triangleleft s_1$ then $exp\text{-}s(Z)$ is $exp\text{-}s_1(Z) \wedge dataorig(Z, t)$,
4. if s is $s_1 \triangleright t$ then $exp\text{-}s(Z)$ is $exp\text{-}s_1(Z) \wedge datadest(Z, t)$,
5. if s is $s_1.s_2$ then
$$exp\text{-}s(Z) \text{ is } (\exists X_1)(\exists X_2) (exp\text{-}s_1(X_1) \wedge exp\text{-}s_2(X_2) \wedge concat(Z, X_1, X_2)).$$

The transformation $T(\varphi)$ of path formula (without fixpoint) φ into a first order formula, is defined inductively.

1. if φ is a path expression s then $T(\varphi)$ is $(\exists Z) exp\text{-}s(Z)$,
2. if φ is $t_1=t_2$ where t_1 and t_2 are path variables [7] then $T(\varphi)$ is $concat(t_1, t_2, \epsilon)$,
3. if φ is $t_1=t_2$ where t_1 and t_2 are both label terms or data terms then $T(\varphi)$ is $t_1=t_2$,
4. φ is $X \in s$ then $T(\varphi)$ is $(\exists Z) (exp\text{-}s(Z) \wedge concat(X, Z, \epsilon))$,
5. if φ is $(\phi \wedge \psi)$ (resp. $(\phi \vee \psi)$, $\neg\phi$, $(\exists x) \phi$, and $(\forall x) \phi$) then $T(\varphi)$ is $(T(\phi) \wedge T(\psi))$ (resp. $(T(\phi) \vee T(\psi))$, $\neg T(\phi)$, $(\exists x) T(\phi)$ and $(\forall x) T(\phi)$).

The transformation T maps a fixpoint path expression $\mu^+_{s_{X_1},\ldots,s_{X_n}}(\varphi)$ into a relational fixpoint expression $\mu^+_T(\psi(T))$ where $\psi(T)$ is defined by:

$$(concat(X_1, \epsilon, \epsilon) \wedge \ldots \wedge concat(X_n, \epsilon, \epsilon))$$
$$\vee (\exists s_{X_1})\ldots(\exists s_{X_n}) (T(\varphi) \wedge T(s_{X_1}, \ldots, s_{X_n}))$$

Example. The transformation of the fixpoint path expression $\mu^+_{s_X}(\varphi)$ where φ is $X \in s_X.a$ is the relational fixpoint expression $\mu^+_T(\psi(T))$ where $\psi(T)$ is

$$concat(X, \epsilon, \epsilon) \vee (\exists s_X) (T(\varphi) \wedge T(s_X))$$

and $T(\varphi)$ is

$$(\exists Z)[((\exists X_1)(\exists X_2) concat(s_X, X_1, \epsilon) \wedge edge(X_2) \wedge label(X_2, a)$$
$$\wedge concat(Z, X_1, X_2)) \wedge concat(X, Z, \epsilon)]$$

$\square$

---

[7] If t_1 or t_2 or both t_1 and t_2 are ground paths, the translation is a little more complex although it does not entails difficulties.

The use of the build-in predicate *concat* in the above proof is hiding the computation of simple paths. This entails that our translation is not purely relational. This cannot be otherwise because some of our path queries are exponential as (pure) relational queries are polynomialy computable.

Note also that given a relational query over the relational schema given in the above proof, it is not always possible to find an equivalent path query. This is essentially due to the "pointwise" flavor of our path fixpoint operator to be opposed to the "globality" of the relational fixpoint operator.

We now investigate the inverse translation, from relational queries to path queries.

Theorem 2. *There exists a translation T mapping instances over any relational schema onto db-graphs and mapping Fixpoint (resp. While) queries onto Path-Fixpoint (resp. Path-While) queries such that:*

if q_{rel} is a Fixpoint (resp. While) query and r is an instance over a relational schema then

$$T(q_{rel}(r)) = (T(q_{rel}))(T(r)).$$

Proof. The transformation of an instance r over a relation schema $\mathcal{R}$ into a db-graph is summarized by the example of figure 4. In order to translate a relational query $\{(X_1, \ldots, X_n) \mid \varphi\}$ into a path query, we need to capture the active domain of φ. We chose to do that by augmenting the db-graph $T(r)$ by $T(const)$ where *const* is an instance over a unary relation schema CONST(ATT) collecting the constant occurring in φ.

Example. Let us consider the relational instance of figure 4 and let the relational query be $\{(X, Y) \mid R(X, Y) \wedge \neg(X = \text{``}e\text{''}) \wedge \neg(Y = \text{``}f\text{''})\}$. The db-graph of figure 4 representing this instance is augmented by the graph representing the instance $\{const(e), const(f)\}$.

Like in the previous proof, for sake of simplicity, we do not detail, all restrictions that should naturally be taken while "choosing" variable names and we abusively use the same notation for a variable X in a first order formula and its "translation" in a path expression or formula.
The transformation of a relational query $q_{rel} = \{(X_1, \ldots, X_n) \mid \varphi\}$ is the path query defined by:

$$\{(X_1, \ldots, X_n) \mid radom(X_1) \wedge \ldots \wedge radom(X_n) \wedge T(\varphi)\}$$

The path formula $radom(X)$ is meant to capture the domain of the relational instance and is defined by : $(\exists v)\ X \in tuple.v$.

The path formula $T(\varphi)$ which is the transformation of a first order formula φ is defined inductively as follows:

1. if φ is $R(t_1, \ldots, t_n)$ and R is a relation schema whose attributes are $A_1 \ldots A_n$ then $T(\varphi)$ is $(\exists U)\ (U \in \text{``}R\text{''}.tuple \wedge \phi_1 \wedge \ldots \wedge \phi_n)$ where

$$\phi_i = \begin{cases} (\exists \alpha)\ (t_i \triangleright \alpha \wedge (\exists X)\ (X \in U.A_i \wedge X \triangleright \alpha)) & \text{if } t_i \text{ is a variable} \\ (\exists X)\ (X \in U.A_i \wedge X \triangleright a) & \text{if } t_i \text{ is the constant } a \end{cases}$$

2. if φ is $t_1 = t_2$ and t_1 is variable and t_2 is constant then $T(\varphi)$ is $t_1 \triangleright t_2$,
3. if φ is $t_1 = t_2$ and t_1 and t_2 are variables then $T(\varphi)$ is $(\exists \alpha)(t_1 \triangleright \alpha \wedge t_2 \triangleright \alpha)$,
4. if φ is $(\phi \wedge \psi)$ (resp. $(\phi \vee \psi)$) then $T(\varphi)$ is $(T(\phi) \wedge T(\psi))$ (resp. $(T(\phi) \vee T(\psi))$),
5. if φ is $\neg \phi$ then $T(\varphi)$ is $\neg T(\phi)$,
6. if φ is $(\exists x)\ \phi$ then $T(\varphi)$ is $(\exists x)\ (radom(x) \wedge T(\phi))$,
7. if φ is $(\forall x)\ \phi$ then $T(\varphi)$ is $(\forall x)\ (\neg radom(x) \vee T(\phi))$.

The transformation of a relational fixpoint expression $\mu_T^+(\varphi(T))$ where Free$(\varphi) = \{X_1, \ldots, X_n\}$ is the fixpoint path expression

$$\mu_{s_{X_1}, \ldots, s_{X_n}}^+ (radom(X_1) \wedge \ldots \wedge radom(X_n) \wedge T(\varphi))$$

where T is the transformation defined above augmented by:

8. if φ is $T(t_1, \ldots, t_n)$ then $T(\varphi)$ is $\phi_1 \wedge \ldots \wedge \phi_n$ where

$$\phi_i = \begin{cases} (\exists \alpha)\ (s_{X_i} \triangleright \alpha \wedge t_i \triangleright \alpha \wedge \neg(s_{X_i} = \epsilon)) & \text{if } t_i \text{ is a variable} \\ s_{X_i} \triangleright a \wedge \neg(s_{X_i} = \epsilon) & \text{if } t_i \text{ is the constant } a \end{cases}$$

Example. Let us consider the relational fixpoint expression $\mu_{good}^+(\varphi(T))$ where φ is $(\forall X)\ (\neg R(X, Y) \vee good(X))$, that computes the set of nodes in the relation R that are not reachable from a cycle. The associated path fixpoint expression is $\mu_{s_Y}^+(\psi)$ where ψ is

$$(\exists u)\ Y \in tuple.u$$
$$\wedge\ (\forall X)\ (\neg\ ((\exists u)\ X \in tuple.u)$$
$$\vee\ (\neg((\exists U)\ U \in \text{``}R\text{''}.tuple$$
$$\wedge\ (\exists \alpha_1)\ (X \triangleright \alpha_1 \wedge (\exists X_1)\ (X_1 \in U.\text{``}A\text{''} \wedge X_1 \triangleright \alpha_1))$$
$$\wedge\ (\exists \alpha_2)\ (Y \triangleright \alpha_2 \wedge (\exists Y_1)\ (Y_1 \in U.\text{``}B\text{''} \wedge Y_1 \triangleright \alpha_2)))$$
$$\vee\ (\exists \alpha)\ (s_Y \triangleright \alpha \wedge X \triangleright \alpha \wedge \neg(s_Y = \epsilon))))$$

$\square$

Acknowledgments

This work was partially supported by the GDR I3. We thank the anonymous reviewers for their valuable remarks and suggestions.

References

1. S. Abiteboul, R. Hull, and V. Vianu. *Foundations of Databases.* Addision-Wesley, 1995.
2. Serge Abiteboul. Querying semistructured Data. In *ICDT*, pages 1–18, 1997.

3. Serge Abiteboul, Dallan Quass, Jason McHugh, Jennifer Widom, and Janet L. Wiener. The Lorel Query Language for Semistructured Data. *International Journal on Digital Libraries*, 1(1):68–88, 1997.

4. Serge Abiteboul and Victor Vianu. Queries and Computation on the Web. In *ICDT*, 1997.

5. Serge Abiteboul and Victor Vianu. Regular Path Queries with Constraints. In *Proceedings of the Sixteenth ACM SIGACT-SIGMOD-SIGART Symposium on Principles of Database Systems*, Tucson, Arizona, 12–15 May 1997.

6. Bernd Amann and Michel Scholl. Gram : A graph data model and query language. In *4th ACM Conf. on Hypertext and Hypermedia*, pages 138–148, 1992.

7. P. Buneman. Semistructured Data. In *Proceedings of the Sixteenth ACM SIGACT-SIGMOD-SIGART Symposium on Principles of Database Systems*, pages 117–121, Tucson, Arizona, 12–15 May 1997.

8. Peter Buneman, Susan Davidson, Gerd Hillebrand, and Dan Suciu. A query language and optimization techniques for unstructured data. *SIGMOD Record (ACM Special Interest Group on Management of Data)*, 25(2), 1996.

9. Vassilis Christophides, Serge Abiteboul, Sophie Cluet, and Michel Scholl. From Structured Documents to Novel Query Facilities. In Richard T. Snodgrass and Marianne Winslett, editors, *Proceedings of the 1994 ACM SIGMOD International Conference on Management of Data*, pages 313–324, Minneapolis, Minnesota, 24–27 May 1994.

10. M. Consens and A. Mendelzon. GraphLog: a Visual Formalism of Real Life Recursion. In *Proc. 9th ACM Symp. on Principles of Database Systems*, pages 404–416, 1990.

11. Mariano P. Consens and Alberto O. Mendelzon. Expressing Structural Hypertext Queries in GraphLog. In *ACM Hypertext'89 Proceedings*, Information Retrieval II, pages 269–292, 1989.

12. M. Fernandez, D. Florescu, A. Levy, and D. Suciu. A Query Language for a Web-Site Management System. *SIGMOD Record (ACM Special Interest Group on Management of Data)*, 26(3):4–11, 1997.

13. J. Frohn, G. Lausen, and H. Uphoff. Access to Objects by Path Expressions and Rules. In Jorgeesh Bocca, Matthias Jarke, and Carlo Zaniolo, editors, *20th International Conference on Very Large Data Bases, September 12–15, 1994, Santiago, Chile proceedings*, pages 273–284, Los Altos, CA 94022, USA, 1994. Morgan Kaufmann Publishers.

14. David Konopnicki and Oded Shmueli. W3QS: A Query System for the World-Wide Web. In *VLDB*, pages 54–65, 1995.

15. L. V. S. Lakshmanan, F. Sadri, and I. N. Subramanian. A declarative language for querying and restructuring the Web. In IEEE, editor, *Sixth International Workshop on Research Issues in Data Engineering: interoperability of non traditional database systems: proceedings, February 26–27, 1996, New Orleans, Louisiana*, pages 12–21. IEEE Computer Society Press, 1996.

16. A. O. Mendelzon, G. A. Mihaila, and T. Milo. Querying the World Wide Web. *International Journal on Digital Libraries*, 1(1):54–67, 1997.

17. A. O. Mendelzon and T. Milo. Formal Models of Web Queries. In *Proceedings of the sixteenth ACM Symposium on Principles of Database systems*, pages 134–143, 1997.

18. Alberto O. Mendelzon and Peter T. Wood. Finding Regular Simple Paths in Graph Databases. *SIAM Journal on Computing*, 24(6):1235–1258, December 1995.

19. R. Milner. *Communication and concurrency*. Prentice Hall, 1989.

20. D. Quass, A. Rajaraman, Y. Sagiv, and J. Ullman. Querying Semistructured Heterogeneous Information. *Lecture Notes in Computer Science*, 1013:319–344, 1995.

21. J. Van den Bussche and G. Vossen. An Extension of Path Expressions to Simplify Navigation in Object-Oriented Queries. *Lecture Notes in Computer Science*, 760:267–282, 1993.

Incremental Maintenance of Hypertext Views

Giuseppe Sindoni*

Dipartimento di Informatica e Automazione
Università di Roma Tre
Via della Vasca Navale, 79
00146 ROMA - ITALY

sindoni@dia.uniroma3.it
http://poincare.dia.uniroma3.it:8080/~sindoni

(EXTENDED VERSION)

Abstract. A materialized hypertext view is a hypertext containing data
coming from a database and whose pages are stored in files. A Web site
presenting data coming from a database is an example of such a view,
where the hypertext pages are HTML files. Even if the most popular
approach to the generation of such sites is the virtual one, there is also a
rationale for a materialized approach. This paper deals with the maintenance issues required by these derived hypertext to enforce consistency
between page content and database state. Hypertext views are defined
as nested oid-based views over the set of base relations. A specific logical
model is used to describe the structure of the hypertext and a nested
relational algebra extended with an oid invention operator is proposed,
which allows to define views and view updates. A manipulation language
has also been defined, which allow to update the hypertext to reflect
the current database state. Incremental maintenance is performed by an
algorithm that takes as input a set of updates on the database and automatically produces the hypertext update instructions. Dependencies
between database and hypertext are maintained by a suitable auxiliary
data structure, together with logs of database updates. The motivation
of this study is the development of the Araneus Web-Base Management
System, a system that provides both database and Web site management.

1 Introduction

The great success of the Web among user communities is imposing the hypertext paradigm as a privileged means of data communication and interchange
in distributed and heterogeneous environments. An ever-increasing number of
Web sites are becoming huge repositories of data, often coming from existing

---

* This work was partially supported by Ministero dell'Università e della Ricerca Sci-
entifica and Consiglio Nazionale delle Ricerche.

databases. There is hence an emerging need to investigate the relationships between structured data, such as those usually managed by DBMSs, and *semistructured* data, such as those that can be found into a hypertext.

In particular, part of the related research activities are addressing the problems connected with the automatic generation of a Web site as a view over a number of underlying data sources [8, 16, 17, 28, 29]. Some commercial database management systems also offer such functionality [2, 5].

1.1 Rationale for Materialized Hypertext

The most common way of automatically generating a derived hypertext is mainly based on the dynamic construction of virtual pages after a client request. Usually, the request is managed by a specific program (for example a Common Gateway Interface in HTML files) or is described using a specific query language whose statements are embedded into pages. These pages are often called *pull pages*, because it is up to the client browser to *pull out* the interesting information. The pull approach unfortunately has some major drawbacks:

1. it involves a certain degree of DBMS overloading, because every time a page is requested by a client browser, a query is issued to the database for extracting the relevant data;
2. it introduces some platform-dependence, because the embedded queries are usually written in a proprietary language and the CGIs need to be compiled on the specific platform;
3. it hampers site mirroring, because, if the site needs to be moved to another server, either the database needs to be replicated, or some network overload is introduced, due to remote queries.

Lately, a new approach is becoming more and more important among the Web operators, which is based on the concept of *materialized hypertext view*: a derived hypertext whose pages are actually stored by the system on a server or directly on the client machine, using a mark-up language like HTML. This approach overcomes the above disadvantages because: *(i)* pages are static, so the http server can work on its own; *(ii)* there is no need to embed queries or script calls in the pages, standard sites are generated; finally *(iii)*, because of their standardization, sites can be mirrored more easily.

The pages of a materialized hypertext are often called *push pages*, to remember the fact that it is the information delivering system that generates pages and stores them. The so-called "Web channels" (see for example [6, 3, 4]) are heavily based on this *push technology* and they are assuming an ever increasing importance among Web users.

1.2 The Problem

Unfortunately, some additional maintenance issues are required by a materialized hypertext, to enforce consistency between page contents and the current database state. In fact, every time a transaction is issued on the database, its updates must efficiently and effectively be extended to the derived hypertext. In particular, *(i)* updates must be *incremental,* i.e. only the hypertext pages that are dependent of database updates must be updated and *(ii)* all the database updates must propagate to the hypertext, as it will be clarified in the follow.

A similar problem has been studied in the context of materialized relational database views [20] and even extended to nested data models [24, 25]. However, the heterogeneity due to the different data formats makes the hypertext view context different and introduces some new issues. Each page is in fact stored, as a marked-up text file, possibly on a remote server. Then, direct access to the single values into the pages is not allowed. This means that, whenever a page needs to be updated, it needs to be completely regenerated from the new state of the database. Moreover, consistency between pages must be preserved and, as it will be illustrated in the sequel, this is almost the same as preserving consistency between objects.

The problem of dynamically maintaining consistency between base data and derived hypertext is the *hypertext view maintenance problem*[1].

The are a number of related issues:

- different maintenance policies should be allowed (*immediate* or *deferred*);
- this implies the design of auxiliary data structures to keep track of database updates; the management of these structures overloads the system and they have to be as light as possible;
- finally, due to the particular network structure of a hypertext, not only has the consistency between the single pages and the database to be maintained, but also the consistency between page links.

1.3 Contributions

This paper deals with such issues, introducing a manipulation language for a specific class of derived hypertext; an auxiliary data structure for *(i)* representing the dependencies between the database tables and hypertext and *(ii)* logging database updates; and finally, an algorithm for automatic hypertext incremental maintenance.

Hypertext views are defined as *nested oid-based views* over the set of base relations. The reference model is the ARANEUS Data Model (ADM [8]), which, essentially, is a subset of the ODMG standard object model and which allows to describe *structured hypertext* as are usually those derived from a database. A *weaving algebra* (WALG), which is essentially a nested relational algebra extended with an oid-generation operator, is the abstract language to describe hypertext generation and update.

An auxiliary data structure allows to maintain information about the dependencies between database tables and hypertext pages. It is based on the concept

---

[1] The same problem has been addressed in the framework of the STRUDEL project [16] as the problem of *incremental view updates for semistructured data*.

of *view dependency graph*, presented for the first time in [21], which is extended to the maintenance of the class of hypertext described by ADM.

Finally, incremental page maintenance can be performed by an algorithm that takes as input a set of changes on the database and produces a minimal set of update instructions for hypertext pages. The algorithm can be used whenever hypertext maintenance is required

1.4 Paper Organization

The paper is organized as follows. Sec. 2 explains briefly the ADM model and the WALG algebra. In Sec. 3 the derived hypertext maintenance problem is formalized and generation and update functionality are presented for the class of hypertext described by WALG. Sec. 4 presents an algorithm for incremental maintenance of that class of views, together with an auxiliary data structure. Sec. 5 presents a brief overview of previous work in the fields of view maintenance and WEB-based management systems. Finally, Sec. 6 concludes.

2 Defining Hypertext Views

In order to describe hypertext structure and mappings between database and derived views, a specific model and an algebra for hypertext views are used.

Their basic features are described by the following example concerning the scheme of a simple University department database, from which the department Web site is derived[2].

```
Person(Name, Position, E-mail);
PersonInGroup(Name, GName);
ResearchGroup(GName, Topic);
Course(CName, Description);
CourseInstructor(CName, IName);
Lessons(CName, IName, LDate);
```

2.1 A Data Model for Web Hypertext

The reference data model for hypertext views is a subset of the ARANEUS Data Model (ADM), and it will be described in the following, with the help of the scheme of Fig. 1, which gives a graphical intuition of how the model can be used to describe the logical structure of a hypertext.

ADM is a page-oriented model, because page is the main concept. Each hypertext page is seen as an object having an identifier (its URL) and a number of attributes. The structure of a page is abstracted by its *page scheme* and each

---

[2] Here it is assumed that the same course may have more than one instructor and that it must to be possible to represent the fact that a course has an instructor who hasn't still scheduled any lesson.

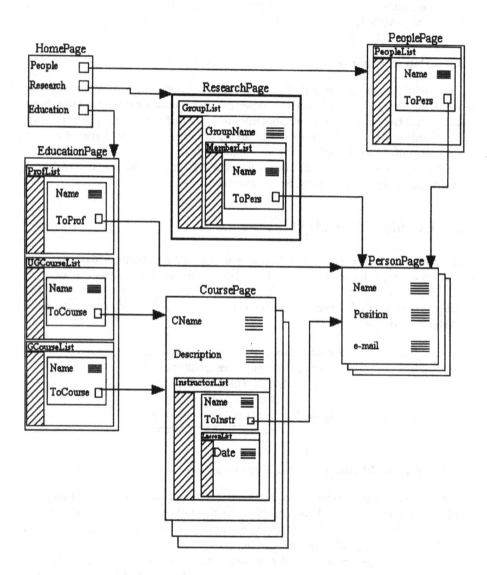

Fig. 1. A portion of a University Department WEB scheme.

page is an instance of a page scheme. The notion of page scheme may be assimilated to the one of relation scheme, in the relational data model, or object class, in object oriented databases. In Fig. 1 for example, home pages of persons are described by the **PersonPage** page scheme.

Each **PersonPage** instance has three simple attributes (**Name**, **Position** and **E-mail**). Pages can also have complex attributes: lists, possibly nested at an arbitrary level, and **links** to other pages. The example shows the **CoursePage** page scheme, having a list attribute (**InstructorList**). Its elements are pairs, formed by a link to an instance of **PersonPage** and the corresponding anchor (**Name**), and a nested list (**LessonList**) of lesson dates. The reader interested in the details of the full model, may see [8].

It is worth to put into evidence that to each page scheme, a template is associated, which contains all graphical page presentation details. It is thus possible to separate the description of the structure of a page from its presentation, in the spirit of XML [7].

2.2 An Algebra for Derived Hypertext Description

With WALG, the weaving algebra, it is so possible to describe a mapping between the database and a materialized hypertext view according to the ADM model. WALG is essentially a nested relational algebra extended with an URL invention operator, which allows an identifier manipulation mechanism to create complex hypertext structures, in a manner similar to the one presented by the authors of [22].

The operators of the algebra work on nested relations and return nested relations, as follows:

- *nest* [12], $\nu_{A \leftarrow B}$, is an operator that groups together tuples which agree on all the attributes that are not in a given set of attributes, say B. It forms a single tuple, for every such group, which has a new attribute, say A, in place of B, whose value is the set of all the B values of the tuples being grouped together;
- *generate* URL, $\text{URL}_{I \leftarrow K}$, is an operator that adds a new attribute to a (nested) relation. The value of I for each tuple of R is uniquely determined by the values of of the attributes in K in the tuple. Thus, it is a Skolem function of these values. The system interprets this values as URLs. The special attribute URL in $\text{URL}_{I \leftarrow K}$ means that the system uses the value of the attribute URL as a page URL for the (nested) tuple. In any other case, the value of I is interpreted as an URL that already exists, thus is a link from this nested tuple (viewed as a page) to another page. I serves as the anchor of the link.
- other relational operators are extended to the nested relational model, for example in the way illustrated in [12].

For example, the WALG expression corresponding to the **CoursePage** view, i.e. to all the **CoursePage** instances (pages), is the following.

$$CoursePage =$$
$$\nu_{InstructorList\leftarrow(IName,ToInstr,LessonList)}$$
$$\nu_{LessonList\leftarrow LDate}$$
$$URL_{URL\leftarrow CName,ToInstr\leftarrow IName}$$
$$\pi_{CName,Description,IName,LDate}$$
$$(Course \bowtie CourseInstructor \bowtie Lessons)$$

(1)

Here `CourseInstructor.IName` and `Course.CName` are the URL attributes, i.e. the attributes whose values are the arguments of the oid generation function. The invention mechanism guarantees the integrity of the generated hypertext: the values of the `ToInstr` attribute and the corresponding URLs are generated by the application of a Skolem function to the same base values.

The weaving algebra is an abstraction of an implemented language, called PENELOPE [8, 27], which allows to define the structure of a Web site according to its ADM model.

3 Maintaining Materialized Hypertext

It has so far been illustrated how the WALG algebra can be used for describing the mapping between a database and a derived hypertext. A manipulation language is then needed to populate the site with page scheme instances and to maintain those instances when database tables are updated. The language is based on invocations of algebra expressions. Moreover, whenever a transaction is issued on the underlying database, hypertext pages become *obsolete*, that is, their current content does not correspond to the current database state. An extension to the system is then needed, in order to enforce, in an incremental manner, consistency between database and hypertext.

3.1 A Manipulation Language for Web Hypertext

In order to perform page creation and maintenance, a simple language has been defined, which is composed of two instructions: `GENERATE` and `REMOVE`. They allow to manipulate hypertext pages and they can refer to the whole hypertext, to all instances of a page scheme or to pages that satisfy a condition.

The `GENERATE` statement has the following general syntax:

```
GENERATE ALL | <PageScheme>
[WHERE    <Condition>].
```

The semantics of the `GENERATE` statement is essentially to create the proper set of pages, taking data from the base tables as specified by the page scheme definitions. The `ALL` keyword allows the generation of all the instances of each page scheme. ''`PageScheme`'' is the name of an ADM page scheme. So, for example, the execution of

```
GENERATE CoursePage;
```

creates all the `CoursePage` page scheme instances, according to Expr. 1.

Finally, it is possible to generate only a subset of a page scheme instances, according to a boolean condition on the attributes of the base tables whose values are involved in the URLs generation, as it will be clarified in the following.

The `REMOVE` statement has a similar syntax:

```
REMOVE ALL | <PageScheme>
[WHERE <Condition>].
```

It allows to remove the specified sets of pages from the hypertext. ''Condition'' is again a boolean condition on the attributes of the base tables whose values are involved in the URLs generation.

3.2 Incremental Page Maintenance

The following example will illustrate the hypertext maintenance problem and clarify the semantics of the manipulation primitives.

Let us have a transaction inserting the new instructor `Turlow` into the Database course staff together with the scheduled lessons: the corresponding inserted tuples are [`Databases, Turlow`] in the `CourseInstructor` table and {[`Databases, Turlow, 15-4-1998`], [`Databases, Turlow, 17-4-1998`]} in the `Lessons` table. This transaction will affect the `CoursePage` view, because the view definition involves some of the `CourseInstructor` and `Lessons` attributes (see Expr. 1). The Web site pages need to be updated accordingly.

The simple "brute force" approach to the problem would simply regenerate the whole hypertext on the new state of the database, clearly performing a number of unnecessary page creation operations. A more sophisticated approach may regenerate only the instances of the `CoursePage` scheme, again unnecessarily regenerating all the pages relative to courses different from the `Databases` one. The optimal solution is hence to regenerate only the page instance corresponding to the `Databases` course.

The corresponding WALG expression follows. It describes the regeneration of the `Databases` course page. The selection condition in fact, extracts only tuples which values are presented in the `Databases` course page.

$$
\begin{aligned}
CoursePage^{Reg} = \\
\nu_{InstructorList \leftarrow (IName,ToInstr,LessonList)} \\
\nu_{LessonList \leftarrow LDate} \\
URLURL \leftarrow CName,ToInstr \leftarrow IName \\
\pi_{CName,Description,IName,LDate} \\
\sigma_{CName="Databases"} \\
(Course \bowtie CourseInstructor \bowtie Lessons)
\end{aligned}
\tag{2}
$$

The database transaction is extended by the following manipulation statement:

```
GENERATE CoursePage
WHERE    Course.CName = 'Databases';
```

Let us now consider a scenario of deletion.

Suppose the **Lessons** table contains several tuples about Databases lessons and one of them is deleted. The resulting nested relation will still contain a tuple for the **Databases** course, as the database deletion involves a nested value in the hypertext. Hence, the corresponding page should not be removed from the hypertext, but simply regenerated, from the new state of the base tables. The corresponding WALG expression is the same as Expr. 2.

The transaction is again extended by:

```
GENERATE CoursePage
WHERE     Course.CName = 'Databases';
```

which is executed on the updated database, hence regenerating the **Databases** course page containing the remaining lesson dates.

On the contrary, suppose we remove the whole Theoretical Computer Science course from the database. The resulting nested relation will not contain anymore tuples for the **Theoretical Computer Science** course, hence, the corresponding page should be actually removed from the hypertext:

```
REMOVE CoursePage
WHERE   Course.CName = 'TheoreticalCS'.
```

From the **WHERE** condition, the corresponding URL is generated:

$$CourseUrl^{Rem} = \text{URL}_{\text{URL} \leftarrow CName} \atop {\sigma_{CName = "TheoreticalCS"} \atop (Course)} \tag{3}$$

and the corresponding page is removed from the hypertext.

Essentially, each database deletion that involves values of URL attributes, corresponds to removing the pages whose URL is created from those values.

To summarize the important points about the two examples:

- addition of tuples may require *addition* of pages or *regeneration* of pages;
- deletion of tuples may require *deletion* of pages or *regeneration* of pages.

The main maintenance problems in this framework, are: *(i)* to automatically produce the proper conditions for the **GENERATE** and **REMOVE** statements and *(ii)* to distinguish database updates corresponding to page removals, from database updates corresponding to page replacements. They are solved by allowing the system to log deletions from each base table and to maintain information about which base tables are involved in URL generation of each page scheme instances.

In the following, an auxiliary data structure for managing such information will be presented. The structure is used by an incremental maintenance algorithm able to produce all the statements to update a page scheme instances, starting from a set of database updates.

4 A Framework for Automatic Incremental Page Maintenance

The overall aim of this work is to provide a tool for relieving a Web administrator of all the run-time page maintenance problems. In particular, an algorithm and an auxiliary data structure have been designed, which are suitable to be used both for *immediate* maintenance and *deferred* maintenance.

Immediate maintenance of hypertext pages is performed when each database transaction is immediately extended with the manipulation statements to update pages that are dependent on the transaction.

When the hypertext is maintained with a deferred approach, its update operations are postponed at a later moment and possibly activated by a triggering mechanism. Deferred maintenance involves problems of site quality analysis, concurrency control and transaction overhead, which will be subjects of further research.

4.1 Design Requirements

The design of the maintenance algorithm and data structure has then been focused on the following main requirements:

- basing the algorithm on the (re)generation or removal of a whole nested tuple (i.e. page) as the atomic maintenance operation: database modifications are propagated to the hypertext by executing page manipulation operations, as it will be clarified in the follow;
- designing an algorithm to asynchronously maintain the instances of a given page scheme, in such a way that it may be used either for immediately extending a database transaction on which the page scheme depends, or for deferred maintenance after a condition triggering.
- creating a *core data structure* to maintain essential information about nested object views and to log database updates, in order to allow deferred maintenance also.

4.2 The Page Scheme Dependency Graph

The system has then been designed to effectively manage the sets of inserted and deleted tuples of each base relation since the last hypertext maintenance. These sets will be addressed as Δ^+ and Δ^-. Δ have been introduced for the first time and in a different context by the authors of [18], and their nature and use in this framework will be clarified in the sequel.

The auxiliary data structure is a graph that allows to maintain information about dependencies between base relations and derived views. It is conceptually derived from the *view dependency graph* defined in [24], which is extended to maintain information about oid attributes, i.e. the attributes of each base relation whose values are the arguments of the oid generation operator. In Fig. 2, part of the dependency graph for the example site of Fig. 1 is depicted. There are two kinds of nodes representing respectively the base relations and the derived page schemes. Edges represent the dependency of a page scheme from a base relation, i.e. the fact that the relation is involved in the generation of the page scheme instances. If an attribute of the base relation is involved in the oid generation, its name is quoted in the edge label. Moreover, for each base relation, the current Δ are explicitly stored[3]. Finally, each view node has a pointer to both the Δ of each of its base tables: it points the entry from which the next maintenance operation has to start, i.e. the first of the tuples corresponding to updates that have not been yet propagated to that page scheme instances. Of course, when maintenance of a page scheme is immediate, there is no need to manage those pointers for that view.

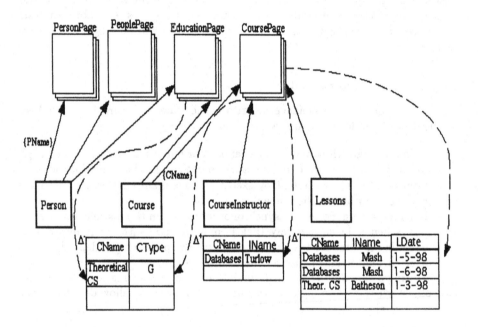

Fig. 2. A Portion of the Dependency Graph for the University Department WEB Scheme.

In Fig. 2 for example, the **CoursePage** view is connected with its base relations (**Course**, **CourseInstructor** and **Lessons**) and the connection with the **Course** relation is labeled with the name of the URL attribute (**CName**). The view has also pointers to the Δ of each relation. In particular, each pointer refers to the first Δ entry that has to be used for the next view maintenance. Here, a "snapshot" is depicted where all the Theoretical Computer Science tuples were deleted from the base tables; the tuple [**Databases, Turlow**] was

---

[3] For the sake of simplicity, in Fig. 2 not all the Δ are depicted.

inserted into the `CourseInstructor` table; and the tuples {[`Databases`, `Mash`, `1-5-98`], [`Databases`, `Mash`, `1-6-98`]} were also deleted from the lessons table. All these updates are still waiting to be propagated to the relevant hypertext views.

The portion of a Δ starting from the tuple pointed by a view will be addressed as the *Waiting Portion* of the Δ for that view. After each maintenance operation, the pointers are moved to the end of the Δ. An overall Δ update operation is needed of course, to delete from Δ all the tuples that are not anymore concerned by view maintenance operations.

The structure is light enough to be maintained without excessive overhead for the system because Δ entries are independent of the number of views. The pointer mechanism allows in fact to "share" each Δ among all the views over the same relation. Moreover, at run-time, the number of updates is usually small with respect to relations.

Note that it is possible to adopt a different maintenance approach for each view. One can decide for example to regenerate the `CoursePage` instances after each transaction on the base tables, to keep students early aware of lessons dates and changes; while adopting a batch approach, for example doing maintenance at the beginning of each course session, for the unique instance of the `EducationPage`.

4.3 An Algorithm for the Maintenance of Page Scheme Instances

The algorithm design has then been based on page regeneration as the single maintenance operation. Each maintenance transaction corresponds essentially to the regeneration and/or removal of the instances of a page scheme. That is, given a page scheme, the algorithm produces all the needed manipulation statements to update the page scheme instances with respect to the tuples contained in the Δ^+ and Δ^- of the relation.

The algorithm produces essentially two kinds of page update statements: **REMOVE** statements and **GENERATE** statements, whose semantics have been described in Sec. 3.1. In Sec. 3.2, one of the main problems in maintaining the nested views in case of deletions has been pointed out: some deletions correspond to nested tuple (i.e. pages) updates, while some others correspond to actual nested tuple deletions, that is, page removals. The capability of managing the Δ^- of base relations allows also to provide an efficient solution to this problem.

Now, let an URL–*relation* (with respect to a page scheme) be a base relation in which at least one of the attributes are involved in the generation of the URLs of the instances of the page scheme. For what has been illustrated in Sec. 3.2, each tuple in each Δ^- of an URL–relation corresponds to the removal of at least one page[4]. Then, for each URL relation (UR_i) the remove condition can be produced using the names of the URL attributes (UA_j) and their values in the waiting portion of the Δ^- of the relation (UV_k):

---

[4] A page scheme may have in general more than one URL relation.

$$UR_i.UA_1 = UV_1 \text{ AND } \ldots\text{AND } UR_i.UA_n = UV_1$$
$$\text{OR}$$
$$\ldots$$
$$\text{OR}$$
$$UR_i.UA_1 = UV_m \text{ AND } \ldots\text{AND } UR_i.UA_n = UV_m$$

where m is the number of tuples in the waiting portion of the Δ^- and n is the number of URL attributes of the relation. The algorithm produces one such condition for each URL relation (in the sequel they will be addressed as $U\Delta^-C_i$) and uses them for the production of the following update instructions:

REMOVE $< PageScheme >$
WHERE $U\Delta^-C_1$;
$\ldots$
REMOVE $< PageScheme >$
WHERE $U\Delta^-C_p$;

where p is the number of URL relations.

After page deletions, the pointers from the page scheme to the Δ^- of the URL–relations must to be moved to the end of the Δ^- itself to keep track that maintenance has been performed on that page scheme.

The Δ^- of base relations that are not involved in URL creation, together with all the Δ^+, contribute to determine the set of pages to be generated again, as it will be clarified in the sequel. For each of such Δ, the proper regeneration conditions are produced and they contribute to form the **WHERE** condition for the **GENERATE** statements.

Let us start with inserted tuples. If the instances of a page scheme are generated starting from a collection of base relations $(R_1, \ldots, R_q)$, then the tuples inserted into a table (say R_i) appear in the Δ^+ of the table, which is joined with the other base tables to give a new relation $(R\bowtie_i)$. From this relation the system, using the names of the URL attributes coming from the dependency graph, is able to extract the condition (Δ^+C_i) to use for incremental regeneration of the page scheme instances with respect to $R\bowtie_i$:

$$R\bowtie_i.UA_1 = UV_1 \text{ AND } \ldots\text{AND } R\bowtie_i.UA_n = UV_1$$
$$\text{OR}$$
$$\ldots$$
$$\text{OR}$$
$$R\bowtie_i.UA_1 = UV_m \text{ AND } \ldots\text{AND } R\bowtie_i.UA_n = UV_m$$

The generated statements to maintain the view with respect to inserted tuples are then the following:

```
GENERATE  < PageScheme >
WHERE     U Δ⁺C₁;
...
GENERATE  < PageScheme >
WHERE     U Δ⁺C_q;
```

They generate the page scheme instances, using the conditions to regenerate only the pages corresponding to inserted tuples, as described by Expr. 2. The construction of the condition and the generation of update statements is repeated for each $U\Delta^+$ of the base relations.

The case for deletions is similar but with a slight subtlety. As it has been illustrated, deletions on URL base tables correspond to physical deletions of hypertext files. Deletions on base tables whose attributes are not involved in URL generation, must correspond to the regeneration of the pages that contain the deleted values, which have to disappear from those pages. Then, Δ^- of URL relations must not be taken into account for condition generation, because its entries have already been propagated as page removals: tuples deleted from the URL relations correspond to page removals as previously illustrated. The system will generate only $(q - p)$ conditions $(NU\Delta^+C_i)$ corresponding to the non–URL base relations of the page scheme and, consequently, only $(q - p)$ **GENERATE** statements.

There is anyway some redundancy that may arise in such a maintenance process.

Modifications. Value modifications are handled as deletions followed by insertions. Hence, if a table tuple is updated, an entry is inserted in its Δ^- and one in its Δ^+. Two different cases must be distinguished.

1. **The table is involved in URL generation.** A condition is produced for the corresponding **REMOVE** statement, and a different condition is produced for the **GENERATE** statement. The page identified by the old URL is correctly removed and then a new page is regenerated, which is identified by a new URL.
2. **The table is not involved in URL generation.** The same condition is produced from the Δ^- and Δ^+ entry and two identical **GENERATE** statement are produced.

Different updates generating the same condition. If two tuples inserted into (or deleted from) different tables originate the same condition, again, two identical **GENERATE** statement are produced.

These drawbacks can be avoided by the following optimization:

1. generation conditions are produced all at once;
2. duplicates are eliminated from generation conditions before producing the **GENERATE** statements.

The maintenance algorithm is based on the previously illustrated principles. Its definition and description follow.

INPUT The Page Scheme Dependency Graph of a derived hypertext, the underlying database and the WALG definition of the page scheme whose instances are to be maintained.

OUTPUT The maintenance statements for the page scheme instances.

Sketch of the algorithm

1. build conditions deriving from Δ^- of URL tables $(U\Delta^-C_i)$;
2. produce

> **REMOVE** $< PageScheme >$
> **WHERE** $U\Delta^-C_1$;
>
> $\ldots$
>
> **REMOVE** $< PageScheme >$
> **WHERE** $U\Delta^-C_p$;

3. move to the bottom the pointers from the view node to the Δ^- of the URL tables;
4. build conditions deriving from Δ^- of non–URL base tables $(NU\Delta^-C_i)$;
5. build conditions deriving from Δ^+ of all the base tables (Δ^+C_i);
6. eliminate duplicates from $NU\Delta^-C_i \cup \Delta^+C_i$;
7. produce

> **GENERATE** $< PageScheme >$
> **WHERE** $NU\Delta^-C_1$
>
> $\ldots$
>
> **GENERATE** $< PageScheme >$
> **WHERE** $NU\Delta^-C_r$
>
> $\ldots$
>
> **GENERATE** $< PageScheme >$
> **WHERE** Δ^+C_1
>
> $\ldots$
>
> **GENERATE** $< PageScheme >$
> **WHERE** Δ^+C_s;

> where r and s are the number of remaining URL and non–URL conditions after duplicate elimination.

8. move to the bottom the pointers from the view node to each Δ^+ and Δ^- of non–URL tables;
9. delete from each Δ all the tuples that are in no more Waiting Portion.

Conditions are produced in the way illustrated in Sec. 4.3.

The algorithm meets the following requirements:

- each database update is propagated to the hypertext, because insertions and deletions are logged, and conditions are produced from logs;
- hypertext maintenance is incremental, because *(i)* each database update is propagated to the dependent views only, *(ii)* the use of conditions allows to restrict page (re)generation to the relevant pages only and *(iii)* the set of (re)generated pages is minimal, because conditions redundancy is avoided;
- finally, deletions corresponding to page removals are distinguished from those corresponding to page generations, thanks to information held by the Page Scheme Dependency Graph.

5 Discussion of Related Work

Materialized Views. The principle of incremental maintenance has been previously explored by several authors in the context of materialized database views [10, 9, 11, 21, 26, 19, 20, 24, 25, 30].

Gupta and Mumick [20], provide an useful overview of problems, techniques and implementations of materialized views. Unfortunately, the specific issues connected with nested and oid-based views are not discussed.

The authors of [10] were the first ones to introduce the concept of materialized view on relational databases. They propose an incremental maintenance algorithm for SPJ views[5] and they introduce a method to automatically find out if a given view is independent of a database update. Those principles are extended and carried through in [9], where the emphasis is on the view independence problem. Though a similar approach could be used in the context of hypertext views, for detecting which page scheme is affected by a database update, the explicit representation of dependencies between each page scheme and its base tables has been preferred to avoid SPJ view limitation and for efficiency reasons.

Ceri and Widom [11] propose a facility to automatically derive production rules to maintain a materialized view. The idea of having a manipulation language to propagate updates to views is similar to the one presented in this paper, which extends that idea to the maintenance of hypertext views.

The authors of [21] propose the *Counting Algorithm* for incremental materialized views maintenance. Though their major aim was to provide a framework to deal with the management of view duplicates, their proposal has been considered as a starting point by successive works aimed at maintaining materialized views in nested data models.

Kawaguchi and others [24, 25] discuss materialized views defined over a nested data model. They use a Datalog-like view definition language and they extend the Counting Algorithm of [21] to handle views over nested base tables. The present proposal deals with issues arising in the different context of nested oid-based views that are stored as hypertext pages (i.e. text files). In particular: each page (view tuple) is a nested object and a different maintenance approach is considered, which (re)generates the whole set of update-interested pages.

---

[5] In SPJ views the only allowed relational operators are Selection Projection and Join.

The orthogonal problem of deferring maintenance operations, thus allowing the definition of different policies, has been studied by the authors of [13, 23] and [14]. One of the future directions of this project will explore such issues in the framework of hypertext views.

Hypertext View Generation. The motivation of this work is the development of the ARANEUS Web Base Management System [1]: a system for managing collections of highly structured data and semistructured data.

A number of systems have been proposed to deal with the contemporary presence of structured and semistructured data. Some of them specifically address the problem of generating a Web site as a view over a set of data sources [16, 15, 17, 28, 29]. None of them support incremental maintenance and their view generation mechanism lacks of the notion of site scheme. They are either based on a graph-based model [16, 28, 29], or on a model derived from hypermedia authoring [15, 17].

Finally, there are some commercial database systems (see, for example, [2, 5]) providing Web page generation facilities. They are however based mainly on pull techniques and they also lack of the notion of site scheme.

6 Conclusions and Future Work

One of the most important problems in managing information repositories where structured and semistructured data live together is to provide applications with the ability of managing materialized hypertext views.

Contributions. This paper has presented a solution for the maintenance of such views, which is based on a specific data model for Web sites and on an algebra for mapping pages on base data according to the site model. This approach resulted particularly suitable for defining a framework for incremental updates of the views. In fact, the capability of formally defining mappings between base data and a derived hypertext has allowed to easily define hypertext updates in the same formalism.

In order to provide the system with the ability of propagating database updates to the relevant pages, a Data Manipulation Language has been defined, which allows to automatically generate or remove a derived site or a specific subset of its pages. The presence of a DML for pages allowed the definition of an algorithm for their automatic maintenance. The algorithm makes use of a specific data structure that keeps track of view-table dependencies and that logs table updates. Its output is a set of DML statements to be executed in order to update the hypertext.

Future Work. These proposals are still under implementation. The current task is to provide the system with immediate maintenance capabilities, thus directly extending each database transaction.

The algorithm will later be used for the implementation of different view maintenance policies. It will be allowed to defer maintenance to a later time and to perform it in batch mode by using the table update logs and implementing proper triggering mechanisms.

There are a number of connected problems that may deserve further investigations.

- Defining the most suitable maintenance policy for each page class involves a site analysis process to extract data about page accesses and, more generally, data about site quality and impact.
- If a deferred policy is chosen for a given class of pages, this causes part of the hypertext to become temporarily inconsistent with its definition. Consequently, transactions that read multiple page schemes may not execute in an efficient manner. The concurrency control problem need to be extended to the context of hypertext views and suitable algorithms have to be developed. In particular, the problem of avoiding *dangling links*, i.e. links pointing nowhere because the formerly target page has been removed, should carefully be addressed.
- Performance analysis are needed in order to show how, in both the above approaches, transaction overhead and view refresh time are affected. The results of these analysis should be used to define a set of *system-tuning* parameters to be used by site administrators for optimization purposes.

Acknowledgements

The author would like to thank Alessandro Masci and Paolo Merialdo for some useful discussions on preliminary drafts and previous versions of the paper. Thanks also to all the ISE people at Rutherford Appleton Laboratory for interesting discussions about the topics of the paper. Thanks finally to the anonymous referees for having helped so much in improving the overall quality of the paper.

References

[1] The ARANEUS Project Home Page. http://poincare.dia.uniroma3.it:8080/-Araneus.

[2] Informix Home Page. http://www.informix.com.

[3] Microsoft Webcast. http://www.eu.microsoft.com/ie/ie40/features/-chan-webcasting.htm.

[4] Netscape Netcaster Release Notes. http://www.netscape.com/ko/eng/-mozilla/4.0/intl/relnotes.html.

[5] Oracle Home Page. http://www.oracle.com.

[6] PointCast Home Page. http://www.pointcast.com.

[7] XML Page at W3C. http://www.w3.org/TR/PR-xml.html.

[8] P. Atzeni, G. Mecca, and P. Merialdo. To Weave the Web. In *International Conf. on Very Large Data Bases (VLDB'97), Athens, Greece, August 26-29*, pages 206–215, 1997. http://poincare.dia.uniroma3.it:8080/Araneus/.

[9] J.A. Blakeley, N. Coburn, and P. Larson. Updating derived relations: Detecting irrelevant and autonomously computable updates. *ACM Transactions on Database Systems*, 14(3):369–400, September 1989.

[10] J.A. Blakeley, P. Larson, and F.W. Tompa. Efficiently updating materialized views. In *ACM SIGMOD International Conf. on Management of Data (SIGMOD'86), Washington, D.C.*, pages 61–71, 1986.

[11] S. Ceri and J. Widom. Deriving production rules for incremental view maintenance. In *Seventeenth International Conference on Very Large Data Bases (VLDB'91)*, pages 577–589, 1991.

[12] L. Colby. A recursive algebra and query optimization for nested relations. In *ACM SIGMOD International Conf. on Management of Data (SIGMOD'89), Portland*, pages 273–283, 1989.

[13] L. Colby, T. Griffin, L. Libkin, I. Mumick, and H. Trickey. Algorithms for deferred view maintenance. In *ACM SIGMOD International Conf. on Management of Data (SIGMOD'96), Montreal, Canada*, pages 469–480, 1996.

[14] L. Colby, A. Kawaguchi, D. Lieuwen, I. Mumick, and K. Ross. Supporting multiple view maintenance policies. In *ACM SIGMOD International Conf. on Management of Data (SIGMOD'97), Tucson, Arizona*, pages 405–416, 1997.

[15] G. Falquet, J. Guyot, and L. Nerima. Language and tool to specify hypertext views on databases. In *Proceedings of the Workshop on the Web and Databases (WebDB'98) (in conjunction with EDBT'98)* http://poincare.dia.uniroma3.-it:8080/webdb98, 1998.

[16] M. Fernandez, D. Florescu, J. Kang, A. Levy, and D. Suciu. STRUDEL – a Web site management system. In *ACM SIGMOD International Conf. on Management of Data (SIGMOD'97), Tucson, Arizona*, 1997. Exhibits Program.

[17] P. Fraternali and P. Paolini. A conceptual model and a tool environment for developing more scalable, dynamic, and customizable Web applications. In *VI Intl. Conference on Extending Database Technology (EDBT'98), Valencia, Spain, March 23-27*, 1998.

[18] S. Ghandeharizadeh, R. Hull, and D. Jacobs. Heraclitus: Elevating deltas to be first-class citizens in a database programming language. *ACM Transactions on Database Systems*, 21(3):370–426, September 1996.

[19] T. Griffin and L. Libkin. Incremental maintenance of views with duplicates. In *ACM SIGMOD International Conf. on Management of Data (SIGMOD'95), San Jose*, 1995.

[20] A. Gupta and I. S. Mumick. Maintenance of materialized views: Problems, techniques and applications. *Data Engineering, IEEE Computer Society*, 18(2):3–18, 1995.

[21] A. Gupta, I.S. Mumick, and V.S. Subrahmanian. Maintaining views incrementally. In *ACM SIGMOD International Conf. on Management of Data (SIGMOD'93), Washington, D.C.*, pages 157–166, 1993.

[22] R. Hull and M. Yoshikawa. On the equivalence of database restructurings involving object identifiers. In *Tenth ACM SIGACT SIGMOD SIGART Symp. on Principles of Database Systems*, pages 328–340, 1991.

[23] A. Kawaguchi, D. Lieuwen, I. Mumick, D. Quass, and K. Ross. Concurrency control theory for deferred materialized views. In *Sixth International Conference on Data Base Theory, (ICDT'97), Delphi (Greece), Lecture Notes in Computer Science*, pages 306–320, 1997.

[24] A. Kawaguchi, D. Lieuwen, I. Mumick, and K. Ross. View maintainance in nested data models. In *Workshop on Materialized Views: Techniques and Applications (in conjunction with ACM SIGMOD 1996)*, pages 72–83, 1996.

[25] A. Kawaguchi, D. Lieuwen, I. Mumick, and K. Ross. Implementing incremental view maintainance in nested data models. In *Sixth Intern. Workshop on Database Programming Languages (DBPL'97), Estes Park, Colorado, August 18-20*, 1997.

[26] A.Y. Levy and Y. Sagiv. Queries independent of updates. In *International Conf. on Very Large Data Bases (VLDB'93), Dublin*, pages 171–181, 1993.

[27] G. Mecca, P. Atzeni, A. Masci, P. Merialdo, and G. Sindoni. The Araneus Web-base management system. In *ACM SIGMOD International Conf. on Management of Data (SIGMOD'98), Seattle, Washington*, 1998. Exhibition Section.

[28] F. Paradis and A. M. Vercoustre. A language for publishing virtual documents on the Web. In *Proceedings of the Workshop on the Web and Databases (WebDB'98) (in conjunction with EDBT'98)* http://poincare.dia.uniroma3.it:8080/webdb98, 1998.

[29] G. Simeon and S. Cluet. Using YAT to build a Web server. In *Proceedings of the Workshop on the Web and Databases (WebDB'98) (in conjunction with EDBT'98)* http://poincare.dia.uniroma3.it:8080/webdb98, 1998.

[30] D. Vista. *Optimizing Incremental View Maintenance Expressions in Relational Databases*. PhD thesis, University of Toronto, 1997.

Using YAT to Build a Web Server*

Jérôme Siméon and Sophie Cluet

INRIA, BP 105, 78153 Le Chesnay, France
{Jerome.Simeon,Sophie.Cluet}@inria.fr
http://www-rocq.inria.fr/verso/{Jerome.Simeon,Sophie.Cluet}/

Abstract. Integration of heterogeneous data sources in a Web environment has become a major concern of the database community. Novel architectures, data models and query languages have been proposed but the complementary problem of data conversion has been less studied. The YAT system provides a means to build software components based on data conversion in a simple and declarative way. We show that the YAT system can also be used to create integrated Web views over heterogeneous data sources very easily. Only minor changes were required for YAT to provide data integration (as opposed to data conversion) in a Web environment. Finally, we report on our experience while building the Verso Web site using YAT.

1 Introduction

Many semistructured data models (e.g. [18,8,1,3]) and appropriate query languages (e.g. [7,2,12]) have been proposed in the last few years. All of them have been designed as a means to integrate heterogeneous, more or less regular data. We pursued a complementary approach and focused on a system to support data conversion (as opposed to integration). The main motivations for this work were: (i) data conversion is an important part of the global integration problem and has been kept hidden in other proposals (usually managed by hand-made wrappers), (ii) existing semistructured models do not consider ordered collections which is crucial to many existing formats, especially in documents (e.g. HTML, SGML or XML), (iii) conversion languages for semistructured data require some typing capacities that are currently lacking in other proposals, and finally, (iv) query languages do not provide the rich restructuring capabilities required to perform data conversions.

In this paper, we describe how the YAT system [10,11], that we built for data conversion, can also be used for data integration in a Web environment. Essential features such as query decomposition and optimisation, persistence or view maintenance are still missing. Yet, we show that, as it is, the YAT system is very well suited to develop quickly, in a simple and declarative way, sophisticated Web views over heterogeneous data sources.

---

* This work is partially supported by the OPAL project (Esprit IV project number 20377) and the AFIRST association (Association Franco-Israélienne pour la Recherche Scientifique et Technique).

The YAT system relies on a data model allowing a rich and uniform representation of data and a rule based language called YATL. The YAT system provides a graphical interface, a library of basic import/export wrappers and standard conversion programs, an interpretor for the language, some type-checking facilities, as well as various mechanisms to combine or compose programs. Its originality, as compared to other similar approaches, can be summarized as follows:

YAT vs other semistructured based systems: As already existing semistructured data models (e.g., [18,8,1]), we rely on a simple representation of graphs to capture data coming from heterogeneous sources. But YAT also provides (i) the possibility to order the outgoing edges from a vertex (in the style of [1]), and most importantly (ii) the ability to capture various levels of representation via a sophisticated type mechanism (as we will illustrate in Section 3 on Web-oriented examples).

The YAT language (YATL) is a declarative, rule based language designed for the specification of conversion/integration programs. Its design is slightly different from that of a query language and for instance, it does not provide query facilities such as generalized path expressions [15,9,2]. On the other hand, it offers more powerful restructuration primitives and explicit Skolem functions, as in [14,17,12], to manipulate identifiers and create complex graphs. Its main originality is in the manipulation of non-set collections, allowing to manage ordering and grouping in collections with duplicates (e.g., list, bag). Both these features are important for most usual formats and essential in HTML.

As opposed to most integration systems, YAT does not yet support advanced functionalities such as persistence or view maintenance. However, we believe that such systems could benefit from the YAT model and conversion language which provide richer modeling and restructuring capacities.

YAT vs other Web targeted systems: Several systems are designed for the management of Web sites over legacy heterogeneous sources. Some proposals rely on semistructured data models (e.g., WebOQL [3], Strudel [12]), others on a document driven approach (e.g., [23,20]). Finally, [4,5] focuses on the maintenance of large sites leaving aside the problems related to the heterogeneity of the input sources.

Because other semistructured approaches like [12] lack the ability to deal with ordered collections, they require two distinct languages: one to describe the integration part of the process, another to specify the generated HTML documents. YATL supports both tasks directly.

A document-driven approach is followed in [23]. It proposes to generate Web sites starting from an editor and allows to define HTML documents with embedded queries over heterogeneous sources. However, this system does not provide integration capabilities but only mapping to HTML, using a rather procedural language.

The ARANEUS Project [4,5] proposes a conceptual and a logical model to design Web sites. The PENELOPE language then allows to specify the generation of HTML pages from relationnal databases. As opposed to this system,

YAT offers a quick and easy-to-use approach which allows to integrate heterogeneous sources but does not consider the maintenance of the generated server.

The paper is organized as follows. In the remainder of the paper, we will use the Verso Group publications Web site as an example to demonstrate the YAT system abilities[1]. In Section 2, we present the architecture and installation procedure of a Web server with the YAT system. The YAT model, which is used for the representation of data from the input sources and of the HTML pages, is introduced in Section 3, while Section 4 shows how to build the HTML view over the original sources using a YATL program. Finally, Section 5 describes how this program is applied and how the HTML view is evaluated. Section 6 concludes the paper and outlines future work.

2 Building a Web Server with YAT

Building a Web server with YAT can be done quickly and easily. To demonstrate this, we use the Verso group publication site as an example. This server is built on top of two heterogeneous sources: (i) an ODMG database management system (namely O_2) stores information about the group researchers (name, contact information, email address etc.) and (ii) XML documents contain the list of the group publications (title, authors, abstract etc.). This set of XML documents is indexed with WAIS [22], providing full text retrieval capabilities to the user.

Figure 1 describes the architecture of the Web site. It is a very standard mediator/wrapper architecture [24]. Wrappers for ODMG, XML (resp. HTML) import (resp. export) information about the connected sources to (resp. from) the YAT middleware model. As will be illustrated in the next section, they implement a straightforward translation from/to YAT. The mediator is used to (i) integrate the input sources and (ii) to specify the conversion from these sources to an HTML YAT representation.

The Web server is built in four steps:

1. *Determine the relevant data sources*
   In our application, we need to access the O_2 DBMS and some XML files.
2. *Connect these sources to YAT supplied wrappers and the wrappers to a YAT mediator.*
   The YAT system provides a library of standard wrappers[2]. Each wrapper supports three kinds of services:
   – Connection/disconnection to/from a source or a mediator,
   – Extraction of meta-information about the connected source (e.g. which model or format, what are available query primitives, etc.),

---

[1] See http://www-rocq.inria.fr/verso/publications/ for a demonstration.
[2] Current list of wrappers covers HTML and XML documents, Object-oriented databases and BibTeX. Consult the YAT system homepage for an updated list of existing wrappers (http://www-rocq.inria.fr/verso/Jerome.Simeon/YAT/).

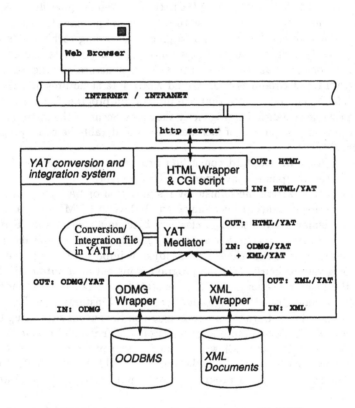

Fig. 1. Architecture of a Web server with YAT

- Import/Export facilities. Each wrapper provides information from its source at different levels of detail. For instance, the ODMG wrapper provides YAT representation of: (i) the ODMG model, (ii) a specific schema or class (for a given database), (iii) actual data (for a given query or object identifier). As will be explained in Section 3, the YAT model imposes no restriction on what the wrappers may generate. For instance, if needed, one could easily import a partially instantiated schema.

3. *Write the integration/conversion program using YATL or its graphical interface.*

This obviously is the most complex part. The Web designer first asks the input/output wrappers for the structure of the data he plans to export/import. This structure can be more or less precise according to his needs (see the wrappers Import/Export facilities above). Then he writes an integration (conversion) program that fits to these data structures. In the example, the program input combines ODMG and XML data structures and the output is HTML compliant. Note that the integration program has also to resolve the possible semantic heterogeneity that may occur in the sources.

YAT provides a number of facilities that considerably help the programmer in this task:

- A library of standard conversion programs (e.g., a generic ODMG to HTML-compliant conversion *à la* O_2Web [16]).
- A customization mechanism by instantiation of YAT programs that allows, for instance, to customize an ODMG to HTML program in order to display a given schema, class or object in a special way. This is done as follows: (i) a generic program is loaded, (ii) a more specific YAT representation of the schema/class/object is imported through the wrapper or given explicitly, (iii) the program is instantiated automatically to fit the given representation. The generated rules can then be modified either manually or through another round of instantiation. For instance, we may instantiate the program again on the output side, using this time a new HTML structure imported from a WYSIWYG editor.
- A mechanism that allows to combine two programs into one. For instance, one may combine the ODMG to HTML and XML to HTML programs to form a program whose input combines ODMG and XML compliant data.

Using these mechanisms, writing a program is, most of the time, only a matter of slightly modifying another existing set of rules. Finally, YAT supports a type-checking module that can be used to verify the coherence of the modified program or trace potential specification deficiencies at run time (e.g., some part of the input data does not match any rule of the program). Because of space limitation, we will not describe all these mechanisms any further, but the reader can consult [10] for a more complete presentation.

4. *Describe the data on which the program is to be executed.*

One last information is missing to execute the YATL program, namely the set of actual data on which it will run. Originally, YAT was designed as a conversion system. Thus, a conversion program was called by a user on some given input data. This is not appropriate for a Web system where HTML data has to be generated on the fly according to what is requested. The current version of YAT, relies on a pragmatic solution to this problem: the user specifies the queries that have to be executed on the sources and their relationship with the program rules (see Section 4 for an example). A more elegant solution would be to describe this kind of mapping at the wrapper level in the style of [19]. This solution requires additional work related to query processing in mediator/wrappers architectures that we are currently considering.

Once these four steps are achieved, the programmer has a running Web server that is accessible through a YAT provided CGI script linked to the HTML output wrapper. To give an idea of the work involved, the specification for the Verso site contains 7 different conversion programs and required a couple of hours work. Some final remarks should be stressed: (i) the YATL language is interpreted and then, it allows to easily test program modifications or to quickly change the layout of pages, as no compilation is required for the mediator that remains generic, (ii) since HTML pages are generated on the fly from the actual data sources, any update is automatically and immediately visible on the Web server.

In the next section, we show how source information (either model/format, schema, data, ...) are represented in the YAT model in an homogeneous fashion, while Section 4 introduces some of the YATL rules that are used in the Verso Web site.

3 The YAT Data Model

A first step towards the creation of our HTML Web view, is to be able to represent the (heterogeneous) data coming from input sources, as well as HTML pages of our Web site. This is the purpose of the YAT middleware model, which allows a uniform and precise representation of the required data.

The YAT data model is similar to other semistructured data models [18, 8], and especially the one proposed in [1]. It consists of named ordered labeled trees that may be unioned (with the $\vee$ symbol) to form a pattern. A set of patterns form a model, which is used to represent external data (ODMG, XML and HTML in our example).

The most original and interesting feature of the YAT model is that it allows to represent data at various levels of detail. For instance, Figure 2 shows several models as exported by wrappers. The three models on the upper part of the figure may be used to represent the O_2 object corresponding to the researcher whose name is Tova Milo. Going from left to right, the models get more and more precise. The first one allows to represent any YAT compliant data. The *Researcher* model represents the O_2 class *researcher* but also all objects belonging to that class. The last model is a representation of the object itself like in usual semistructured data models. Each of these three models is an *instance* of its predecessor(s).

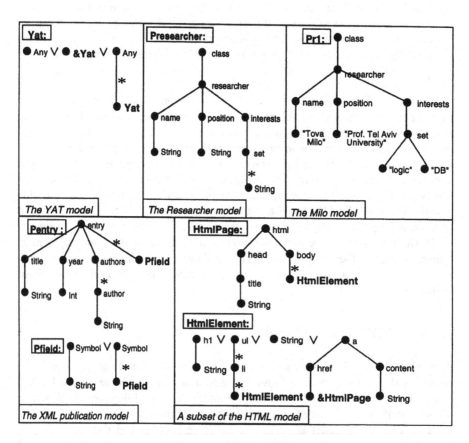

Fig. 2. Some YAT Models

Another interesting example is the XML model in the lower left hand side of the figure. It mixes precise with less precise informations. An XML entry (pattern *Pentry*) is described as being a sequence of fields. The first three fields (i.e., *title, year* and *authors* fields) are precisely described. Then, the remainder of pattern *Pentry* only indicates that they are followed by zero or more additional fields. Each of these fields is described by the *Pfield* pattern, and therefore, has a label of type *Symbol* (the name of the field) and may be composed of either a simple string or of a sequence of other (nested) fields. This example illustrate the YAT model capabilities, not only to describe structured data, but also partially structured data, and especially to be able to fit very preciselly to the knowledge one have of the data.

Finally, the last model allows to represent any HTML data (we only give here a very simplified version of the HTML model). This model fits to the HTML Document Type Definition [21] (i.e. its SGML grammar or DTD). Once again, we represent actual HTML data in the YAT tree model, where internal nodes (e.g. *h1, ul, a*) represent HTML tags and leaf nodes contains strings or references to other pages (in anchors).

Let us now see how these models are constructed and give an intuition of the instantiation mechanism. The nodes of a YAT tree may be labeled with a (i) constant (e.g., "Tova Milo"), (ii) symbol (e.g., *class, researcher, set*), (iii) type annotation (e.g., *String, Symbol*, or *Any* that stands for *any label*), (iv) pattern name (e.g., *Yat*) or (v) reference to a pattern name (e.g., *&Yat*). The edges of a YAT tree may be annoted by an occurrence symbol. In the example, $\star$ is the only occurrence symbol used. It indicates the possibility to replace the annotated edge by an arbitrary number of edges (e.g., the two *set* rooted subtrees).

A model is an instance of another, if one can find a mapping between their edges and nodes. An edge is instantiated according to its occurrence symbol. A node is instantiated according to its label through the following rules:

1. A constant or symbol node can only be instantiated by a node whose label is identical (e.g., the nodes labeled *class*).
2. A type node can be instantiated by a node whose label is a subtype or an instance of that type. E.g., the node labeled *Any* can be instantiated by the nodes labeled *String, Symbol*, "Tova Milo" or *class*. Remark that these two first rules can be merged to one by considering a constant as a special type annotation which only subtype is itself.
3. A node labeled with a pattern name can be instantiated by a tree, instance of that pattern. E.g., the two sub-trees of *Presearcher* and *Pr1* whose roots are labeled *researcher* are instances of the *Yat* labeled node.
4. A node labeled with reference to a pattern name can be instantiated by a node whose label is a reference to an instance of that pattern. E.g. the *&HtmlPage* labeled node is instance of the *&Yat* labeled node because the *HtmlPage* pattern is an instance of the *Yat* pattern.

If we now consider our examples again, pattern *Pr1* is an instance of either the *Yat* pattern or the *Presearcher* pattern. On the one hand, pattern

Presearcher is a (partial) instance of the *Yat* pattern. On the other hand, pattern *Pr*1 is a complete instance as it contains only constants or symbols and no ⋆ annotation and therefore cannot be further instantiated. We will say that *Pr*1 is *ground*. Remark that complete instantiation captures typing (e.g. *Pr*1 is of type *Presearcher*), while partial instantiation captures subtyping (e.g. *Presearcher* is a subtype of *Yat*). Remark also that instantiation here is very similar in spirit to subsumption in [6].

This (more or less precise) information described in the YAT model can be used for various purposes. Exported by the wrappers, it gives the programmer a good idea of the data he manipulates and will help him in writing the integration program. It may also be used, in conjunction with a type inference mechanism to check that a given integration program generates HTML-compliant data (See in [10]) or really matches the input data exported by the wrappers. Indeed, this last mechanism is very useful, finding most of the simple errors the programmer may have done. In next section, we show how to write the YATL integration program (step 3 of Section 2).

4 Integration Using YATL

Now that we are able to describe the structural input (ODMG and XML) and output (HTML) of our application, we need a way to map the former to the later. This is done using YATL, either directly or through its graphical interface. Although, the syntax may look somewhat complicated, note that: (i) most of the time, the programmer only has to modify some existing rules and, from our experience, can master the syntax of the rules rather fast; (ii) the system provides a set of algorithms to derive new programs from existing ones, using program instantiation or composition; and (iii) The programmer has the option to use the graphical interface to modify such rules [10].

YATL is a declarative language that allows to describe complex conversions on graphs. It is a rule-based language, each rule describing a small part of the data conversion process. The body of a rule is used to filter the input data and extract relevant information, while the head of the rule describes what is to be generated. Skolem functors [14, 17, 13] are used for the creation of new pattern names, and give the possibility to generate complex graphs with references. YATL also offers ordering and grouping primitives to manipulate collections with duplicates. Both of these features are frequently used in the generation of a Web site, respectively for the specification of hypertext links, and to describe the page layout, or to generate sorted lists, tables etc. Remark that, as opposed to previous approaches [12, 5, 23], YATL can address directly both the hypertextual and structural aspects of HTML, therefore avoiding the use of two distinct languages.

To illustrate the various capabilities of YATL, we will show how to build a very simple Web site. This site is inspired from the Verso Web site and will contain: (i) two pages which give, respectively, the list of all researchers and the list of all publications, (ii) one page for each researcher in the project, with his name, position and links to his publications, and (iii) one page for each publication with the title, list of authors, year of publication and any available additional information (e.g. the abstract). This can be done with, roughly, one rule per page. Rule *All_Researcher* below is the first rule of our YATL program:

Rule All_Researchers

$$
\begin{aligned}
&\textbf{\textit{HtmlPageAll}}() : \\
&html\langle \to head \to title \to \text{"Verso Researchers"}, \\
&\qquad \to body\langle \to ul \overset{*}{\to} li \to a\langle \to href \to \textbf{\textit{\&HtmlPage}}(N), \\
&\qquad\qquad\qquad\qquad\qquad \to content \to N\rangle\rangle\rangle \\
&\Longleftarrow \\
&\qquad \textbf{\textit{Presearcher}} : \\
&\qquad class \to researcher\langle \to name \to N, \\
&\qquad\qquad\qquad\qquad\quad \to position \to P, \\
&\qquad\qquad\qquad\qquad\quad \to interests \to set \overset{*}{\to} I\rangle
\end{aligned}
$$

This rule creates a single Web page that contains a list all researchers in the database along with pointers to their personal page. This page will be an entry point to the Web site. On the lower part of the rule (i.e., after the $\Longleftarrow$ symbol), the pattern **Presearcher** is used to filter the input data and retrieve the required information through variable bindings (in this example, the researchers names are bound to variable N, position to variable P and interests to variable I). On the upper part, the output pattern describes how the HTML structure is generated. The special annotation '$*$' on the edge of a rule's pattern indicates a collection, allowing to filter (in the body) or create (in the head) nodes with multiple children. We will see how to perform more advanced manipulation with collections later on. The output of the rule is identified by a Skolem function: **HtmlPageAll**(). The fact that this Skolem function has no parameter indicates that only one new pattern will be created, including the transformation of all the input filtered data. Remark that the head of the rule contains a reference to another Skolem function, this time parameterized by the researchers names ($\&HtmlPage(N)$). This allows to create a reference to another pattern created in another rule. Note that the program does not contain URLs as they will be automatically generated from the Skolem functions by the HTML wrapper/CGI script (See Section 5). Note also that we could have used the researcher's identity as a parameter, replacing N by **Presearcher** in the Skolem function. As it is, there will be one reference per researcher name, removing possible duplicates from the original database.

Now, to create the HTML page associated to this reference, we need a second rule. This is the rule *Single_Reasearcher* below:

Rule Single_Reasearcher

$HtmlPage(N)$:
$html\langle \rightarrow head \rightarrow title \rightarrow H1,$
$\quad \rightarrow body\langle \rightarrow h1 \rightarrow H1,$
$\quad\quad\quad \rightarrow$ "Position: ",
$\quad\quad\quad \rightarrow P$
$\quad\quad\quad \rightarrow$ "List of publications: ",
$\quad\quad\quad \rightarrow ul \xrightarrow{*} li \rightarrow a\langle \rightarrow href \rightarrow \& HtmlPublication(T),$
$\quad\quad\quad\quad\quad\quad\quad\quad\quad \rightarrow content \rightarrow T\rangle\rangle\rangle$
$\Longleftarrow$
$\quad\quad \mathbf{Pentry}\ :\ entry\langle \rightarrow title \rightarrow T,$
$\quad\quad\quad\quad\quad\quad\quad\quad \rightarrow year \rightarrow Y,$
$\quad\quad\quad\quad\quad\quad\quad\quad \rightarrow authors \xrightarrow{*} author \rightarrow N,$
$\quad\quad\quad\quad\quad\quad\quad \xrightarrow{*} Pfield\rangle,$
$\quad\quad \mathbf{Presearcher}\ :\ class \rightarrow researcher\langle \rightarrow name \rightarrow N,$
$\quad\quad\quad\quad\quad\quad\quad\quad\quad\quad\quad\quad\quad\quad \rightarrow position \rightarrow P,$
$\quad\quad\quad\quad\quad\quad\quad\quad\quad\quad\quad\quad\quad\quad \rightarrow interests \rightarrow set \xrightarrow{*} I\rangle,$
$\quad\quad H1\ \text{is concat}("\text{Homepage of }", N)$

This rule creates the page associated to one researcher identified by its name. It integrates data from both the O_2 database and the XML documents. Its input is a set of patterns, each of them being an instance of **Pentry** or **Presearcher**, and its output is a new HTML page identified by the **HtmlPage**(N) Skolem function. Remark that Variable N, used in both **Pentry** and **Presearcher** patterns, makes the correspondence between a given researcher in the object database and its publications in the XML file. Another novelty in this rule is the use of an external function 'concat' which calculates the page title $H1$ from the researcher's name N. Among other things, the page of a researcher contains the list of titles of its publications, and a link to page **HtmlPublication**(T) which gives a full description of the selected article. The rule that creates this page is given below:

Rule Single_Publication

$HtmlPublication(T)$:
$html\langle \rightarrow head \rightarrow title \rightarrow$ "Verso publication",
$\qquad \rightarrow body\langle \rightarrow h1 \rightarrow T,$
$\qquad\qquad \rightarrow ul \rightarrow li\langle \rightarrow$ " published in ",
$\qquad\qquad\qquad \rightarrow Y,$
$\qquad\qquad\qquad \rightarrow$ " by ",
$\qquad\qquad\qquad \overset{I}{\rightarrow} N\rangle\rangle\rangle$
$\Longleftarrow$
$\qquad\qquad \textbf{Pentry} : entry\langle \rightarrow title \rightarrow T,$
$\qquad\qquad\qquad\qquad \rightarrow year \rightarrow Y,$
$\qquad\qquad\qquad\qquad \rightarrow authors \overset{I}{\rightarrow} author \rightarrow N,$
$\qquad\qquad\qquad\qquad \overset{*}{\rightarrow} Pfield\rangle$

This rule creates a page for each entry in the set of publications, giving it's title, the year it was published and the list of authors[3]. The only novelty in this rule is that we replaced the usual $\star$ annotation for the authors' edge by a variable (I). This serves two goals. First, on the body side of the rule, edge $\overset{I}{\rightarrow}$ indicates that we want to filter a collection, and also that we want to store the rank of the children in variable I. Therefore it allows to keep track of the order in which authors appear. Second, on the head side of the rule, variable I is taken as an ordering criteria, and indicates that the corresponding children in the created pattern should be ordered with respect to the value of I. Therefore, it allows to restore the initial ordering of authors. In our example which deals with bibliographic entries, the order in which authors appear in a publication is a very important semantic information and it is essential not to loose it: YATL allows to do so. The last rule *All_Publications_by_Year* below illustrates again, on an example where grouping is required, the possibilities of YATL for collection manipulation. This rule creates a page with all available publications, grouped by year. Grouping is specified by the $\overset{\|Y}{\rightarrow}$ edge which states that a new child is created for each distinct year Y (grouping) and that the children must be ordered according to the value of Y (ordering). The ordering possibilities of YATL are mandatory to manage Web documents, and are widely used in the Verso publication site to give several views of a given list of publications (ordered by title, by publication date, by authors, etc). Let us conclude this description of YATL with two remarks. First, we already mentioned the possibility for the programmer to check the validity of a given program. Especially, it can be used to verify that the generated data will always be valid HTML[4]. Also, in the context of Web Site management, the possibility to specify templates for the HTML pages using a standard HTML editor should be provided. This is not possible

---

[3] An additional recursive rule would be necessary to retrieve the data from the *Pfield* pattern. We refer the reader to [10] for more information on this issue.

[4] Current implementation of the HTML wrapper uses HTML 3.2 DTD [21].

in current prototype of YAT, that was primarily designed as a general purpose tool, but we plan to support this solution in the future.

Rule All_Publications_by_Year

$HtmlAllPublications()$:
$html\langle \rightarrow head \rightarrow title \rightarrow$ "Verso publications sorted by year",
$\qquad \rightarrow body\langle \rightarrow h1 \rightarrow$ "Verso publications sorted by year",
$\qquad\qquad \rightarrow ul \xrightarrow{[]_Y} li\langle \rightarrow Y,$
$\qquad\qquad\qquad\qquad \rightarrow ul \xrightarrow{*} li \rightarrow a$
$\qquad\qquad\qquad\qquad\qquad \langle \rightarrow href \rightarrow \&HtmlPublication(T),$
$\qquad\qquad\qquad\qquad\qquad\qquad \rightarrow content \rightarrow T\rangle\rangle\rangle$

$\Longleftarrow$

$\qquad$ **$Pentry$** :
$\qquad entry\langle \rightarrow title \rightarrow T,$
$\qquad\qquad \rightarrow year \rightarrow Y,$
$\qquad\qquad \rightarrow authors \xrightarrow{*} author \rightarrow N,$
$\qquad\qquad \xrightarrow{*} Pfield\rangle$

Now, the specification of the Site is finished, and we only need to explain how to connect the rules to their actual input. The YAT system was first designed for data conversion, assuming that the input data is given by the user. This approach could not be used in the case of the Verso Web site, as we wanted to keep the HTML pages virtual to facilitate updates and maintenance of the site. Moreover, for performance reasons, it is important to load only the necessary data from the database and XML documents when a page is requested. This requires a means to know, for a given page, what data should be extracted from the sources. We choose a simple and practical solution to this problem. In current implementation, each rule is mapped to a set of queries over the data sources. In our running example this is done with the instructions given on figure 3.

The first line of this mapping file should be read as follow: to create page *$HtmlPageAll()$*, send the query `AllResearchers` to the ODMG wrapper. The root statement indicates that `HtmlPageAll()` generates an entry point into our Web server (in our example, one can access the site either through the list of all researchers or the list of all publications). In a similar way, the second instruction states the input needed to generate the page *$\&HtmlPage(N)$* can be obtained by sending two queries, one to the ODMG wrapper and the other one to the XML wrapper etc.

This solution was simple to install and required only very minor changes in the original YAT system. However, in this approach, the Web designer has to know how to query each of the input sources. It is not very elegant and could lead to practical difficulties if the number of sources increases. More elegant solutions for this problem lead to issues related to query processing over heterogeneous sources, see Section 6 for a short discussion on this question.

```
root HtmlPageAll() :-
    ODMG(AllResearchers);

HtmlPage(N) :-
    ODMG(select x
         from x in AllResearchers
         where x.name = $N),
    XML($N);

HtmlPublication(T) :-
    XML($T);

root HtmlAllpublications() :-
    XML(true);
```

Fig. 3. Query description of sources

5 Evaluation of the HTML View

We finally want to show how the different components work together. In this section, we explain how the evaluation of a Web page is done. At first, the user is given a set of entry points to the Web site. For instance, such an entry point is the following URL:

`http://myserver/cgi-bin/cgiwrapper?p0`

where p0 is the pattern name corresponding to *HtmlPageAll*(). When the user sends this URL to the http server, the following operations are performed (as illustrated on Figure 4):

1. the http server launch the `cgiwrapper` cgi script, passing the pattern name p0 as an argument, requesting the appropriate HTML page;
2. the cgi script/HTML wrapper maps this name to the corresponding Skolem function (here *HtmlPageAll*()), and asks the mediator to send the corresponding *pattern*;
3. the mediator consults the *mapping file* to know which sources must be accessed and how to query these sources. In our example, the simple query "Allresearchers" must be sent to the ODMG wrapper;
4. the ODMG wrapper passes this query to the real O_2 database, which returns the set of following objects (where o1, o2, ... are O_2 object identifiers):

```
o1 = tuple(name: "Tova Milo",
           position: "Prof. Tel Aviv University",
           interests: set("logic","DB"));
o2 = tuple(...
```

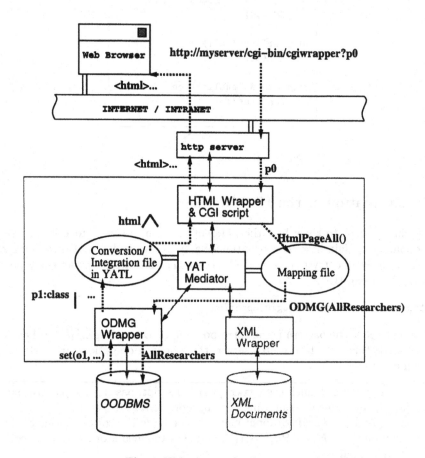

Fig. 4. Web page evaluation process

5. the result of this query is translated back into the middleware model by the ODMG wrapper and passed to the mediator as the following set of patterns (where $Pr1$, $Pr2$, ... are pattern names mapped to object identifiers o1, o2, ...):

$Pr1$:
$class \rightarrow researcher\langle \rightarrow name \rightarrow$ "Tova Milo",
$\rightarrow position \rightarrow$ "Prof. Tel Aviv University",
$\rightarrow interests \rightarrow set\langle \rightarrow$ "logic",
$\rightarrow$ "DB"$\rangle\rangle$

...

6. on this input, the YATL program can be executed by the mediator. As was already described in Section 4, input patterns are matched over the body of the rules, and a corresponding HTML page is generated in the YAT middleware model. In our current example, we apply rule *All_Researchers*, creating the new following pattern:

$HtmlPageAll()$:
$html\langle \rightarrow head \rightarrow title \rightarrow$ "Verso Researchers",
$\rightarrow body\langle \rightarrow ul\langle \rightarrow li \rightarrow a\langle \rightarrow href \rightarrow \&HtmlPage($"Tova Milo"$)$,
$\rightarrow content \rightarrow$ "Tova Milo"$\rangle$
$... \rangle\rangle\rangle$

7. finally, the output HTML pattern is converted a last time into a real HTML stream, which is sent back to the http server as follow:

```
<HTML><HEAD><TITLE>Verso Researchers</TITLE></HEAD>
<BODY>
<UL>
<LI><A HREF="http://myserver/cgi-bin/cgiwrapper?p1">Tova Milo</A>
...
</UL>
</BODY>
</HTML>
```

During this last conversion, Skolem functions that occur in the result are mapped to URLs containing the appropriate pattern names, generated by the wrapper (here p1, p2 ...). Therefore, these new URLs can be sent back, allowing the user to navigate in the generated HTML pages.

Note that this evaluation is far from optimal. For instance, during the evaluation of page $HtmlPageAll()$ it is not necessary to retrieve all the information concerning the researchers as only the names are used. We also believe that a large part of the computation could be pushed down to the data sources, allowing to take advantage of existing optimizers in these sources. In a context of distributed sources, parallel evaluation could also be investigated. Indeed a lot of work remains regarding the optimization of this process.

6 Conclusion

In this paper, we described how the YAT system, designed primarily for data conversion, can favorably be used to implement a Web site over heterogeneous data sources. This approach has been applied successfully on the Verso group Web site at INRIA, and the system turned out to be very simple and practical to use. Amongs the nicest features of the system, let us cite: (i) the possibility to verify conversion programs, (ii) the virtual approach that makes updates to the site directly visible and (iii) the fact that changing the HTML view (i.e. the YATL program) can be done without recompiling any of the components of the system, therefore greately facilitating the task of the Web administrator.

From this experience, we believe that the YAT system is a good step towards a complete data integration system. However, some issues should be addressed to achieve this goal. The major difficulty is related to the evaluation process as described in Section 5. A solution could be to provide a generic and standard way for wrappers to export query capabilities of the source the wrap, and for mediators to take advantage of these information for the view evaluation. It would allow to suppress the mapping file that we are currently using and automatically send appropriate queries to the data sources. Some other interesting issues are: incremental view maintenance, mixed materialized/virtual approach or update propagation. A lot of work also remains to provide optimal evaluation. In the context of Web Site management, support for HTML templates and document-driven approaches like in [23] could also be provided. We plan to work in these directions in the future.

References

1. S. Abiteboul, S. Cluet, and T. Milo. Correspondence and translation for heterogeneous data. In *Proceedings of International Conference on Database Theory (ICDT)*, Delphi, Greece, January 1997.
2. S. Abiteboul, D. Quass, J. McHugh, J. Widom, and J. L. Wiener. The lorel query language for semistructured data. *International Journal on Digital Libraries*, 1(1):68–88, April 1997.
3. G. Arocena and A. Mendelzon. Weboql: Restructuring documents, databases, and webs. In *Proceedings of IEEE International Conference on Data Engineering (ICDE)*, Orlando, February 1998.
4. P. Atzeni, G. Mecca, and P. Merialdo. To weave the web. In *Proceedings of International Conference on Very Large Databases (VLDB)*, pages 206–215, Athens, Greece, August 1997.
5. P. Atzeni, G. Mecca, and P. Merialdo. Design and maintenance of data-intensive web sites. In *Proceedings of the International Conference on Extending Database Technology*, pages 436–450, Valencia, Spain, March 1998.
6. P. Buneman, S. B. Davidson, M. Fernandez, and D. Suciu. Adding structure to unstructured data. In *Proceedings of International Conference on Database Theory (ICDT)*, Delphi, Greece, January 1997.
7. P. Buneman, S. B. Davidson, G. Hillebrand, and D. Suciu. A query language and optimization techniques for unstructured data. In *Proceedings of ACM SIGMOD Conference on Management of Data*, pages 505–516, Montreal, Canada, June 1996.

8. P. Buneman, S. B. Davidson, and D. Suciu. Programming constructs for unstructured data. In *Proceedings of International Workshop on Database Programming Languages*, Gubbio, Italy, 1995.
9. V. Christophides, S. Abiteboul, S. Cluet, and M. Scholl. From structured documents to novel query facilities. In *Proceedings of ACM SIGMOD Conference on Management of Data*, pages 313–324, Minneapolis, Minnesota, May 1994.
10. S. Cluet, C. Delobel, J. Siméon, and K. Smaga. Your mediators need data conversion! In *Proceedings of ACM SIGMOD Conference on Management of Data*, pages 177–188, Seattle, Washington, June 1998.
11. S. Cluet and J. Siméon. Data integration based on data conversion and restructuring. Technical report, Verso database group - INRIA, October 1997. http://www-rocq.inria.fr/verso/Jerome.Simeon/YAT/.
12. M. Fernandez, D. Florescu, J. Kang, A. Y. Levy, and D. Suciu. Catching the Boat with Strudel: Experiences with a Web-Site Management System. In *Proceedings of ACM SIGMOD Conference on Management of Data*, pages 414–425, Seattle, Washington, June 1998.
13. M. F. Fernandez, D. Florescu, A. Y. Levy, and D. Suciu. A query language for a web-site management system. *SIGMOD Record*, 26(3):4–11, September 1997.
14. R. Hull and M. Yoshikawa. Ilog: Declarative creation and manipulation of object identifiers. In *Proceedings of International Conference on Very Large Databases (VLDB)*, pages 455–468, Brisbane, Australia, August 1990.
15. M. Kifer, W. Kim, and Y. Sagiv. Querying object-oriented databases. In *Proceedings of ACM SIGMOD Conference on Management of Data*, pages 393–402, San Diego, California, June 1992.
16. O_2 Technology, Versailles. *The O_2 Web Reference Manual version 4.6*, September 1996.
17. Y. Papakonstantinou, S. Abiteboul, and H. Garcia-Molina. Object fusion in mediator systems. In *Proceedings of International Conference on Very Large Databases (VLDB)*, pages 413–424, Bombay, India, September 1996.
18. Y. Papakonstantinou, H. Garcia-Molina, and J. Widom. Object exchange across heterogeneous information sources. In *Proceedings of IEEE International Conference on Data Engineering (ICDE)*, pages 251–260, Taipei, Taiwan, March 1995.
19. Y. Papakonstantinou, A. Gupta, H. Garcia-Molina, and J. D. Ullman. A query translation scheme for rapid implementation of wrappers. In *Proceedings International Conference on Deductive and Object-Oriented Databases (DOOD)*, volume 1013 of *Lecture Notes in Computer Science*, pages 97–107. Springer-Verlag, Singapore, December 1995.
20. F. Paradis and A.-M. Vercoustre. A language for publishing virtual documents on the web. In *International Workshop on the Web and Databases (WebDB'98)*, Valencia, Spain, March 1998.
21. D. Raggett. HTML 3.2 reference specification. W3C Recommendation, January 1997. http://www.w3c.org/TR/REC-html32.
22. University of Dortmund. *freeWAIS-sf*, 0.5 edition, 1995.
23. A.-M. Vercoustre, J. Dell'Oro, and B. Hills. Reuse of information through virtual documents. In *Second Australian Document Computing Symposium*, pages 55–64, Melbourne, Australia, April 1997.
24. G. Wiederhold. Mediators in the architecture of future information systems. *Computer*, 25(3):38–49, March 1992.

Languages and Tools to Specify Hypertext Views on Databases[1]

G. Falquet, J. Guyot, L. Nerima

Centre universitaire d'informatique, University of Geneva, Switzerland
falquet I guyot I nerima @cui.unige.ch
http://cuiwww.unige.ch/db-research/hyperviews

Abstract. We present a declarative language for the construction of hypertext views on databases. The language is based on an object-oriented data model and a simple hypertext model with reference and inclusion links. A hypertext view specification consists in a collection of parameterized node schemes which specify how to construct node and link instances from the database contents. We show how this language can express different issues in hypertext view design. These include: the direct mapping of objects to nodes; the construction of complex nodes based on sets of objects; the representation of polymorphic sets of objects; and the representation of tree and graph structures. We have defined sublanguages corresponding to particular database models (relational, semantic, object-oriented) and implemented tools to generate Web views for these database models.

1   Introduction

The hypertext navigation paradigm [4] has proven highly efficient for easily sharing and accessing information without having to learn any specific query language or having to know the information storage structure (see for example most of the on-line help systems of recent software products or the World-Wide-Web global information system 4.). Moreover, database systems become universally used for storing, retrieving, and processing large amounts of data in an efficient and secure way. This lead to the development of so-called "database publishing" tools which make the content of a database accessible through a Web interface or to data browsing tools.

A hypertext view is a (virtual) hypertext derived from the database relations or classes. From the view concept it borrows the idea of a view definition language that specifies how to compute the view. But instead of producing a derived database element (class) it produces nodes and links that form a hypertext. The aim of a hypertext view are:

- to represent a part of the content of a database and
- to replace traditional query operations (selections, joins, projections) by a reasonable number of navigation steps in the hypertext.

The last goal implies that the hypertext structure must be carefully designed. For instance, it is not sufficient to simply map each database object onto a hypertext node and

1. This work was partially supported by the Swiss National Science Foundation, grant no. 21-45791.95

each object relationship to a hypertext link. We have defined a language and implemented tools to simplify and study the task of producing hypertext views.

The rest of this paper is organized as follows: In the next section we present our hypertext view definition language for object-oriented databases. In section 3 we analyze several issues that arise when designing hypertext views and we show how they can be handled with our language. In section 4 we present the formal syntax and semantics of the language and in section 5 we compare our approach with others.

2   The Models and the Hypertext View Definition Language

Building hypertext views consists essentially in mapping database objects to hypertext objects. We chose simple database and hypertext models to base the view definition language on. These models can then be easily mapped to other database and hypertext models to build concrete tools. For instance, we have implemented concrete tools for viewing relational databases and O2 databases on the Web.

2.1   The Database Model

The database model is an object-based model which is a subset of the O2 database model [11][1]. In this model each object has an identity (oid) and a value. We only consider objects whose value are tuples [name$_1$: value$_1$, name$_2$: value$_2$, ..., name$_n$: value$_n$] where each name$_i$ is an attribute name and each value$_i$ is either: an atomic value (of type integer, boolean, float, string, etc.); or a reference to another object; or a collection of references (set, list, bag). A *database schema* is a set of class definitions which are composed of a class name and a type (we do not consider methods) and an inheritance relationship. The type of a class constrains the values of its objects. A *database instance* is a set of objects and a set of named collections. Each object is an instance of a class and its value belongs to its class type. A named collection is a set (or list) of objects which are instances of a class or of one of its subclasses.

2.2   The hypertext model

We consider a simple hypertext model whose structural part is composed of nodes, anchors, and links.

Each *node* has a unique identity and a content.

The *content* of a node is a sequence of *elements* which may be character strings, images, etc.

An *anchor* is an element or a sequence of elements within the content of a node, it serves as a starting or ending point of a link.

A *link* is defined by its starting and ending anchors and by its category which is either 'reference' or 'inclusion'. Reference links are intended to create a navigation structure within the nodes. Inclusions links are intended to create nested structures that represent complex contents (structured documents).

This model can easily be mapped to the Web model. The only problem comes from inclusion links because, in HTML, the <A HREF...> tag corresponds to reference links and there are no inclusion links (except for images, with the IMG tag). The approach we took when creating tools for the Web, was to represent in a single HTML page the content of a node and of all its subnodes and to use embedded list tags to show the inclusion structure (Fig. 2 shows an example).

2.3 The Hypertext View Definition Language

A hyperview specification consists of set of node schemes which specify the collection from which the node's content is to be drawn; the selection and ordering criteria; the elements that form the content; and links to other nodes. A node definition takes the following form:

```
node <node-name> [ <parameters> ] is
        <field-list>
   from <collection>
   selected by <expression>
   ordered by <expression>
```

Each <field> of the <field-list> can be either a literal constant (string, integer, etc.) or an attribute name. Fields may contain presentation functions (bold(), italic(), break(), paragraph(), heading1(), etc.) which generate markup tags for the target hypertext system.

Content of a node. The content of a node is based on a collection specified in the from <collection> clause. The sequence of fields specifies how to construct the elements that represent every selected object. For example, let employeesOfDept be defined as:

```
node employeesOfDept[d: Department] is
   " No: ", bold(no), " => " ,
   bold(name), break(),
   " Hire date: ", hire_date
from EMP selected by dept = d
     ordered by emp_name
```

The content of a node instance employeesOfDept[sales] is obtained by
- selecting all the objects in the collection EMP which have the value sales for their attribute dept
- ordering these objects according to the values of attribute name
- for each object creating the sequence of elements corresponding to: the string "No: ", the value of attribute no (surrounded by <B> and </B> tags), the string "=>", etc.

It will appear as shown in Fig. 1[1]

Figure 1. A simple node instance

Reference Links. Links are specified through the href statement. The starting point (anchor) of a link is always a field. The anchor text will form an active element in the starting node which can trigger the navigation to the referenced node. A link specification refers to a node through its schema name and a list of parameter values. It is an expression of the form:

```
href <schema_name> [ <value>, ... ] <field>
```

For instance, consider the following node definition:

```
node dept_in[loc: String] is
  no, ": ", bold (name), " ",
  href employeesOfDept [self] " Employees: "
  ...
from DEPT selected by location = loc
  ordered by no
```

(Note: the pseudo variable *self* iterates over the sequence of selected objects).

The representation of each selected department d will have an anchor text "Employees:" that is the starting point of a link to the node employeesOfDept[d].

Inclusion Links. An inclusion link between two nodes determines a compound-component relationship between these nodes. The target node is to be considered as a sub-node of the source node of the link. This fact should normally be taken into account by the hypertext interface system which should present inclusion links in a particular way (generally by including the sub-node contents within the node presentation). Inclusion

---

1. Illustrations are snapshots of Web pages dynamically generated with the LAZY system. A description of this implementation can be found in http://cui-www.unige.ch/db-research/hyperviews/

links are particularly useful to create multi-level hierarchical nodes to represent complex entities.

The figure below shows an instance of a node dept_in2 which has the same definition as dept_in except for the reference link which is replaced by the inclusion link
include employeesOfDept[self] " Employees:"

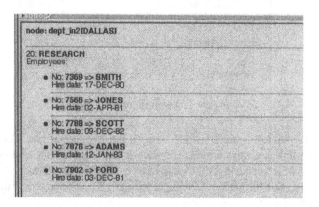

Figure 2. A node with an inclusion link

The content of an included node may depend on a distance parameter. By definition, a node is at distance 0 from itself and a node included in a node at distance i is at distance i + 1. A visibility can be associated with each field of a node schema to indicate the maximum distance from which this field is visible. The content of a node at distance d is composed of all the fields with a visibility greater or equal to d. As we will see in the next section, this mechanism has useful applications such as:

- avoiding infinite inclusion structures (at a given maximum distance all included nodes become empty);
- including summaries or outlines of nodes to reduce the number of navigation steps.

3   Designing Hypertext Views

Hypertext design is a complex problem, which has attracted many research (see [21] for instance). More recently, methodologies have been developed to design hypertext views of databases [2][9][8]. In the case of hypertext views of databases the design can take advantage of the data semantics expressed in the database schema but, as mentioned in [2], the distance between the database schema and the hypertext structure is great. For instance, a good database structure should minimize data redundancy to avoid update anomalies. On the contrary, redundancy may help the hypertext user by reducing the number of navigation steps to reach some information. In database design, the length of logical access paths is not important since the database is generally accessed through application programs or high level interfaces (e.g. forms). In hypertexts, since the basic action is the navigation step, the number of links to traverse is an important criterion to determine the usability of the system.

In this section we will show how our language can be used in several design cases.

3.1 Direct Object Mapping

The most straightforward way to map database entities to a hypertext structure consists in taking each object o of the database to create a hypertext node node(o). In this situation, the attributes with an atomic value form the content of the node. An attribute that refers to another object o' gives rise to a reference link to node(o'). A multivalued attribute generates a link to an index node which in turn points to the nodes representing the individual objects. Thus the structure of the hypertext view is isomorphic (in terms of graph) to the database structure.

The direct object mapping can be specified in the following way: for each collection C of type c with attributes $a_1, ..., a_k$ (atomic), $s_1: D_1, ..., s_r: D_r$ (single valued references), and $m_1: set(E_1), ..., m_t : set(E_t)$ (multi-valued references) define a node schema:

```
node C [me: c] is
   a1, ..., ak
   href D1[s1],
   ...,
   href Dr[sr]
   include E1 Index[m1],
   ...,
   include Et Index[mt]
from C selected by self = me ordered by 1
```

Each instance of this node schema represents a single object of the collection C. Single valued attributes yield references to the node representing the referred object. Multivalued attributes yield inclusions of index nodes which point to all the referred objects. The index nodes have the following schema:

```
node Ei Index [e: set Ei] is
   href Ei[self]
from e
```

3.2 Mapping Homogeneous Sets of Objects to Nodes

In order to reduce the number of navigation steps, the hypertext designer may wish to present several (or all) objects of a collection in a single node. This type of presentation is directly supported by the language since each node represents a subset of a collection (from <collection>) specified by a predicate (selected by <predicate>).

For instance, a node instance employeesOfDept[s] (defined in 2.3) represents all the employees of department s (from EMP selected by d = dept). Thus a reference link to employeesOfDept[s] can lead in a single step from a node representing department s to a node representing all its employees.

3.3 Derived Links

Since the selection predicate of a node is not limited to reference attributes, it is possible to create new (computed) links that do not appear explicitly in the database schema. This is shown on the following example:

```
node CitiesNear[c: Coordinates] is
  name, ...
from CITIES selected by
  location.distance(c) < 100

node City is
  name, population, ...
  href CitiesNear[location] "nearby cities"
from CITIES ...
```

The reference link from City to CitiesNear leads from a node representing a city c to a node representing all the cities which are less than 100km from c.

3.4 Mapping Sets of Heterogeneous Objects to Nodes

In the previous section we have shown how to define nodes by selecting sets of objects from the same collection. We now consider aggregation nodes which are made of objects coming from different collections. In this case grouping occurs along the inter-collection axis instead of the within-collection axis.

This type of node construction is particularly useful to reconstruct complex entities which have been decomposed and represented as several interrelated objects stored in different collections. It is natural to group all the objects that represent a complex entity in a single hypertext node. The node's content can be organized hierarchically to reflect the structural composition of the complex object. The main advantage of this mapping lies in its compact presentation of related information, thus avoiding navigation operations among the different components of the complex entity.

To create aggregation nodes we use inclusion links that point to subnodes. The following example shows the construction of a complex node with a nested structure to represent courses stored in a university database.

Database schema:

```
class Course(                    class Offering(
   code : String,                   code : String,
   title : String,                  course : Course,
   credits : Int,                   semester : String
   description : String,         )
   prerequisites : set(Course) )
```

```
class Professor(                    class Teaching(
   name : String,                      offering : Offering,
   ...                                 professor : Professor
)                                   )

COURSES : set(Course); OFFERINGS : set(Offering);
TEACHINGS : set(Teaching); PROFESSORS : set(Professor);
```

Node schemes:

```
node Course [c : Course]  is
   heading1(code, " * ", title),
      "credits: ", credits,
   heading3("Description"),
      description,
   heading3("Prerequisites"),
      include Prereqs [prerequisites] ,
   heading3("Offerings"),
      include Offerings[self]
from COURSES
   selected by self = c ordered by code


node Prereqs [pre : set Course]
      list_type: enumeration(" ")
   is
      href course[self] code, " (", title, ")"
from pre


node Offerings[c : course]
      list_type: definition
   is
      bold(code), " (", semester, ") ",
      include  Teaching[self]
from OFFERINGS
      selected by course = c order by code


node Teachings[o : Offering]
      list_type: enumeration(" ")
   is
      include ProfessorName[professor]
from TEACHINGS
      selected by offering = o


node ProfessorName [p : Professor]
      list_type: none
   is
      href Professor[self] name
from PROFESSORS
```

The Course node is the top of the nested structure, it contains data coming directly from Course objects (credits, description) and it includes nodes Prereqs and Offerings which contains the lists of prerequisites and offerings respectively. The node Offerings displays information about particular offerings for this course (code, semester). It includes a node Teaching which displays the list of professor names for this offering. Note that the "list_type" statement allows to specify different types of presentations (bullet lists, definition lists, enumerations with a separator character, etc.). Figure 3 shows a typical instance of Course.

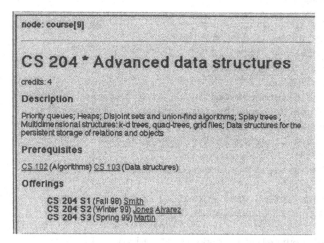

Figure 3. A node with a nested structure

Aggregation can also occur on objects which are not related in the database. For instance, a university home page may point to courses, research, and social events which are not related entities of the database.

3.5 Recursive Inclusions (Static and Dynamic)

The following node schema is recursive since it has an inclusion link to itself

```
node EmpWithMgr [e : Emp ] is
   " No: ", bold(no), " => " , bold(name),
   break(), " Hire date: ", hire_date,
   include EmpWithMgr [manager]
from Employees selected by self = e
   ordered by empno
```

However this does not generate a cyclic inclusion structure at the instance level since the graph of the *manager* relation is acyclic (i.e. there is no cycle at the data level). Fig. 4 shows an instance of that node schema.

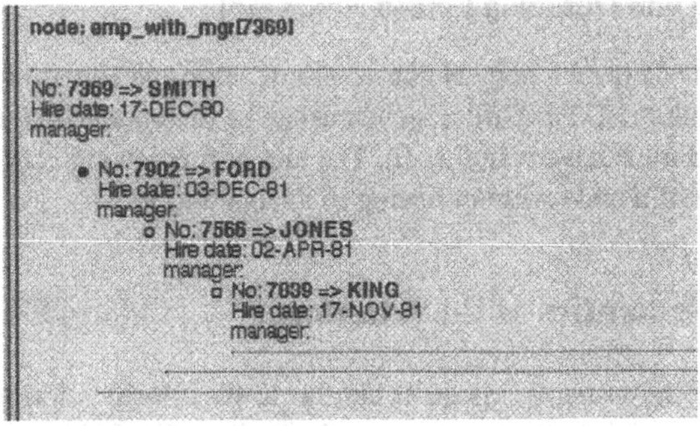

Figure 4. Recursive inclusions of nodes

When there are cycles in the data, the visibility distance mechanism prevents the creation of recursive inclusions at the instance level. Since each field in a node definition has a maximum visibility distance, it implies that there is a level of inclusion from which all the included nodes become empty.

Thus, recursive inclusion can be employed to specify hypertext views that represent data having a tree or graph structure. This representation may significantly reduce the number of navigation steps, compared to the direct object mapping.

3.6 Representing Specialized Entities (Union Nodes)

Collections may contain objects of different classes which are subclasses of the collection's class. To represent such polymorphic sets one can use the inclusion mechanism. A top node is used to represent the common attributes, it has inclusion links to specific nodes used to represent the specific parts. Each specific node selects only the objects which have a given type.

```
// generic node
node emp [e: employee] is
   name, address, ... // common attributes
   include driver[self]
   include secretary[self]
from EMP

// specific nodes
node driver [e: employee] is
   max_km, license_no, ...
from EMP/Driver selected by self=e

node secretary[s: employee] is
   ...
from EMP/Secretary selected by self=s
```

An expression of the form *collection/class* represents all the objects in *collection* which are instances of *class* or instances of a subclass of *class*.

3.7 Previewing and Outlining Linked Nodes [10]

Previewing a node M from a node N consists in including in N part of the content of M and a reference link to M. The partial inclusion can be obtained with the visibility mechanism (some field must have visibility 0). The aim of previewing is to give information about the content of a node without having to navigate to it.

4 Formal Semantics of the Language

The definition of the semantics is quite similar to the specification of database query languages but it must also take into account the notion of node identity which is necessary to specify the semantics of links. The identity of a node instance is a triple (*schema name*; *actual parameter values, inclusion level*). This differs from the semantics of usual query languages which do not create new objects as the result of a query.

To formally define the semantics of the definition language we must specify, for a given database instance, how to interpret a node instance expression in terms of nodes, links, anchors and contents (the complete syntax of the language is given in appendix). To keep the description small, we will suppose that the semantics of arithmetic and logic expressions is given and we will not take into account presentation functions.

Let D be the node definition:

node N $[p_1:T_1, p_2: T_2, ..., p_k: T_k]$
$f_1, ..., f_n$
from C
selected by $S(self, p_1, p_2, ..., p_k)$
ordered by $O(self, p_1, p_2, ..., p_k)$

where each field f_j is

level l_j [(**href** | **include**) $N'_j[expr'_1, expr'_2, ..., expr'_{sj}]$] e_j

The interpretation of a node instance expression $E = N[expr_1, expr_2, ..., expr_k]$ at a given inclusion depth d is composed of a *node identity* $\mathbf{I_{id}}(E, d)$, a *node content* $\mathbf{I_C}(E, d)$, and a *set of links* $\mathbf{I_L}(E, d)$.

The identity of a node consists of the node's name, the value of its parameters and its inclusion depth.

$$\mathbf{I_{id}}(E, d) = (N, [\mathbf{I}(exp_1), \mathbf{I}(exp_2), ..., \mathbf{I}(exp_k)], d).$$

In order to define the content of the node, we first define the set of objects from which the content will be drawn:

$$S_0 = \{o \in C \mid \mathbf{I}(S)(o, \mathbf{I}(expr_1), \mathbf{I}(expr_2), ..., \mathbf{I}(expr_k)) = true\}.$$

It is the set of objects o that belong to C and satisfy the predicate S.

Then S_1 is a sequence $<o_1, o_2, ..., o_r>$ such that

$$o_i \in S_1 <=> o_i \in S_0 \text{ and}$$

$$I(O)(o_i, I(expr_1), I(expr_2), ..., I(expr_k)) \leq I(O)(o_{i+1}, I(expr_1), I(expr_2), ..., I(expr_k)).$$

Thus S_1 is the set S_0 ordered by the expression O.

The content $I_C(E, d)$ of the node is the sequence of elements obtained by concatenating the sequences $<I_C((f_1, o_i, d), ..., I_C(f_n, o_i, d)>$ ($i = 1, r$) where $I_C(f_j, o_i, d)$ is the content of field f_j for object o_i at depth d. It is defined as follows:

- I_C (**level** l_j <link-specification> e_j, o_i, d) = <empty> if the visibility level l_j is less than d,
- I_C (**level** l_j <link-specification> k, o_i, d) = k if k is a constant,
- I_C (**level** l_j <link-specification> a, o_i, d) = $o_i.a.toString()$ if a is an attribute name (where *toString* is a method that maps an object to its string representation).

The set of links $I_L(E, d)$ is the union of the sets $\{I_L((f_1, o_i, d), ..., I_L(f_n, o_i, d)>$ ($i = 1, r$) where

- I_L(**level** l_j e_j, o_i) = the null link
- I_L(**level** l_j **href** $N'_j[expr'_1, expr'_2, ..., expr'_{sj}]$ e_j, o_i) is a reference link with starting node id: $I_{id}(E, d)$ (the id of this node instance), ending node id: $I_{id}(N'_j[expr'_1, expr'_2, ..., expr'_{sj}], d)$, starting anchor: $(i-1)n + j$ (the sequence number of this element),
- I_L(**level** l_j **include** $N'_j[expr'_1, expr'_2, ..., expr'_{sj}]$ e_j, o_i) is an inclusion link with starting node id: $I_{id}(E, d)$ ending node id: $I_{id}(N'_j[expr'_1, expr'_2, ..., expr'_{sj}], d+1)$ starting location: $(i-1)n + j$

5 Comparison with Related Work

Database publishing. Several ways have been explored to publish the content of databases on the Web. The procedural approach consists in writing database programs that generate HTML pages (e.g. Oracle Web Server [14], CGI scripts, Java/JDBC server-side applications, etc.). Another approach consists in automatically generating HTML pages from the database schema (e.g. O2Web [23]).

This last approach corresponds to the direct object mapping described in section 3.1. It can be improved by defining a collection of views over the database and generating the hypertext from these views; it is also possible to overload generic methods with specific ones. However, it is not clear that features like (recursive) inclusion links can be easily expressed with this technique.

Toyama and Nagafugi [18] define and extension of the SQL query language to present the result of a query as a structured document (e.g. HTML, LaTeX). They introduce connectors and repeaters in place of the SQL target list of a query.

Virtual documents. The virtual document approach consists in extending a document definition language with database querying features. For instance, database queries can be embedded into HTML pages [13]. In [15] Paradis and Vercoustre propose a prescription language to specify the static and dynamic content of a virtual document. The static content is expressed with the usual HTML tags. The dynamic content is obtained by evaluating queries on (heterogeneous) data sources. The language has operators to select and combine information from different query results.

Web site management. In [8], Fernandez et al. describe a system to produce a Web-site (a set of HTML pages) from different data sources integrated through a graph based data model. A specific query language (STRUQL) is used to query the data graph and construct a graph that forms the content of the Web-site. A second language (HTML-template language) is used to specify the presentation of each object.

In [16] Siméon and Cluet extend the YAT system to build HTML pages. The YATL language allows to specify graph conversions between the input data model (ODMG objects, XML documents, ...) and the output model (HTML pages) viewed as graphs.

Methodology for the Design of Web Applications. The Araneus methodology proposed by Atzeni et al. [2] distinguishes three levels: the hypertext conceptual level (Navigation Conceptual Model); the hypertext logical level (Araneus Data Model); and the presentation level (HTML templates). It is possible to analyze our language with respect to these levels. The conceptual level corresponds to node names, reference links, base collections, and selection predicates. The logical level (internal node structure) corresponds to the specification of node fields (constants, attributes and inclusion links). A node with a complex ADM type can be represented by a hierarchy of included nodes (see 3.4). Finally, the markup functions (or strings with HTML tags) define the generated document's markup which will be used to present the document.

In [9] Fraternali and Paolini introduce the HDM-lite methodology which is an adaptation of the Hypermedia Design Methodology for Web applications. Their navigation model includes navigation modes (index, guided tour, showall, ...) to help navigating within collections of objects.

6 Conclusion

Language properties. The language we have presented has several properties that are important to develop hypertext views: it is non-procedural, it has the capacity to restructure the database information, i.e. to present it in different forms (corresponding to different points of view), it has the capacity to create structured node contents (complex hierarchical nodes or structured documents), it has the capacity to create orientation structures like indices, outlines, node previews, etc., it has a node identification scheme that enables other applications to access the generated nodes and that permits to store hypertext views independently of the database.

A view definition is relatively robust with respect to schema updates since every node schema depends only on its base collection. In addition, a node schema depends only on the name and the parameter of the node it refers to. Thus node schemes can be changed without affecting the rest of the hypertext view.

From a more theoretical point of view, we have already shown in [7] that select-project-outer-join queries can be represented by nodes with inclusion links. To represent select-project-join queries it is necessary to slightly modify the semantics of inclusion links.

Prototypes. We have developed several tools to generate hypertext views. The LAZY system generates Web pages over a relational database, it implements a subset of the described view language. The implementation relies on two components: a node definition compiler and a node server connected to a HTTP server. The compiler translates node definitions into relational views and stored procedures. The node server dynamically generates HTML pages by querying the generated views and/or calling the stored procedures. We are currently working on a portable implementation of the node server, written in Java and based on JDBC.

The MetaLAZY tool is an implementation of the hypertext view language for a semantic data model. It translates a semantic data schema into a relational schema and generates LAZY nodes for this schema. It uses multiple levels of inclusion to hide the auxiliary relations that represent many-to-many relationships.

We have also developed a tool to produce materialized hypertext views over an O_2 database. These views consist in sets of HTML pages that can be stored on external media (CD-ROM, etc.) independently of the database.

Future plans include the addition of navigation modes [9] to node schemes and mechanisms to update the database through hypertext views.

Aknowledgement

We would like to thank the anonymous referees for their insightful and valuable comments.

7 References

1. S. Abitboul, R. Hull, V. Vianu. *Foundations of Databases*, Addison-Wesley, 1995.

2. P. Atzeni, G. Mecca, P. Merialdo. "Design and Maintenance of Data-Intensive Web Sites".In Proc. of the EDBT'98 Conf., Valencia, 436-450, 1998

3. T. Barsalou, N. Simabela, A. Keller, G. Wiederhold. "Updating Relational Databases through Object-Based Views". In Proc. ACM SIGMOD, Denver, 248-257, 1991.

4. T. Berners-Lee, R. Cailliau, A. Luotonen, H. Frystyk Nielsen, A. Secret. "The World-Wide Web". Comm. of the ACM, Vol. 37, No. 8, 76-82, 1994..

5. S. Bobrowski. *Oracle7 Server Concepts Manual*, Oracle Corp., Redwood City, CA, 1992.

6. J. Conklin. "Hypertext: An Introduction and Survey". IEEE Computer, Vol. 20, No. 9, 17-42, 1987.

7. G. Falquet, L. Nerima, J. Guyot. "A Hypertext View Specification Language and its Properties". CUI Technical report #102, University of Geneva, 1996.

8. M. Fernandez, D. Florescu, J. Kang, A. Levy, D. Suciu. "Catching the Boat with Strudel: Experiences with a Web-Site Management System". In Proc. ACM SIGMOD Conf., Seattle, 414-425, 1998.

9. P. Fraternali, P. Paolini. "A Conceptual Model and a Tool Environment for Developping More Scalable, Dynamic, and Customizable Web Applications". In Proc. of the EDBT'98 Conf., Valencia, 421-435, 1998.

10. S. Ichimura, Y. Matsushita. "Another Dimension to Hypermedia Access". In Proc. of the Hypertext'93 Conf., Seattle, 63-72, 1993.

11. C. Lécluse, P. Richard, F. Velez. "O2, an Object-Oriented Data Model ". In Proc. ACM SIGMOD, Chicago, 1988.

12. J. Nanard, M. Nanard. "Shoud Anchors Be Typed Too? An Experiment with MacWeb". In Proc. of the Hypertext'93 Conf., Seattle, 51-62, 1993

13. T. Nguyen, V. Srinivasan. "Accessig Relation al Databases from the World Wide Web". In Proc. ACM SIGMOD Conf., 529-540, 1996.

14. Oracle Inc. home page: http://www.oracle.com

15. F. Paradis, A-M. Vercoustre. "A Language for Publishing Virtual Documents in the Web". In Proc. of the WebDB Workshop, Valencia, 1998.

16. J. Siméon, S. Cluet. "Using YAT to Build a Web Server". In Proc. of the WebDB Workshop, Valencia, 1998.

17. J. Teuhola. "Tabular Views on Object Databases". Tech. Rep. R-93-11, University of Turku, Finland, 1993

18. M. Toyama, T. Nagafuji. "Dynamic and Structured Presentation of Database Contents on the Web", In Proc. of the EDBT'98 Conf., Valencia, 451-465, 1998.

19. C. A. Varela, C. C. Hayes. "Zelig: Schema–Based Generation of Soft WWW Database". In Proc. W3 Conf., 1994.

20. *Special Issue: Advanced User Interfaces for Database Systems*. SIGMOD Record, Vol. 21, No. 1, 1992.

21. Special section: Hypermedia Design, CACM, Vol. 38, No. 8, 1995.

22. "The O2 System". Comm. of the ACM, Vol. 34, No. 10, 1991

23. "O2 Web Presentation", O2Technology, Versailles, France, 1995.

Appendix

Syntax of the LAZY language

HypertextView = **define** { Node-schema } **end**

Node-schema = **node** node-name ["[" Parameter-list "]"]
     List-Markup
     is
     Field-list
     from collection ["/" type-name]
     [**selected by** Expression]
     [**ordered by** Expression-list]

Field-list = Field { "," Field }

Field = [Level] [Link-spec] Markup-Element

Markup-element = Element I Markup "(" Markup-element ")"

Element = ε I Constant I attribute-name

Link-spec = (**href** I **include**) node-name ["[" Expression-list "]"]

Parameter-list = Parameter { "," Parameter }

Parameter = [**set**] param-name ":" type-name

Expression-list = Expression { "," Expression }

Expression = Term I Term Op Term

Term = Atom I "(" Expression ")"

Atom = Constant I attribute-name I **self**

Op = "=" I "<" I ">" I "+" I "-" I **and** I **or** I ...

Constant = string I number

Markup = **bold** I **italic** I **break** I ... I **heading1** I **heading2** I ...

List-markup = list_type: (**ordered** I **unordered** I **definition** I **enumeration** I **none**) [(separator)]

Level = **level** "0" I ... I "9"

WebSuite—A Tool Suite For Harnessing Web Data

Catriel Beeri, Gershon Elber, Tova Milo, Yehoshua Sagiv, Oded Shmueli,
Naftali Tishby, Yakov Kogan, David Konopnicki, Pini Mogilevski, Noam Slonim

Abstract. We present a system for searching, collecting, and integrating Web-resident data. The system consists of five tools, where each tool provides a specific functionality aimed at solving one aspect of the complex task of using and managing Web data. Each tool can be used in a stand-alone mode, in combination with the other tools, or even in conjunction with other systems. Together, the tools offer a wide range of capabilities that overcome many of the limitations in existing systems for harnessing Web data. The paper describes each tool, possible ways of combining the tools, and the architecture of the combined system.

1 Introduction

The *World-Wide Web* (WWW) is a readily-available domain of heterogeneous information sources. Its rapid growth and widespread use have transformed it to the central, if not universal, repository of data on essentially any topic. Unfortunately, current WWW technologies, including Web browsers and search engines, do not satisfactorily address the many problems that arise when trying to access this repository. Some of these problems are:

- Web data is weakly typed. Formats, are often missing or are loose; many formatting decisions and logical organization are left to the discretion of the data owners. This makes extraction of the desired parts of data a difficult task.
- There often exist many sources with data on a topic. Locating them is a difficult problem. Search engines often provide grossly inaccurate answers. Even when the location of the data is approximately known, a tiresome exhaustive manual browsing is often needed to accurately pinpoint it.
- A data source may contain only partial data on a topic, and distinct sources may contain complementary data, possibly with some overlap, or with contradictions. This poses a difficult data integration problem.
- Additionally, formats in data sources may differ widely from strict structures in databases. Web clients therefore need to be able to handle and translate between many different formats.

To illustrate some of these problems, consider searching for bibliographical data, say on topics in Computer Science. Such data is found in many locations. Search engines sometimes help locating them, often not. Locations may be approximately known, e.g. under a university or department home page, but exact locations are site-dependent and may be difficult to pinpoint. Documents are often only weakly structured using HTML tags, and the inner logical organization is user dependent. Thus, automatic extraction of, say, article titles, becomes a difficult task.

Every developer of Web applications has to deal with, at least, some of the above issues [6, 7, 9, 11–14, 16, 21, 34, 35]. A problem in many of the efforts undertaken in the past is that they adopt a 'complete system' approach. Thus their solutions are often tailored to a specific application, rather than being general. Additionally, by being parts of complete systems, solutions cannot be used independently, or utilized for other applications. In this paper, we report on a different approach undertaken in a project by the authors. Rather than focusing on building one specific Web application, we chose to build a *set of tools*, where each tool addresses one specific task. Each tool can be used in a stand-alone mode, in combination with the other tools, or even in conjunction with other systems. We believe that given a set of such tools, with generic, easy to use. interfaces, specific Web applications can then be built by a "mix and match" approach, by combining some of the tools together. Thus, the set of tools is 'greater' then the sum of its parts. The goals of our project were first, to construct useful tools, and second, and more importantly, to show that a combination of these tools enables us to easily build powerful complex Web systems. Six tools were developed in this work:

- A global database server, W3GDB, that provides a global integrated database view of data sources.
- A statistical-learning mechanism, W3LEARN, for classifying, analyzing and tagging loosely structured data.
- A data translator, W3TRANS, for defining data translations among data formats.
- A query engine and a query language, W3QS and W3QL, for querying the Web.
- A personal information manager, PIM, to manage a user's data.
- A virtual reality generator, VRG, to support the creation of more natural data manipulation interfaces.

(Some of these tools have been described in other publications.) The emphasis in this paper is in describing how they can be combined in various ways to help users address the problems described above. For this, we describe in some detail four of the tools, and then we describe an example application that combines them into a useful system for search, extraction, and use of bibliographic data. We also consider how these tools can provide services needed by others. Two of the tools, PIM and VRG are described only briefly. The first is similar in spirit to many commercial tools that are becoming available now. The second is a more visionary project that is only now reaching the stage where integration with other tools can be seriously considered.

2   The Global Database (W3GDB)

The global-database tool (W3GDB) provides a single, unified view of Web-resident data. Naturally, the global database cannot encompass all the data on the Web, and it is more realistic to assume the existence of a global database for each coherent slice of the Web. The application described in Section 6, for example, has a global database with information about publications. The purpose of the global database is to provide the capability of posing queries as if the user has to deal with a *single* database system and not with a myriad of information sources all over the Web. The W3GDB tool provides a conceptual schema, cast in the relational model, and the user can formulate any relational query using the relations of the conceptual schema (also referred to as the *global relations*). However, the global relations are *not* materialized. Instead, each *information source* on the Web is represented as a separate *local database*, and the relations of that local database, called *local relations*, are the ones that are actually materialized. In fact, other tools of our system are used to find new information sources and translate their data into appropriate local databases.

Thus, there is a single conceptual schema that is used to formulate queries, but there are many different local databases that are needed to answer those queries. One task of the W3GDB tool is to translate queries on the global database into queries on the local databases and evaluate them. But W3GDB also serves as a natural entry point into the system and as a coordinator that invokes other tools when needed. The reason is that using the global relations to formulate a query is the easiest way of finding information, and only if this approach does not yield the desired information, should the user start the more elaborate process of looking for additional information sources, translating them into local databases, mapping those databases into the global one and, finally, resubmitting the query to W3GDB in order to get a more accurate answer to his/her query.

In summary, the functionalities provided by W3GDB are as follows. First, the ability to formulate queries against the global relations (i.e., the conceptual schema). Second, an evaluation of those queries with respect to the local relations representing the various information sources. Third, the ability to define a local database for a new information source; that is, define the local relations of that local database and, by invoking other tools of the system, create actual data for those relations from the information source. Fourth, the ability to define the mapping between the new local relations and the global relations.

Providing the above functionalities, while at the same time cooperating smoothly and easily with the other tools in a way that covers all aspects of *querying and integrating* heterogeneous information sources, is a source of some conflicting requirements. For one, the whole idea behind the two-level approach of local and global relations is to offer maximum flexibility in describing information sources vs. the rather rigid and coherent global schema that is more convenient for a casual user. But if this flexibility is used liberally, it may mean that a lot of effort would have to be invested into translating information sources into local relations. The reason is that in the W3TRANS tool, a separate translation program would have to be written for each output format. In our case, an instance of an output format is just an instance of a local schema (i.e., a schema of a local database). So, if there is a lot of variations among the local schemas, then many different translation programs would have to be written. Similarly, for each local database, there is a need to define a mapping between the local relations and the global ones. That mapping depends on the local schema. So, once again, many different mappings would have to be defined if there is a lot of variations among the local schemas. This is not just time consuming, but also error prone. In what follows we discuss remedies for these problems.

2.1 Mapping Local Relations to Global Relations

Our approach to the definitions of local relations and their mappings to the global relations is characterized by the ability to reuse those definitions from one information source to another when those sources are of a similar nature (e.g., contain listings of publications). In that respect, our approach is different, for example, from the approach of the pioneering Information Manifold work [28] that advocates local relations that fit as much as possible the structure of the data found at the information source. In particular, in the Information Manifold, local relations should be defined so that they will not have null values. For W3GDB, we have developed an approach that permits null values, and consequently, there is more flexibility in using the same local schema for different information sources.

We use Datalog rules in order to map local relations to the global ones. For example, the following rules define the global relations g_1 and g_2 in terms of the local relation l; note that there may be additional rules for g_1 and g_2 that define them in terms of other local relations (of the same or different information source).

$$g_1(X, Z) :- l(X, Z, Y).$$
$$g_2(Z, Y) :- l(X, Z, Y).$$

Given the above rules, the problem is how to represent a tuple of l that has only partial information. As an example, suppose that some tuple of l has values for the first and third columns, but not for the second one. We can handle missing information by means of null values that are expressed as logical terms (similarly to the way of defining logical object id's in F-logic [24]). So, for example, $l(a, f_2(l(a, null, b)), b)$ is a tuple of l with the values a and b in the first and third columns, respectively, and the null value $f_2(l(a, null, b))$ in the second column. Note that the term representing the null value is generated by applying the functor f_2 to the tuple itself, and f_2 is a functor that is associated exclusively with the second column of l. This guarantees the uniqueness of null values (note that $null$ is considered a constant symbol), and assures that, when a query is evaluated, different null values are not "accidentally" equated to yield superfluous tuples that should not be in the answer to the query.

A second feature of our approach is the ability to map some information into the global relations by encoding it directly into the mapping rules, without having to insert it first into the local relations. Typically, we use this feature to insert information that is source dependent. For example, we may want to have for each publication an attribute *Institute* that specifies the institute in which that publication was found. The information about the institute's name is not written explicitly in listings of publications; rather, it is found in a URL or in some other Web page. Therefore, the easiest way to do it, in our system, is through the mapping rules, as in the following example.

$$g_1(X, Z, Y, Institute) :- l(X, Z, Y), \ Institute = \text{'Tel-Aviv University'}.$$

Inserting information directly in the mapping rules enables us to apply the same translation program of W3TRANS for generating l, regardless of the institute in which the information source was found.

It should be emphasized that W3GDB is not restricted just to the approach described above. It can also incorporate the approach based on view usability, as done in the Information Manifold. In fact, a hybrid approach that combines the two (i.e., view usability and the one described above) is also possible. Similarly, W3GDB can also incorporate algorithms that take into account binding patterns [38].

2.2 Experience with the System

The above approach has proven to be very useful in the application of querying publications (which is described in Section 6). We defined one local schema that contains all the information we expect to find about publications. Therefore, the data translation tool (W3TRANS) had to be programmed only once (i.e., only one translation program had to be written). Similarly, the rules defining the mapping between the local and global relations needed only minimal changes when moving from one information source to another. Typically, we had to change the names of local relations and some information that is specific to an information source (e.g., the name of the institute in which the publications were found).

The global-database tool (W3GDB) is implemented in Sicstus Prolog as a server that is available to clients via the TCP/IP protocol. Currently, local relations are transferred to W3GDB as text files, and they are not maintained to reflect updates in the information sources.

2.3 A Brief Comparison with Related Work

Our approach is similar to that of the Information Manifold [28] in the sense that it describes information sources as local relations and maps those local relations to the global ones. Other systems (e.g., TSIMMIS [22] and HERMES [41]) concentrate on translating queries directly rather than by mapping local relations to global ones. But there are some important differences between our approach and the Information Manifold. We can easily handle null values, and therefore, our approach makes it quite easy to use the same local schema for information sources of a similar nature. The local schema does not have to be an exact reflection of the structure of the data found at an information source. Instead it may be just an "upper bound" of what we expect to find there. Null values are filled in automatically when a tuple for a given relation has only partial information. Similarly, the mapping between the local and global relations does not change much when moving from one information source to another. Thus, the overhead in adding new information sources that are similar to existing ones is minimal.

A second important difference is in the mapping rules. In our approach, global relations are expressed in terms of local relations, and therefore, translating a query on the global relations into a query on the local relations is straightforward and is done by means of rule substitutions. In the Information Manifold, local relations are expressed as *views* of the global relations, and therefore, evaluating a query requires sophisticated algorithms for view usability [29] that are either inefficient (i.e., exponential) or nonexistent in the general case. The Information Manifold uses a heuristic approach to solve the view-usability problem.

3   Statistical Categorization and Tagging (W3LEARN)

This tool can deal with fuzzy, noisy, and irregular input. This is essential in dealing with the large variety and diversity of information sources over the Web. The methodology we apply to deal with the natural and noisy nature of the web data files is that of statistical pattern recognition, or statistical learning from examples.

In learning from examples, an unknown input-output relation ("rule") is being *randomly* sampled to provide a set of *training examples*. From these training examples, a *learning algorithm* generates an *hypothesis* relation, from an *hypotheses class*, that approximates the original input-output rule. Much is known by now about the quality of this approximation for many rules and hypotheses classes. In particular, under certain technical conditions we can guarantee good performance (low classification error) *outside* of the training sample, on arbitrary data taken from the same distribution as the training data. This essential property of machine learning is known as *generalization*. In this section we describe the application of statistical learning techniques to two generic and fundamental problems often encountered when Web data ia accessed, and demonstrate our solutions of the problems for classification and tagging of bibliography source, see Section 6.

3.1   Statistical File Categorization

The first issue addressed by statistical learning techniques is automatic file categorization, that is, deciding on the type of data contained in a file among several file categories such as latex, html, ... It is assumed that initial training data, i.e. typical examples of files from each category, is provided by the user or by another classifier.

We developed a new algorithm for automatic extraction of efficient statistical signatures that enable sequential statistical hypothesis testing of two (or more) text categories [40].

The method is based on automatic identification of a small set of strings that provide maximal statistical discriminability of the given categories. Such strings are characterized by their different occurrence frequencies in different categories, while still being frequent enough to be observed in short text excerpts. Quantitatively, such strings are detected by large contribution to the cross-entropy between the strings distributions in the different categories.

In the training phase the algorithm generates a "dictionary" of strings, often but not always words, which are statistically discriminative among the different categories. The discrimination power of each such string is determined by its contribution to the cross-entropy of the string distributions in the two categories,

$$D[p_1|p_2] = \sum_x p_1(x) \log \frac{p_1(x)}{p_2(x)} , \qquad (1)$$

where x is a string in the dictionary and $p_i(x)$ its estimated probability in the i-th category. Such strings can be automatically detected by parsing the training data using text compression algorithms, similar to the Lempel-Ziv algorithm. This pairwise measure is extended to several categories using Bayes law.

A small example of such a dictionary is given in the table below, which is a small part of the Computer Science bibliography tagging dictionary. The training complexity amounts to two passes through the training strings, keeping only strings which are sufficiently informative. The cross-entropy, estimated from the training data, also provides estimates of the test size and level of confidence of the categorization.

String	Distribution
(a)	0.004132 0.491736 0.475207 0.004132 0.004132 0.004132 0.004132
(abstract)	0.045455 0.590909 0.045455 0.045455 0.045455 0.045455 0.045455
(acm)	0.007143 0.007143 0.935714 0.007143 0.007143 0.007143 0.007143
(adaptation)	0.357143 0.071429 0.071429 0.071429 0.071429 0.071429 0.071429
(almost)	0.071429 0.357143 0.071429 0.071429 0.071429 0.071429 0.071429
(alcom)	0.023810 0.023810 0.785714 0.023810 0.023810 0.023810 0.023810

The above table shows a short segment of the tagging dictionary. Each column corresponds to a specific category. Each string is shown with its empirical probability in the different tagging categories.

3.2 Automatic Statistical Tagging

The second technique we developed is automatic segmentation of text into fields with statistically distinguishable signatures, such as bibliography items. The segmentation method is similar to the text categorization problem of the previous section, but here the segments are much shorter (a few words) and additional structural and syntactic information must be employed. This additional information comes from the temporal order of the items and from knowledge of the possible field separators. The essence of the difficulty here is in the fast switching between the different statistical sources that determine the various fields. It is not only essential that the fields are statistically well discriminated, but that there is a clear field switch which has to be identified precisely. We apply the technique of hidden Markov models (HMM) to this task. This technique, originally developed for speech recognition, can automatically segment sequences that are generated by different statistical sources by modeling the data as a stochastic function of a Markov chain. In this case the different tagged fields are considered as generated by the hidden states of the Markov chain.

Unlike the more general HMM training problem, where the states are inferred by unsupervised learning, the training in the bibliography case can be easily performed using *"BIBTEX"* files, which are already labeled by the corresponding bibliography fields. This is also our output format. In general, however, such tagging is not available and the unsupervised segmentation method should be used.

The input file to this tool can be (but is not always only) an HTML file which contains bibliography items, such as:

```
<LI> Synchronization power depends on the register size.
Y. Afek and G. Stupp, In Proceeding of the 34th Ann IEEE Symp
on Foundations of Computer Science, pages 196-205, November, 1993.
<A HREF="ftp://ftp.math.tau.ac.il/pub/afek/focs93.ps.gz">

<LI> N. Alon, Y. Matias and M. Szegedy,
<A HREF="ftp://ftp.math.tau.ac.il/pub/noga/AMS.ps.Z"> The
space complexity of approximating the frequency moments,
Proceeding of the 28th ACM STOC, 1996.
```

Notice that fields such as *title, authors,* are not explicitly marked and occur in different orders in items. The output of the segmentation tool on such a file portion looks as follows (and is in the form requested by the W3TRANS tool).

```
<BIB>
<AUTHORS> <AUTHOR>Y. Afek <AUTHOR>G. Stupp
<TITLE>Synchronization power depends on the register size.
<LINK>ftp://ftp.math.tau.ac.il/pub/afek/focs93.ps.gz
<JOURNAL>In Proceeding of the 34th Ann IEEE Symp on Foundations
of Computer Science,
<MONTH>November
<YEAR>1993

<BIB>
<AUTHORS> <AUTHOR>N. Alon <AUTHOR>Y. Matias <AUTHOR>M. Szegedy
<TITLE>The space complexity of approximating the frequency moments,
<LINK>ftp://ftp.math.tau.ac.il/pub/noga/AMS.ps.Z
<JOURNAL>Proceeding of the 28th ACM STOC,
<MONTH>
<YEAR>1996
```

The important ingredient of this tool is that it can handle erroneous, noisy, and irregular input. However, it can also make errors in its labeling, classification and segmentation. It is thus important that the other components of the system, or other users of these tools, are robust enough to deal with statistical tagging mistakes.

4 The Translator (W3TRANS)

A primary motivation for new database technology is to provide support for the broad spectrum of multimedia data available on the network. These data are stored under different formats: a specific database vendor format, SGML or Latex (documents), DX formats (scientific data), Step (CAD/CAM data), etc. Their integration is a very active field of research and development, (see for instance, for a very small sample, [14, 11, 12, 15, 13, 21, 34, 35, 6, 16, 7]).

A key observation is that, often, the application programs used by organizations can only handle data of a specific format. (e.g. Web browsers, like Netscape, expect files in HTML format, and relational databases expect relations). To enable a specific tool to manipulate data coming from various sources, a translation phase must take place–the data (in the source format) need be mapped to the format expected by the application.

Currently two kinds of tools are available for mapping from one format into another one: (i) specialized tools that perform a default mapping from one format to another (e.g., from Latex to HTML[42]) and (ii) more general tools allowing the user to specify a mapping (e.g., ICA[30]). The tools of the former kind are easy to use but are very limited since they do not allow the user to customize mappings. In fact, the user does not know a priori how the data will be translated [39]. Although more satisfactory, the tools of the latter kind still have many drawbacks: (i) they are very difficult to use, (ii) they often do not keep the correspondences between the various components of the source data and those of the translated data, and they do not provide good support for inverse translations; this makes it very difficult to propagate updates (on the translated data) back to the source, (iii) they do not use a declarative language and thus can hardly be analyzed for optimization or update purposes [20].

The goal is to build a translation tool that will overcome the above shortcomings, and allow easy specification of a mapping via a declarative language.

4.1 System Overview

At the heart of the solution are (1) a middleware data model to which various data sources are mapped, and (2) a declarative language, called TreeLog, for specifying data translation within the middleware model.

The choice of the *middleware* data model is clearly essential—it serves as a common ground for all the data sources, and has to provide a clean abstraction of the different formats in which data are stored. The model we use consists of *ordered labeled trees*. It is simple, yet general enough to capture the essence of the formats we have mentioned. Our model is similar to the one used in [12] and to the OEM model for semi-structured data (see, e.g., [22, 35]). (This is not surprising since the data formats that motivated these works are part of the formats that we intend to support.) A difference is that we view the children of each vertex as ordered. This is crucial to describe lists, an essential component of the DX formats.

Each data source that is to be exposed to the Web community is expected to provide a mapping to/from the middleware format. The representation of each source inside the middleware is very close to the structure of data in the source, so the implementation of such a mapping is fairly easy. For example, a SGML document can be represented by the parse tree of the document. A relational database can be represented by a tree whose root represents the whole database, and having one child for each relation (labeled with the relation name). These nodes will have children representing the tuples in the relation, and having a child for each of the attributes.

The fact that the data representation is close to the source format means that the representation of the various sources inside the middleware can be different. So the translation scheme consists of 3 phases:

(i) In the first phase, data is imported from the source to the middleware data model to yield a forest-like representation that is hiding details unnecessary for the restructuring (e.g., tags or parsing information).

(ii) Then, the data is translated from one abstract representation to the other.

(iii) Finally, the data is exported to the target.

For part (ii) of the translation scheme (translations inside the middleware), we use the *TreeLog* language [8, 32]. It is a rule-based language, with a fixpoint semantics, in the flavor of Datalog. It differs from other rule-based languages in its strong tree-awareness: it provides syntactic constructs to search and build complex trees that represent data.

For lack of space we cannot give here a formal definition of the middleware model and the TreeLog language, nor can we demonstrate how the language is used for defining useful translations. More details and examples of translation programs can be found in [8, 32].

Nevertheless, we would like to point out one significant advantage of the language with respect to updates. Assume some data has been extracted and translated from one format to the other, and then was updated in the target system. To propagate the update back to the source, one needs to know the correspondence among the various pieces of data in the two systems, and also to have an inverse translation, mapping data from the target format to the source. Interestingly it turns out that in most practical cases, translation, correspondences between data elements, and inverse translations, can all be automatically derived from one TreeLog program [8]. This is an important result. It saves on writing different specifications for each sub-component of the data integration task, and also helps in avoiding inconsistent specifications.

4.2   Implementation

The ideas above have been implemented and tested in a prototype system, called *W3TRANS* [4]. It currently supports the HTML, SGML, RELDB (relational format), and O2 (an object oriented system), data formats.

The system is written in Java and built in a client-server architecture. The server stores a set of common translation programs, and is in charge of communicating with the various data sources for importing/exporting data. When a client wants to perform a translation, it connects to the server, and asks for some data to be imported. The server, on behalf of the client, sends the request to the relevant data source. The data (after being mapped to the middleware format) is then sent to the client. The client can either fetch an existing translation program from the server and activate it locally, or write a new program. Once the translation is done, the client asks the server to export the translated data to the appropriate target source. As assistance to the user, both the source and the target data (in their middleware format) can be displayed on a graphic window. Some benefits of the architecture are:

– For security reasons, it is better to grant access to the external sources (part of which are databases), only to one user - which is the W3TRANS server.
– The most extensive computation - the parsing and activation of the TreeLog program, is done at the client. Thus, avoiding a bottleneck at the server.

The architecture also complies with the current Java requirement that all the communication of a Java client (Applet) is done through the server from which the client applet was loaded.

5   W3QL and W3QS

W3QL [27] is a high level query language designed to operate against the WWW. W3QS is a system that provides a W3QL implementation and additional services. W3QL related material may be found at [44]. A complete description of W3QL and W3QS is found in [26]. W3QS is accessible at [45].

W3QL is a SQL-like query language. It enables specifying patterns over the WWW (viewed as a "directed graph") as well as specifying content conditions. Unlike SQL, the W3QL "From List" is a list of paths. Paths may be *unbounded*, i.e. the path's edges may be left unspecified. W3QL allows specifying a limit on the length of unbounded paths. The current W3QL implementation allows only a single path in the "From List".

One can write W3QL queries to specify useful tasks. To get a taste of W3QL's querying abilities, consider the following problem. We'd like to search through a site, say the Data Mining group publications at West University (http:-//www.west.edu/datamining/publications.html) and look for papers in La-tex format that are authored by Smith and Jones. Here is our first cut into the problem:

```
1      Select
2      From n1,11,n2
3      where
4      n1 in {
5      http://www.west.edu/datamining/publications.html
6      };
7      n1: PERLCOND '(n1.content =  /Jones/i) &&
8      (n1.content =  /Smith/i)';
9      n2: PERLCOND ' (n2.format =  /Latex/i)';
10      using ISEARCHd
```

Line 2 specifies a pattern consisting of page n1 pointing via link 11 to page n2. Page n2 should be a Latex file (Line 9) and Page n1 should contain the strings Jones (/i means case independent matching) and Smith (Lines 7-8).

This is not yet what we want, since currently we know that page n1 contains both Jones and Smith, but there is no guarantee that page n2 (the Latex file) is actually co-authored by them. Adding the following condition ensures co-authoring:

```
n2: PERLCOND 'n2.author.content =  /Jones/i
&& n2.author.content =  /Smith/i';
```

The PERLCOND program extracts the author field of the Latex file and verifies that it contains the strings "Jones" and "Smith".

Finally, we may know a starting point at West University but not the exact location of the Data Mining Group. We can modify the first few lines of the above query to search through the West site. The expression (nx,1x) denotes an *unbounded* path of length 1 or more. Therefore the line From n1,11,n2 must be modified to From n0,10,(nx,1x),11,n1,12,n2[1].

The above is merely a simple example of W3QL's capabilities. For example, not always does one know the search starting points, or cares to specify them. In such cases, one may obtain starting points from an established search service (e.g. Infoseek at www.infoseek.com), and proceed from these points. This entails specifying, within a W3QL query, the search service HTTP address and how the query forms (of the search service) are to be filled. Thus, one can use existing search services as database-like indexes.

Among the more important features of W3QL are the ability to specify arbitrary boolean conditions on nodes and links, the ability to use previous form filling activities to navigate through forms (and to prompt the user on encountering new forms), the ability to define (refreshed) views, and the ability to analyze file formats (e.g. checking the author of a Latex file).

---

[1] The query needs to be further modified if we stipulate that the Data Mining group is accessible from West's starting page with a path of length less than 4. For clarity, this further modification is omitted.

5.1 W3QS

W3QS provides a query engine for executing W3QL queries. It provides help buttons, several editing interfaces, and maintenance and display of the user's queries. Additionally, it allow immediate or deferred execution of queries, query editing in the middle of execution, and sophisticated display of query results. Queries may contain sophisticated Perl conditions, see [46], and may navigate through forms, using user-supplied or default responses. W3QS is accessible at [45].

5.2 Summary

One may view W3QL as a mechanism for specifying information retrieval agents (or robots). W3QL searches can be more sophisticated than those provided by search services such as AltaVista or Yahoo. Such services may be used from within W3QL queries.

6 Cooperative Publications Querying—WGDB, W3LEARN, W3TRANS and W3QS

So far we presented four tools, each aiming at solving one specific Web-related problem By combining the tools in different ways, one can build a wide range of applications and overcome many of the limitations in existing systems for utilizing Web data.

To illustrate this, we describe below an application that was built using the tools. The application supports queries about publications of Computer Science researchers. The global database (W3GDB) provides a schema containing information about publications, their titles, authors, etc., and the user can pose queries against that schema. The data for the global database is derived from many local databases, where each local database represents some information source found on the Web. However, the global database does not contain all the relevant information sources that exist on the Web, and part of the application consists of searching for new information sources and incorporating them into the global database. The application relies heavily on graphical user interfaces and HTML forms; these are not shown here, for lack of space. The user interface controls the interaction with the global database, and is also used to connect to the other components of the system (each of those components has its own user interface).

Typically, a user of this particular application starts by posing a query about publications. The query is phrased with respect to the relations of the global database schema. The user interface for phrasing the query is in the style of Query-By-Example. In the first form shown to the user, the list of the relations of the global database schema is presented, and the user is asked to check the relations that will participate in the query. The query is the natural join of the relations checked by the user, and in addition to the natural join, the user is also allowed to specify a selection and a projection. These are facilitated by allowing the user to check attributes that appear in the result (i.e., to specify the projection), and also to specify a selection for each attribute. In this particular example, there is one selection, namely `PubArea = 'Databases'`. Once the definition of the query is completed, the query is submitted for execution.

The query is executed by translating it into queries on the local relations (using the appropriate rules stored in W3GDB), and the user can view the result as a set of tuples. Suppose that the result does not contain sufficient information (e.g., the user was looking for publications coauthored by Milo, but could not find any). In this case, the user should activate other tools of the system in order to find new information sources on the Web that may contain the information he/she is looking for. The search for new information sources starts with a W3QL query. E.g., a query starts a search in a specified page (i.e., specified by its URL) and looks for pages connected to the first one via a single hyperlink that contains the character string `bib`. Moreover, the pages reached in this way should contain the character string `Milo`. Thus, pages are retrieved based on how they are reached as well as their contents. The query (in this case) may seem a bit contrived, but the principle should be clear. The user may combine any condition on the contents of Web pages (e.g., appearance of some keywords in those pages) as well as any condition on the location of those Web pages and how they are connected to other pages on the Web (e.g., search only Web pages that are "close by", i.e. that can be reached by following at most two hyperlinks from some page located on a Web server of a Computer Science Department). Thus, the user is able not just to incorporate knowledge about the contents of the pages he/she is looking for, but also incorporate knowledge on how those pages are interconnected.

The W3QL query is submitted to, and executed by, W3QS. The result is a list of URLs (of the Web pages satisfying the conditions of the query). Next, each document in the result is evaluated by the statistical-learning tool (W3LEARN) to determine whether it consists of a listing of publications. Technically, W3LEARN gives an estimation of the relevance of the data in the document to the subject of interest (i.e., listings of publications, in our case). Note that the statistical-learning tool must have been previously trained on a large sample of documents in order to acquire the capability of discerning between documents that contain listings of publications and those that do not. If the document consists of publications, W3LEARN further analyzes the document and adds tags, according to a predetermined format, for indicating author names, titles, etc.

Now the user should activate the data translation (W3TRANS) tool in order to translate each tagged document into a collection of local relations (representing the publications found in that document). Once W3TRANS is activated, the user is required to specify the formats of the data source and the desired output, and the translation program between those formats. In this specific scenario, all these three parameters are known in advance and can be selected from the appropriate menus. Note that this is not a coincidence. Once W3LEARN has been trained to tag a document, the set of possible tags is known in advance, and therefore the local relations into which the document is to be translated can also be determined in advance (since null values do not present any problem in our system); similarly, the translation program can also be determined in advance once the data-source and output formats are known.

So, after choosing the appropriate formats and translation program, W3TRANS is activated for the given tagged document, and the output is the URL of a file that contains the new local relations (created from that tagged document). Now, these new local relations have to be added to the global database (W3GDB).

To accomplish this task, the user now needs to specify the name of the new collection of local relations, and the URL of the file containing those relations. Next, the user has to define rules that map the local relations to the global ones. Some of the rules used in our case are as follows.

$$glAuthor(AutId, AutName, \_AutLink, \_AutEmail, \_AutPhone, \_AutFax) :-$$
$$tauAuthors(AutId, AutName).$$
$$glPubAutInst(PubId, AutId, InstId, \_GrantNo) :-$$
$$InstId =' TAU', tauPubAuthor(AutId, PubId).$$

Note that variables in the head that do not appear in the body will later be replaced by null values, as described earlier. Since the same local schema is used whenever possible, the rules are almost the same in most (if not all) cases. However, information that is unique to a local source can be inserted through the rules rather than directly into the local relations. For example, the institute ID is inserted through the second rule. The advantage of this approach is that it is much easier to modify the rules for a specific local database than to modify W3TRANS.

After incorporating the new local relations in W3GDB, the original W3GDB query has to be re-submitted, and the result is shown as a list of tuples. Note that an attribute that appears without a value has a null value.

7 The Other Tools

We briefly sketch here the other two tools developed in the framework of our project.

7.1 The Personal Information Manager, (PIM)

Currently, a significant part of the daily work of scientists and other professionals revolves around the manipulation of files, messages, memos, and items of a similar nature. Those include besides regular data, also email and newsgroup data, URL lists, and so on. Many tools now support graphical window-based interfaces. There seems to be a much slower convergence for the data storage and handling component. The main idea of PIM is to base the handling of all such items on a set of core database functionalities, including storage and retrieval, and declarative querying. This has the advantages first that much of the schema and storage organization tasks can be automated, and second that sharing of data and structure (where available and relevant) across all tools and applications employed by a user can be supported. Various programs that serve specific purposes run as clients on top of a layer that offers these core database functionalities. Typical clients include a mailer, a meeting calendar, a tasks-to-do-queue, and so on.

In terms of cooperation with the other tools described above, one can view PIM as residing in a layer *above* the previously described tools, taking advantage of the services provided by them. For example, a PIM client could be used to manage a user's bibliography database. When additional items are needed, the services of other tools of Wesuite are inboked, as described above.

7.2 The Virtual Reality Generator VRG

Virtual reality is not a new idea. We just mention here an important characteristic of this tool, that makes it relevant to the project, and an excellent candidate for future integration. Most of the current technologies of virtual reality services, if used in a widely distributed environment, require the shipping of enormous amount of graphic data. The VRG tool is a notable exception. It is based on a concise language for describing objects, and on an efficient technology for generating the objects. Thus, a VRG server can drive many clients, by maintaining a database of objects and relationships, and sending over the network only instructions for generating objects. The generation is performed at the client's site. This results in extremely fast update of scenes. The central management by a server allows for sharing of scenes and objects between clients, thus making (almost) real-time interaction between clients in a virtual reality possible.

For the specific needs addressed by tools as described above, e.g., maintaining a bibliography database, note that user interfaces to Web data are currently rather limited. The navigational nature of most Web browsers provides a rather narrow visual window, showing only one page at a time. Other visualization paradigms (e.g. [23, 17, 33, 36, 18]) enable the user to work with groups of documents and highlight issues such as the network structure and the documents content. However, they are still rather isolated from the local user environment and the other applications the user is working with. The VRG can be used, for example, to generate a virtual office or library, with shelves and file cabinets, from which books and other bibliographic items can be retrieved. See figure 1, which describes a scene of an office created using a compact prescription of about 5000 bytes. In this scene, data from the web can be mapped (interchanged, and interrogated) on the billboard (right), the phones, the computers and the books (left on the shelf). The left computer displays a real time video sequence while the computer at the center of the scene shows an HTML page of an on line WEB based newspaper. VRG related material may be found at [5].

Fig. 1. AVRG office scene

8 Conclusions

In this paper we presented a system for searching, collecting, integrating and managing Web data. The system consists of five tools, each is aimed at solving one fundamental problem encountered when attempting to utilize Web data. Each tool can be used in a stand-alone mode, in combination with the other tools, or even in conjunction with other systems. The combination of these tools enables the building of complex Web based applications in a flexible way.

We have experimented with the tools, and with mixing and matching them, in constructing combined applications. We believe that, in general, systems that are developed in such a modular fashion can be more powerful than those developed in a monolithic centralized manner. This is because (1) each component is developed by experts in the tool's specific area of application, and thus is state of the art for the specific task, and (2) one can use expertise from a variety of areas (e.g. in our system, AI and Databases) to enrich the system capabilities. This effort points to a fruitful research direction, that of "wrapping applications" out of basic tools that will be available across the network.

The bibliography scenario is an example of a particular kind of cooperation. A W3GDB task is carried out with the aid of W3QS (WWW searching), W3LEARN (source utility determination and tagging) and W3TRANS (format conversion). This type of cooperation is by no means the only one possible. We list several possible modes of cooperation among the tools:

1. Direct W3GDB and W3QS cooperation. W3GDB can utilize W3QS querying capabilities directly for obtaining data from sites that are known to be relevant for a task. It may use W3QS's view mechanism to make sure that certain sources are accessed at pre-determined time intervals and are monitored for changes. It may also utilize W3LEARN to extract certain pieces of information, without using W3TRANS's format transformation capabilities.
2. W3GDB and W3QS may utilize W3TRANS directly, without W3LEARN, in accessing known structured sources or (relational or object oriented) databases.
3. PIM can utilize each of these tools in obtaining and organizing data.
4. W3QS may use W3LEARN for examining information sources, as part of W3QL queries. Here, W3LEARN offers certain services in classifying the types of sources which W3QS can use. Currently, W3QS can recognize only certain information source types (e.g. Postscript or Latex files) on its own. An ability of recognizing and parsing a larger set of source types (e.g. articles on distributed databases) will greatly enhance W3QL's querying ability.

Acknowledgments

Tova Milo thanks Serge Abiteboul and Sophie Cluet for their contribution to the development of the formal foundation of the data translation system W3TRANS.

References

1. W3SQL. http://www.cs.technion.ac.il/~konop/w3qs.html.
2. W3QS. http://www.cs.technion.ac.il/~W3QS.
3. West university. http://www.west.edu/datamining/publications.html.
4. W3TRANS. http://www.math.tau.ac.il/~pinim/w3trans-home.html.
5. VRG. http://www.cs.technion.ac.il/~anda/files/WebSuite.html.
6. S. Abiteboul, S. Cluet, T. Milo. Querying the file. *Proc. of Intl. Conf. on Very Large Data Bases*, Dublin, 1993
7. S. Abiteboul, S. Cluet and T. Milo, A database interface for files update, *Proc. ACM SIGMOD Int. Conf. on Management of Data*, May 1995.
8. S. Abiteboul, S. Cluet, and T. Milo. Correspondence and Translation for Heterogeneous Data. In *Proc. Int. Conf. on Database Theory (ICDT)*, 351–363. 1997.
9. P. Atzeni, S. Labonia, A. Masci, G. Mecca, P. Merialdo and E. Tabet. "The ARANEUS Project," http://poincare.inf.uniroma3.it:8080/Araneus/araneus.html
10. G. Bell, A. Parisi, and M. Pesce. The Virtual Reality Modeling Language: Version 1 Specification. May 1995. http://www.virtpark.com/theme/vrml/.
11. P. Buneman, S. Davidson, K. Hart, C. Overton, and L. Wong. A data transformation system for biological data sources. In *Proc. Int. Conf. on Very Large Data Bases (VLDB)*, pages 158–169, Zurich, Switzerland, 1995.
12. P. Buneman, S. Davidson, and D. Suciu. Programming constructs for unstructured data, May 1996.
13. M.J. Carey et al. Towards heterogeneous multimedia information systems: The Garlic approach. Technical Report RJ 9911, IBM Almaden Research Center, 1994.
14. V. Christophides, S. Abiteboul, S. Cluet, and M. Scholl. From structured documents to novel query facilities. In *Proc. ACM Sigmod, Minneapolis*, 1994.
15. T.-P. Chang and R. Hull. Using witness generators to support bi-directional update between object-based databases. In *Proc. ACM SIGMOD/SIGACT Conf. on Princ. of Database Syst. (PODS)*, San Jose, California, May 1995.
16. M. Consens, T. Milo. Optimizing Queries on Files, *ACM SIGMOD Int. Conf. on Management of Data*, Minneapolis, Minnesota, 301-312,May 1994.
17. F. Das Neves. The aleph: A tool to spatially represent user knowledge about the www docuverse. In *Proc. ACM Hypertext '97*, 1997.
18. Peter Doemel. WebMap – a graphical hypertext navigation tool. In *Proceedings of the 2nd Int'l World Wide Web Conference*, Chicago, October 1994. http://www.ncsa.uiuc.edu/SDG/IT94/Proceedings/Searching/doemel/-www-fall94.html.
19. Excite Inc. Excite: Main page. 1996. http://www.excite.com.
20. A. Feng and T. Wakayama. Simon: A Grammar Based Transformation System of Structured Documents, *Proc. Int. Conf. Electronic Publishing*,1994.
21. J.C. Franchitti and R. King. Amalgame: a tool for creating interoperating persistent, heterogeneous components. *Advanced Database Systems*, pages 313–36, 1993.
22. H. Garcia-Molina, D. Quass, Y. Papakonstantinou, A. Rajaraman, Y. Sagiv, J. D. Ullman, and J. Widom. "The TSIMMIS Approach to Mediation: Data Models and Languages," to appear in a special issue of the *International Journal of Intelligent Information Systems;*
23. M. Hemmje. Lyberworld - a visulalization user interface with full text retrieval. In *Proceedings of SIGIR 94*, 1994.

24. M. Kifer, G. Lausen, and J. Wu. "Logical Foundations of Object-Oriented and Frame-Based Languages," *JACM*, Vol. 42, No. 4, pp. 741–843, 1995.
25. T. Kirk, A. Y. Levy, Y. Sagiv, and D. Srivastava. "The Information Manifold," *AI Spring Symp.*, 1995.
26. Konopnicki, D., Shmueli, O., Information Gathering in the World-Wide Web: The W3QL Query Language and the W3QS system. ACM TODS, to appear.
27. Konopnicki D., and O. Shmueli. W3QS: A Query System for the World-Wide Web. In *Proceedings of 1995 VLDB Conference*, , Zurich, Switzerland, September 1995.
28. A. Levy, A. Rajaraman, and J. Ordille. "The World-Wide Web as a Collection of Views: Query Processing in the Information Manifold" *Proc. Workshop on Materialized Views: Techniques and Applications*, Montreal, Canada, pp. 43–55, 1996.
29. A. Y. Levy, A. O. Mendelzon, Y. Sagiv, and D. Srivastava. "Answering Queries Using Views," *Proc. 14th PODS*, 1995.
30. A. Mamrak, C. O'Connell, Technical Documentation for the Integrated Chameleon Architecture: *ftp.ifi.uio.no /pub/SGML/ICA*, 1992.
31. A. Mendelzon, G. Mihaila, and T. Milo. Querying the world wide. In *Proc. of PDIS'96*, 1996.
32. P. Mogilevski. Integration and Translation of Heterogeneous Data. M.Sc Thesis, Tel-Aviv University. 1997.
33. S. Mukherjea and J.D. Foley. Visualizing the World Wide Web with the Navigational View Builder. *Computer Networks and ISDN Systems*, 27:1075–1087, 1995.
34. Y. Papakonstantinou, H. Garcia-Molina, and J. Ullman. Medmaker: A mediation system based on declarative specifications. Available at db.stanford.edu/pub/papakonstantinou/1995/medmaker.ps.
35. Y. Papakonstantinou, H. Garcia-Molina, and J. Widom. Object exchange across heterogeneous information sources. In *Int'l Conf. on Data Engineering*, 1995.
36. J.E. Pitkow and K.A. Bharat. WebViz: A tools for World Wide Web access log analysis. In *Proc. 1st Int'l World Wide Web Conf.*, Geneva, Switzerland, May 1994. http://www1.cern.ch/PapersWWW94/pitkow-webvis.ps.
37. D. Quass, A. Rajaraman, Y. Sagiv, J. D. Ullman, and J. Widom. "Querying Semistructured Heterogeneous Information," (Proc. 4th Int. Conf., DOOD'95, Singapore, Dec. 1995, T. W. Ling, A. O. Mendelzon, and L. Vieille (Eds.)), LNCS 1013, Springer, pp. 319–344, 1995.
38. A. Rajaraman, Y. Sagiv, J. D. Ullman. "Answering Queries Using Templates With Binding Patterns," *Proc. 14th PODS*, 1995.
39. K. Shoens, A. Luniewski, P. Schwartz, J. Stamos, and J . Thomas. The rofus system: Information organization for semi-structured data. In *Proc. of the 19th Int. conf. on Very Large Databases, VLDB93*, pages 97–107, 1993.
40. N. Slonim and N. Tishby, *Automatic statistical categorization and segmentation of text*, HUJI Technical Report, To appear.
41. V.S. Subrahmanian, S. Adali, A. Brink, R. Emery, J. Lu, A. Rajput, T. Rogers, R. Ross, and C. Ward. "HERMES: A Heterogeneous Reasoning and Mediator System. Tech. Report, U. of Maryland, 1995.
42. J. Walker. HTML Converters. In *http://www2.ncsu.edu/bae/people/faculty/walker/hotlist/htmlconv.html*, 1994.
43. Yahoo Inc. Yahoo: Main page. 1996. http://www.yahoo.com.
44. W3QS Home Page. http://www.cs.technion.ac.il/~konop/w3qs.html.
45. The W3QS System. http://www.cs.technion.ac.il/~W3QS.
46. PERLCOND Home Page. http://www.cs.technion.ac.il/~konop/perlcond.html.

Extracting Patterns and Relations
from the World Wide Web

Sergey Brin

Computer Science Department
Stanford University
sergey@cs.stanford.edu

Abstract. The World Wide Web is a vast resource for information. At the same time it is extremely distributed. A particular type of data such as restaurant lists may be scattered across thousands of independent information sources in many different formats. In this paper, we consider the problem of extracting a relation for such a data type from all of these sources automatically. We present a technique which exploits the duality between sets of patterns and relations to grow the target relation starting from a small sample. To test our technique we use it to extract a relation of (author,title) pairs from the World Wide Web.

1   Introduction

The World Wide Web provides a vast source of information of almost all types, ranging from DNA databases to resumes to lists of favorite restaurants. However, this information is often scattered among many web servers and hosts, using many different formats. If these chunks of information could be extracted from the World Wide Web and integrated into a structured form, they would form an unprecedented source of information. It would include the largest international directory of people, the largest and most diverse databases of products, the greatest bibliography of academic works, and many other useful resources.

There has been considerable work on integrating a number of information sources using specially coded wrappers or filters [Tsi,MOS97]. However, these can be time-consuming to create and are usually used for tens, not thousands of sources. In this paper, we address the problem of extracting a relation from the thousands of sources that may hold pieces of the relation on the World Wide Web. Our goal is to discover information sources and to extract the relevant information from them either entirely automatically, or with very minimal human intervention.

In this paper, we consider the problem of extracting a relation of books – (author,title) pairs from the Web. Intuitively, our solution works as follows. We begin with a small seed set of (author, title) pairs (in tests we used a set of just five books). Then we find all occurrences of those books on the Web. From these occurrences we recognise patterns for the citations of books. Then we search the Web for these patterns and find new books. We can then take these books and find all their occurrences and from those generate more patterns. We can use these new patterns to find more books, and so forth. Eventually, we will obtain a large list of books and patterns for finding them.

2 The Duality of Patterns and Relations

The method we propose is called DIPRE - Dual Iterative Pattern Relation Expansion. It relies on a duality between patterns and relations which we explain below.

2.1 The Problem

Here we define our problem more formally:

Let D be a large database of unstructured information such as the World Wide Web. Let $R = r_1, ..., r_n$ be the target relation. Every tuple, t, of R occurs in one or more times in D. Every such *occurrence* consists of all the fields of t, represented as strings, occurring in close proximity to each other in D (in the case of the Web, this means all the fields are near each other, on the same Web page).

In the test problem we examine in this paper, the target relation R is the set of books - (author, title) pairs that occur on the Web. Clearly, this is not well defined. However, given a potential author and title and where they are mentioned on the Web, a human can generally tell whether this is a legitimate book.

If we compute an approximation, R' of R then the coverage is $\frac{|R' \cap R|}{|R|}$ and the error rate is $\frac{|R' - R|}{|R'|}$. Our goal is to maximize coverage and minimize the error rate. However, a low error rate is much more critical than high coverage. Given a sufficiently large database, D, a recall of just 20% may be acceptable. However, an error rate over 10% would likely be useless for many applications.

Typically, we cannot actually compute R. Therefore, we cannot not know the precise values of coverage and error rate. However, we can sample the error rate by having a user check random elements of R'. Coverage is much more difficult to estimate.

2.2 Patterns

Intuitively, a pattern matches one particular format of occurrences of tuples of the target relation. Ideally the pattern is specific enough not to match any tuples that should not be in the relation, however, in practice a few false positives may occur. Patterns may have various representations. In our work we used a very limited class of regular expressions. More formally:

Let p be a pattern. Then $M_D(p)$ is the set of tuples that match p in D and $|p|_D$ is the number of elements in $M_D(p)$. Then the coverage of $p, C_D(p, R) = |M_D(p) \cap R|/|R|$ and the error rate of p is $E_D(p, R) = |M_D(p) - R|/|M_D(p)|$.

For a set of patterns, $P = p_1, ..., p_k$, we define $M_D(P) = \bigcup_{p \in P} M_D(p)$. We extend $C_D(P, R)$ and $E_D(P, R)$ analogously. Alternative definitions of $M_D(P)$ may require a tuple to match multiple patterns (see Section 6).

2.3 Pattern Relation Duality

An important observation is that given a set of patterns, P with high coverage and low error rate, we can construct a very good approximation to R simply by finding all matches to all the patterns. Thus, given a good set of patterns, we can build a good set of tuples. However, we also wish to have the converse property - given a good set of tuples, we can build a good set of patterns. We can do this by finding all occurrences of the tuples in D and discovering similarities in the occurrences. The combination of the ability to find tuples from patterns and patterns from tuples gives us great power and is the basis for the technique we propose in this paper.

3 Dual Iterative Pattern Relation Extraction

Dual Iterative Pattern Relation Extraction - DIPRE is a technique for extracting relations which makes use of pattern-relation duality. It works as follows:

1. $R' \leftarrow$ Sample
   Start with a small sample, R' of the target relation. This sample is given by the user and can be very small. In our tests, we used a list of five books with authors.
2. $O \leftarrow$ FindOccurrences(R', D)
   Then, find all occurrences of tuples of R' in D. In our experiments, these were nearby occurrences of the author and the title of a book in text. Along with the tuple found, keep the context of every occurrence (url and surrounding text).
3. $P \leftarrow$ GenPatterns(O)
   Generate patterns based on the set of occurrences. This is the tricky part of the algorithm. Roughly speaking, this routine must generate patterns for sets of occurrences with similar context. The patterns need to have a low error rate, so it is important that they are not overly general. The higher the coverage of the patterns the better. However, a low coverage can be compensated for with a larger database.
4. $R' \leftarrow M_D(P)$. Search the database for tuples matching any of the patterns.
5. If R' is large enough, return. Else go to step 2.

3.1 Controlling Expansion

The above process is not necessarily very stable and may stray away from R. In particular, several bogus tuples in $M_D(P)$ can lead to several bogus patterns in P in the next iteration. This in turn can cause a whole slew of bogus tuples. For this reason the GenPatterns routine must be careful to minimize the amount of damage caused by a potential bogus tuple (or several small tuples). Another measure of safety is to define $M_D(P)$ more stringently so as to require tuples to match multiple patterns in P. This second measure has not been necessary in the tests we have performed but may be necessary in future tests. Finally, various threshholds may need to fluctuate as the relation expands.

4 Finding Authors and Titles

For our experiments we chose to compute a relation of (Author,Title) pairs from the World Wide Web. This problem lends itself particularly well to DIPRE because there are a number of well-known books which are listed on many web sites. Many of the web sites conform to a reasonably uniform format across the site.

4.1 Patterns for Books

In order to use DIPRE to find books, it is necessary to define what patterns consist of. The definition of a pattern largely determines the success of DIPRE. However, for our tests we used a very simple definition of a pattern. It requires further investigation to determine whether more sophisticated definitions of patterns work better.

We defined a pattern as a five-tuple: *(order, urlprefix, prefix, middle, suffix)* where *order* is a boolean value and the other attributes are strings. If *order* is true, an *(author,title)* pair matches the pattern if there is a document in the collection (the WWW) with a URL which matches `urlprefix*` and which contains text that matches the regular expression:
`*prefix, author, middle, title, suffix*`

The *author* is restricted to:
`[A-Z][A-Za-z .,&]`^{5,30}`[A-Za-z.]`
The *title* is restricted to:
`[A-Z0-9][A-Za-z0-9 .,:'#!?;&]`^{4,45}`[A-Za-z0-9?!]`
If *order* is false, then the title and author are switched.

4.2 Occurrences

We also have to define how an occurrence is structured since it should have a correspondance to the definition of a pattern. An occurrence of an *(author,title)* pair consists of a seven-tuple:
(author, title, order, url, prefix, middle, suffix)
The *order* corresponds to the order the title and the author occurred in the text. The *url* is the URL of the document they occurred on. The *prefix* consists of the m characters (in tests m was 10) preceding the author (or title if the title was

first). The *middle* is the text between the author and title and the *suffix* consists of the m characters following the title (or author).[1]

4.3 Generating Patterns for Books

An important component of the DIPRE procedure is the GenPatterns routine which takes a set of occurrences of books and converts them into a list of patterns. This is a nontrivial problem and there is the entire field of pattern recognition devoted to solving the general version of this problem. For our purposes, however, we use a simple set of heuristics for generating patterns from occurrences. As long as there are few false positives (patterns that generate nonbooks) this is sufficient. Each pattern need only have very small coverage since the web is vast and there are many sources of information so the total coverage of all the patterns can still be substantial.

Suppose we are given a set of occurrences and we wish to construct a specific a pattern as possible that matches all of them. We can do this as follows:

1. Verify that the *order* and *middle* of all the occurrences is the same. If not, it is not possible to generate a pattern to match them all. Set *outpattern.order* and *outpattern.middle* to *order* and *middle* respectively.
2. Find the longest matching prefix of all the urls. Set *outpattern.urlprefix* to that prefix.
3. Set *outpattern.prefix* to the longest matching suffix of the *prefix*'s of the occurrences.
4. Set *outpattern.suffix* to the longest matching prefix of the *suffix*'s of the occurrences.

We denote this routine GenOnePattern(O).

Pattern Specificity A pattern generated like the above can be too general or too specific. We are not concerned about it being too specific since there will be many patterns generated and combined there will be many books. However, the pattern may be too general and may produce many nonbooks.

To combat this problem we attempt to measure the *specificity* of the pattern. The *specificity* of a pattern p roughly corresponds to $-\log(P(X \in M_D(p)))$ where X is some random variable distributed uniformly over the domain of tuples of R.[2] For quick computation, we used the following formula for the *specificity* of a pattern ($|s|$ denotes the length of s):

specificity$(p) = |p.\text{middle}||p.\text{urlprefix}||p.\text{prefix}||p.\text{suffix}|$

---

[1] The prefix and suffix could actually be less than m characters if the line ends or starts close to the occurrence but this is a restriction of the current implementation and it is unclear whether it has a positive or negative effect.

[2] If the domain is infinite like the space of all strings, the uniform distribution may not be sensible and a different distribution should be used.

We reject any patterns with too low a *specificity* so that overly general patterns aren't generated. More specifically, we insist that specificity$(p)n > t$ where n is the number of books with occurrences supporting the pattern p and t is a threshhold. This ensures that all the strings of a pattern are nonempty (otherwise the *specificity* is zero). Also we require that $n > 1$ since basing a pattern on one example is very error-prone.

Algorithm for Generating Patterns Here, we present the algorithm for Gen-Patterns(O). It takes advantage of the algorithm GenOnePattern(O) introduced in Section 4.3.

1. Group all occurrences o in O by *order* and *middle*. Let the resulting groups be $O_1, ... O_k$.
2. For each group O_i, $p \leftarrow$ GenOnePattern(O_i). If p meets the specificity requirements then output p. Otherwise:
   - If all o in O_i have the same URL then reject O_i.
   - Else, separate the occurrences o in O_i into subgroups grouped by the character in their urls which is one past $p.urlprefix$. Repeat the procedure in step 2 for these subgroups.

This routine uses a simple further subdivision based on the url when the pattern generated is not sufficiently specific. One can also imagine using the prefix or the suffix.

We have described a simple technique for generating patterns from lists of occurrences books. One can imagine far more sophisticated techniques and this is the subject of further research. However, as is indicated by the results (Section 5) even this simple scheme works well.

4.4 Performance Issues

There are two very demanding tasks DIPRE - finding occurrences of books given a long list of books and finding pattern matches given a list of patterns. Both of these operation must take place over a very large database of Web documents.

For the first task, finding occurrences of books, we first pass the data through two fgrep filters. One only passes through lines that contained a valid author and the other only passes through lines that contained a valid title. After this it is the task of a program written in Python to actually check that there are matching authors and titles in the line, identify them and produce occurrences as output. Several alternative approaches involving large regular expressions in Flex and in Python were attempted for this purpose but they quickly exceeded various internal bounds.

For the second task, we use just a Python program. Every pattern is translated into a pair of regular expressions, one for the URL, and one for the actual occurrence. Every URL is first tested to see which patterns apply to it. Then the program tests every line for the relevant regular expressions. This approach is quite slow and needs to be improved. Future versions are likely to use Flex or the rex C library. This task can be made somewhat easier by targeting just the URL's which match the patterns and we made some attempt to do this. However, the data is not structured to make that completely trivial and we wish the techniques we develop to be general enough to be able to handle no restrictions on URL's.

The generation of patterns from occurrences is not much of a performance issue at this point in time because there are only thousands of occurrences generated. As larger tests are run this will become more important. Currently, the occurrences are sorted using gsort by *order* and *middle*. Then a Python program reads through the resulting list and generates patterns as described in Section 4.3.

5 Experiments

While the experiments performed so far have been very limited, due to time constraints they have produced very positive results. Many more experiments are in progress.

5.1 Web Data Used in Experiments

For data we used a repository of 24 million web pages totalling 147 gigabytes. This data is part of the Stanford WebBase and is used for the Google search engine [BP] and other research projects. As a part of the search engine, we have built an inverted index of the entire repository.

The repository spans many disks and several machines. It takes a considerable amount of time to make just one pass over the data even without doing any substantial processing. Therefore, in these we only made passes over subsets of the repository on any given iteration.

An important note for this project is that the repository contains almost no web pages from Amazon [Ama]. This is because their automatically generated urls make crawling difficult.

5.2 Pattern Relation Expansion

Isaac Asimov	The Robots of Dawn
David Brin[3]	Startide Rising
James Gleick	Chaos: Making a New Science
Charles Dickens	Great Expectations
William Shakespeare	The Comedy of Errors

Fig. 1. Initial sample of books.

URL Pattern	Text Pattern
`www.sff.net/locus/c.*`	`<LI><B>`*title*`</B> by` *author* `(`
`dns.city-net.com/ĩmann/awards/hugos/1984.html`	`<i>`*title*`</i> by` *author* `(`
`dolphin.upenn.edu/d̃cummins/texts/sf-award.htm`	*author* `||` *title* `|| (`

Fig. 2. Patterns found in first iteration.

We started the experiment with just 5 books (see Figure 1). These produced 199 occurrences and generated 3 patterns (see Figure 2). Interestingly, only the first two of the five books produced the patterns because they were both science fiction books. A run of these patterns over matching URL's produced 4047 unique (author,title) pairs. They were mostly science fiction but there were some exceptions. (See Figure 3.)

H. D. Everett	The Death-Mask and Other Ghosts
H. G. Wells	First Men in the Moon
H. G. Wells	Science Fiction: Volume 2
H. G. Wells	The First Men in the Moon
H. G. Wells	The Invisible Man
H. G. Wells	The Island of Dr. Moreau
H. G. Wells	The Science Fiction Volume 1
H. G. Wells	The Shape of Things to Come: The Ultimate Revolution
H. G. Wells	The Time Machine
H. G. Wells	The War of the Worlds
H. G. Wells	When the Sleeper Wakes
H. M. Hoover	Journey Through the Empty
H. P. Lovecraft & August Derleth	The Lurker at the Threshold
H. P. Lovecraft	At the Mountains of Madness and Other Tales of Terror
H. P. Lovecraft	The Case of Charles Dexter Ward
H. P. Lovecraft	The Doom That Came to Sarnath and Other Stories

Fig. 3. Sample of books found in first iteration.

A search through roughly 5 million web pages found 3972 occurrences of these books. This number was something of a disappointment since it was not a large blowup as had happened in the first iteration. However, it would have taken at least a couple of days to run over the entire repository so we did not attempt to generate more. These occurrences produced 105 patterns, 24 of which had url prefixes which were not complete urls. A pass over a couple million urls produced 9369 unique (author, title) pairs. Unfortunately, there were some bogus books among these. In particular, 242 of them were legitimate titles but had an author of "Conclusion". We removed these from the list. This was the only manual intervention through the whole process. In future experiments, it would be interesting to see whether leaving these in would produce an extraordinary amount of junk.

For the final iteration, we chose to use the subset of the repository which contained the work books. This consisted of roughly 156,000 documents. Scanning for the 9127 remaining books produced 9938 occurrences. These in turn generated 346 patterns. Scanning over the same set of documents produced 15257 unique books with very little bogus data. (See Figure 4)

This experiment is ongoing and hopefully, a larger list of books will be generated soon. The current one is available online [Bri].

5.3 Quality of Results

To analyse the quality of the results, we picked twenty random books out of the list and attempted to verify that they were actual books by searching on Amazon [Ama], the Visa Shopping Guide for books [Vis], the Stanford online library catalog, and the Web.[4] As a measure of the quality of the results, 19 of the 20 were all bonafide books. The remaining book was actually an article - "Why I Voted for a User Car", by Andrew Tobias.

The big surprise was that a number of the books were not found in some or all of the sources except for the Web. Some of these books were online books; some were obscure or out of print; some simply were not listed on some sites for no apparent reason. In total, 5 of the 20 books were not on Amazon which claims to have a catalog of 2.5 million books.

Other than the article mentioned above, there are a few visible problems with the data. Some books are mentioned several times due to small differences such as capitalization, spacing, how the author was listed (for example "E.R. Burroughs" versus "Edgar Rice Burroughs"). Fortunately, however, authors are quite particular about how their name is listed and these duplications are limited. In several cases, some information was appended to the author's name such as publication date.

6 Conclusions

Our general goal is to be able to extract structured data from the entire World Wide Web by leveraging on its vastness. DIPRE has proven to be a remarkable tool in the simple example of finding lists of books. It started with a sample set of 5 books and expanded it to a relatively high quality list of over 15,000 books with very minimal human intervention. The same tool may be applied to a number of other domains such as movies, music, restaurants, and so forth. A more sophisticated version of this tool is likely to be able to extract people directories, product catalogs, and more.

---

[4] Unfortunately, the Library of Congress search system was down at the time of these tests.

Henry James	The Europeans
Henry James	The Golden Bowl
Henry James	The Portrait of a Lady
Henry James	The Turn of the Screw
Henry James	Turn of the Screw
Henry John Coke	Tracks of a Rolling Stone
Henry K. Rowe	Landmarks in Christian History
Henry Kisor	Zephyr
Henry Lawson	In the Days When the World Was Wide
Henry Longfellow	The Song of Hiawatha
Henry Miller	Tropic of Cancer
Henry Petroski	Invention On Design
Henry Petroski	The Evolution of Useful Things
Henry Roth	Call It Sleep
Henry Sumner Maine	Ancient Law
Henry Tuckerman, Lindsay, Phila	Characteristics of Literature
Henry Van Dyke	The Blue Flower
Henry Van Dyke, Scrib	Days Off
Henry Van Loon	Life and Times of Pieter Stuyvesant
Henry Wadsworth Longfellow	Paul Revere's Ride
Henry Wadsworth Longfellow	Evangeline
Henry Wadsworth Longfellow	The Song of Hiawatha
Herbert Donald	Lincoln
Herbert M. Hart	Old Forts of the Northwest
Herbert M. Mason, Jr	The Lafayette Escadrille
Herbert R. Lottman	Jules Verne: An Exploratory Biography
Herbert Spencer	The Man Versus the State
Herman Daly	For the Common Good
Herman Daly	Valuing the Earth
Herman E. Kittredge	Ingersoll: A Biographical Appreciation
Herman Haken	Principles of Brain Functioning
Herman Hesse	Demian
Herman Hesse	Siddhartha
Herman Hesse	Sidharta
Herman Melville	Bartleby, the Scrivener
Herman Melville	Billy Budd
Herman Melville	Billy Budd
Herman Melville	Moby Dick
Herman Melville	The Confidence Man
Herman Melville	The Encantadas, or Enchanted Isles
Herman Melville	Typee: A Peep at Polynesian Life
Herman Weiss	Sunset Detectives
Herman Wouk	War And Remembrance
Hermann Hesse	Klingsor's Last Summer
Hermann Hesse	Knulp
Hermann Hesse	Rosshalde
Hermann Hesse	Strange News From Another Star
Herodotus	Histories
Herodotus	The Histories
Herodotus	The History of Herodotus
Herschel Hobbs	Pastor's Manual
Hetschel	First Stage: Moon
Hiaasen	Stormy Weather
Hilaire	Surivals and New Arrivals
Hilaire	The Great Heresies
Hilary Bailey	Cassandra: Princess of Troy
Hilary Norman	The Key to Susanna
Hilbert Schenck	Chronosequence
Hilbert Schenck	The Battle of the Abaco Reefs
Hilda Conkling	Poems by a Little Girl
Hilda Hughes	Shudders
Hilda Hughes	When Churchyards Yawn
Hillerman	A Thief of Time
Hillerman	Skinwalkers
Hillerman	Talking God
Hiram Corson	Introduction to Browning
Hjalmar Hjorth Boyesen	Boyhood in Norway
Hjalmar Hjorth Boysen	Tales From Two Hemispheres

Fig. 4. Sample of books in the final list.

6.1 Scalability and Steady State

There are several challenges to the scalability of this method. One is the performance required to scan for large numbers of patterns and tuples over a huge repository. Improvements in the underlying algorithms and implementation are likely to solve this problem in the very near future.

A potentially more difficult obstacle is whether DIPRE can be kept from diverging from the target as it expands the relation. For example, since it really used only the two science fiction books which were in the seed sample, why did it not produce a large list of science fiction books. Clearly, it gravitated to a compilation of all books and even a few scatterred articles managed to enter the relation. Keeping this effect under control as the relation expands is nontrivial but there are several possibilities.

Connection to Singular Value Decomposition One possibility is to redefine of $M_D(P)$ to require multiple patterns to match a tuple. A more extreme version of this is to assign a weight to every tuple and pattern. A matching tuple is assigned a weight based on the weights of the patterns it matches. A generated pattern is assigned a weight based on the weights of the tuples which match it. If this is done linearly, this technique breaks down to a singular value decomposition of the tuple-pattern matrix (multiplied by its transpose). This is analogous to Latent Semantic Indexing [DDF+90] which is done on the document-word matrix. In this case, the eventual steady state is the dominant eigenvector. Unfortunately, this is independent of the initial sample which is clearly not desirable. Nonetheless, the relationship to LSI is compelling and bears further investigation.

The independence of the steady state from the initial state above may also be a problem even without the use of weights. There are several possible solutions. One is to run only through a limited number of iterations like we demonstrated in this paper. Another solution is to make sure that the transformation of tuples to patterns to tuples is nonlinear and has some local steady states which depend on the initial state. This can be accomplished through the use of the initial sample R' in the computation of GenPatterns. In this case, the user may also provide an $\bar{R}'$, a list of counterexamples.

6.2 Implications of Automatic Extraction

One of the most surprising results of this experiment was finding books which were not listed in major online sources such as the book "Disbanded" by Douglas Clark [Cla] which is published online or "The Young Gardeners' Kalendar" by Dollie Radford [Rad04] an obscure work published in 1904. If the book list can be expanded and if almost all books listed in online sources can be extracted, the resulting list may be more complete than any existing book database. The generated list would be the product of thousands of small online sources as opposed to current book databases which are the products of a few large information sources. Such a change in information flow can have important social ramifications.

References

[Ama]   Amazon home page. http://www.amazon.com.

[BP]   Sergey Brin and Larry Page. Google search engine. http://google.stanford.edu.

[Bri]   Sergey Brin. List of books. http://www-db.stanford.edu/~sergey/booklist.html.

[Cla]   Douglas Clark. *Disbanded*. Benjamin Press, 69 Hillcrest Drive, Bath Ba2 1HD, UK. http://www.bath.ac.uk/~exxdgdc/poetry/library/di1.html.

[DDF+90] Scott Deerwester, Susan Dumais, Goerge Furnas, Thomas Landauer, and Richard Harshman. Indexing by latent semantic analysis. *Journal of the American Society for Information Science*, 41(6):391–407, 1990.

[MOS97]   Workshop on management of semistructured data. http://www.research.att.com/~suciu/workshop-papers.html, May 1997.

[Rad04]   Dollie Radford. *The Young Gardeners' Kalendar*. Alexander Moring, Ltd., London, 1904. http://www.indiana.edu/~letrs/vwwp/radford/kalendar.html.

[Tsi]   Tsimmis home page. http://www-db.stanford.edu/tsimmis/tsimmis.html.

[Vis]   Visa shopping guide for books. http://shopguide.yahoo.com/shopguide/books.html.

WUM: A Tool for Web Utilization Analysis

Myra Spiliopoulou[1] and Lukas C. Faulstich[2] *

[1] Institut für Wirtschaftsinformatik, HU Berlin
[http://www.wiwi.hu-berlin.de/~myra], [myra@wiwi.hu-berlin.de]
[2] Institut für Informatik, FU Berlin
[http://www.inf.fu-berlin.de/~faulstic], [faulstic@inf.fu-berlin.de]

Abstract. The navigational behaviour of users in the web is essential for the providers of information, services and goods. Search engines can help a user find a provider of interest, but it is the proper organization of the provider's site that stimulates the user's propensity to consume. To verify whether the site is effectively organized, knowledge on the navigation patterns occuring during visits to the site must be obtained. Our Web Utilization Miner WUM can assist in obtaining this knowledge. WUM is a mining system for the discovery of navigation patterns. A navigation pattern is a directed graph that summarizes the traversal movements of a group of visitors and satisfies certain human-centric criteria that make it "interesting". Instead of focussing the mining process on the statistically dominant but not always interesting patterns, WUM supports the specification of *interestingness* criteria on their structure, content and statistics.
WUM provides a declarative mining language, MINT, with which the human expert can specify interestingness criteria on the fly. To discover the navigation patterns satisfying the expert's criteria, WUM exploits an innovative aggregated storage representation for the information in the web server log.

1 Introduction

Web sites are most often organized in a way the providers consider appropriate for the majority of the site's visitors. However, our knowledge of the actual navigational behaviour of the visitors is still sparse and fragmentary. Simple access statistics provide only rudimentary feedback, while studies on specific behavioural patterns, e.g. page revisits [12], are of rather ad hoc nature.

Knowledge about the navigation patterns occurring in or dominating the usage of a web site can greatly help the site's owner or administrator in improving its quality. Data mining can assist in this task by effectively extracting knowledge from the past, i.e. from the site access recordings. In [5], the term "web usage mining" is suggested to describe this type of mining activity.

To aid an expert in reorganizing a web site, a web usage miner should provide feedback on (i) access to certain nodes and paths considered of importance, (ii)

* Supported by the German Research Society, Berlin-Brandenburg Graduate School in Distributed Information Systems (DFG grant no. GRK 316).

nodes and paths preferred or avoided by the visitors and (iii) generic traversal behaviour, e.g. trends for backward moves, cycles etc. Miners generating sequential patterns that satisfy certain support or confidence thresholds are not adequate. Rather, we need a tool that can identify navigation patterns satisfying properties specified by the expert in an ad hoc manner. Those properties can concern the statistics or the contents of the pattern but may be as vague as the existence of cycles or the repeated access to some, otherwise undefined, node.

The web miner proposed in [3] simply discovers statistically dominant paths. The "WEBMINER" of [5] provides a query language on top of external mining software for association rules and for sequential patterns. However, the expressiveness of this language is restricted by the input parameters acceptable by the miner. To our knowledge, current miners do not support generic specifications on the structure of the patterns to be discovered, e.g. page revisits, cycles etc.

In this study, we present a mining mechanism that avoids those shortcomings, by incorporating the query processor to the miner. Our Web Utilization Miner WUM (http://www.wiwi.hu-berlin.de/~myra/WUM employs an innovative technique for the discovery of navigation patterns. The information on web traversals is modelled according to a graph-based formalism and aggregated into a materialized view over the web log.

The expert guides the pattern discovery by means of our mining language, MINT. In MINT, she can specify the generic characteristics a pattern should possess to be of potential interest to her. Thus, only patterns having the desired characteristics are constructed, while uninteresting ones are pruned out early.

In this study, we give an overview of WUM and then focus on the functionality it offers by means of MINT. We first present the architecture of WUM. Section 3 describes the process of aggregating web log data into an Aggregated Log, on which mining is applied. In section 5 we describe our mining language MINT and its processing mechanism for the discovery of navigation patterns. The related work is discussed in section 6. We conclude in section 7.

2 The Architecture of WUM

The architecture of our Web Utilization Miner is depicted in Fig. 1. There are two major modules: the *Aggregation Service* prepares the web log data for mining and the *MINT-Processor* does the mining.

The *Aggregation Service* extracts information on the activities of the users visiting the web site and groups consecutive activities of the same user into a transaction. It then transforms transactions into sequences. Its major task is to merge and aggregate those sequences into a tree structure. This process is described informally in the next section.

MINT is the language, in which the experts specifies the interestingness criteria to be satisfied by the mining results. The *MINT-Processor* is the mining core of WUM, responsible for the discovery of navigation patterns from the aggregated information extracted by the *Aggregation Service* from the weblog. The

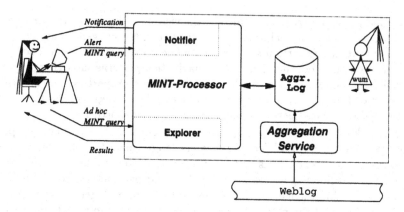

Fig. 1. The architecture of WUM

criteria specified by the expert in MINT are used by the *MINT-Processor* to prune out uninteresting patterns as early as possible.

The *MINT-Processor* can be invoked in two modes: As *Notifier*, it executes preprocessed queries periodically. As *Explorer*, it accepts ad hoc queries. The purpose of the *Notifier* is to discover whether the web access data set shows deviations from the expected usage. Hence, the "alert queries" it executes should correspond to the beliefs of the site's owner on the statistics and structure of the dominant navigation patterns. If those beliefs are not satisfied, the user should be alerted to invoke the *Explorer*, which can help in discovering the actually dominant navigation patterns.

We would like to stress here that WUM, similarly to most miners, is not an expert system. The expertise belongs to its user and is indispensable, on the one hand to describe what is interesting to her, and on the other hand to avoid misinterpretations of the results. In particular, the user should be familiar with the site's content and its intended use. She must possess some expertise on human behaviour in hypermedia environments, so that she may transform the expectations of usage into mining directives and correctly interpret the mining results; these issues are addressed e.g. in [12, 14]. Finally, she should own the appropriate background to properly interpret the statistics of the results.

3 Aggregating Visitor Transactions

The discovery of navigation patterns in WUM is performed on the basis of the information extracted from the web server log after some (currently simple) data cleaning and inserted into the "Aggregated Log". The Aggregated Log contains *aggregated* data on the visitor trails in the site, where a "visitor trail" is a sequence of page requests comprising a visitor transaction.

The Aggregated Log is built by WUM's *Aggregation Service* as explained in the following. Its activities are summarized in Fig. 2. In this figure, we use the shorthands a, b, c, d, e, f for the web pages. We list accesses of three visitors between 11:42 a.m. and 12:34 p.m.

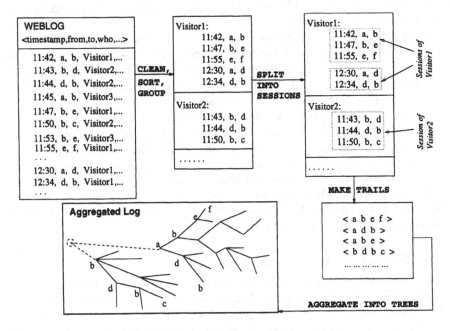

Fig. 2. Construction of the Aggregated Log

3.1 Cleaning the Log and Grouping the Entries into Transactions

The web server log is first "cleaned" by removing entries that should not be taken into account during mining. Such entries may be those recording accesses to image files [4] or accesses performed by a special group of visitors, such as robots. The types of entries to be removed by *Aggregation Service* can be interactively specified in the user interface [15].

The *Aggregation Service* must next decide whether any two subsequent accesses to web pages stem from the same visitor. Methodologies based on the usage of cookies, user registration, exploitation of knowledge on the network's topology etc have been proposed to this purpose [5, 8]. Currently, our *Aggregation Service* assumes that accesses from the same host come from the same visitor. An extended discussion on this issue can be found in [5, 11].

3.2 Identifying the Transactions of a Visitor

In the next step of the process depicted in Fig. 2, consecutive entries of a visitor are grouped into "transactions". A transaction consists of the recorded activities of the visitor within one session. Hence, the *Aggregation Service* decides here whether two subsequent entries belong to the same session of the visitor or not.

We support two criteria for grouping consecutive web page accesses of a visitor into a transaction: (i) a maximal duration or (ii) a maximal elapsed time between any two subsequent page accesses. According to the former criterion, the elapsed time between the first and last entry of a transaction may not exceed a threshold value. According to the latter criterion, two consecutive entries belong to the same transaction if the elapsed time between them is lower than a(nother) threshold. In both cases, if the latest entry occurs at a timepoint beyond the threshold value, it is assigned to a new transaction.

Other criteria for grouping entries into transactions are proposed e.g. in [4]. They can be seamlessly incorporated into the *Aggregation Service* of WUM.

After grouping entries into transactions, transactions are modelled as sequences in the next step. To do so, the *Aggregation Service* removes unnecessary information like the visitor identification and the timestamp. It then merges consecutive entries into a sequence $< fromPage_1, \ldots, fromPage_n, toPage_n >$. We call this sequence a "trail". Note that after the removal of visitor identifiers and timestamps, there are many identical trails.

3.3 Merging Trails into an Aggregate Tree

In the final step, the *Aggregation Service* merges the visitor trails along common prefixes into a tree structure, the "aggregate tree". The "Aggregated Log" is a large persistent aggregate tree composed of all trails. To bypass the fact that not all trails start at the same page, we introduce a dummy root node, from which the merged trails emanate.

A node in an aggregate tree corresponds to the occurence of a page in a trail. Common trail prefixes are identified, and their respective nodes are merged into a tree node. This node is annotated with the number of visitors having reached the node across the same trail prefix. We call this the "support" of the node.

Example 1. At the left side of Fig. 3 we show the topological graph of a tiny web site and a number of trails recorded in the web log. Along with each trail we show the number of visitors that have followed it.

In Fig. 3, a is the first page of trails 1, 4 and 5; by summing up the visitors having traversed them, we compute 21 as the support of a. In trails 1, 4, page b was visited after a; the respective trie node has a support of 11. Note that trails 2, 3, 6 starting at b cannot be merged with trails 1 and 4 starting at a.

In trails 2 and 6, page b has been accessed twice. When constructing the aggregate tree, we see that a total of 13 visitors accessed b (via trails 2, 3, 6), but only 6 of them came back to b, across trails 2 and 6 that have the same prefix. We must distinguish between different occurences of the same page, so that page revisits can be discovered. Hence, during trail merging, the *Aggregation Service* assigns to each page its occurence number.

The aggregate tree of Fig. 3 has a dummy node # as root. This convention allows us to model the Aggregated Log as a single large aggregate tree. The support of # is the total number of entries recorded in the weblog.

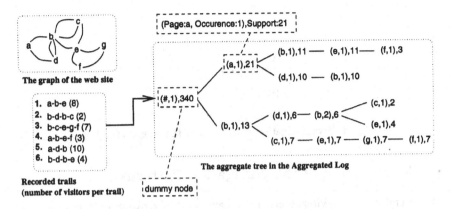

Fig. 3. Merging trails in the Aggregated Log

3.4 Navigation Patterns over the Aggregated Log

On Fig. 3 we can see that trails with different prefixes may still have pages in common. If we merge those trails at their common nodes, we construct an aggregated graph that is no more a tree: In fact, this is a "navigation pattern".

Example 2. Before introducing navigation patterns formally, let's see how they can be constructed from the Aggregated Log of Fig. 3. Suppose we are interested in the navigation patterns between b and e. To construct them, we first discover the branches of the Aggregated Log containing them. From the figure, there is one branch in the subtree rooted at (a,1),21 and two branches rooted at (b,1),13. Note that the branch (b,1),13--(d,1),6--(b,2),6-(e,1),4 reveals that there are *two* navigation patterns between b and e: one between (b,1) and e,1) and one between (b,2) and e,1).

To produce those navigation patterns, we merge the branches at the common nodes. Then, we have to recompute the supports of the "junction" nodes that were produced after the merging. To do so, we just sum up the supports of the original nodes. Hence, the support of (b,1) in the first pattern (Pattern 1) is 11 + 13, produced by summing the support of the node below (a,1),21 and of the node root of the second subtree below the dummy root. Note that (b,1),13 belongs to two branches but is only one node; hence, it is not used twice in the summation. The two navigation patterns are shown in Fig. 4.

Pattern 1 shows that 22 of the 24 visitors of (b,1) have reached e across different routes. 6 of them returned to b. Only 4 of those 6 reached e afterwards. This last fact cannot be deduced from pattern 1; it is assessed from pattern 2.

One might ask why we use a tree structure instead of a navigation pattern as our Aggregated Log. The reason is that trees can be built without information loss, whilst patterns cannot: In our simple example, a closer observation of Pattern 1 reveals that we lost the number of visitors that have accessed e after reaching b for the second time. Hence, navigation patterns are not explicitly stored but extracted from the Aggregated Log by the miner.

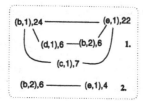

Fig. 4. Two navigation patterns over the Aggregated Log

4   Construction of the Navigation Patterns

By the end of the previous section, we have built navigation patterns by means of examples. To formally describe the notion of navigation pattern and its construction procedure, we must analyze the formalism underlying WUM [10]. Due to space limitations, we rather present a simplified construction method. In particular, instead of defining navigation patterns on the basis of the Aggregated Log, from which they are actually extracted, we define them on the basis of the trails produced by the *Aggregation Service* at an intermediate step.

4.1   Patterns and Pattern Descriptors

We denote by *Trails* the collection of trails extracted by the *Aggregation Service* from the web server log. *Trails* may contain duplicates, so it is not a set but a "bag" (synonym: "multiset"). Hereafter, we refer to the terms "bag" and "multiset" interchangeably and we use $\{\!\!\{\ldots\}\!\!\}$ as the delimiter pair for bags.

Before defining a "navigation pattern", we introduce the formal notion of descriptor for a navigation pattern.

Definition 1. *Let WPO be the set of Web Page Occurences, where a page occurence is a pair comprised of a page URL and an occurence number. Further, let $\star$ be a wildcard denoting a sequence of zero or more nodes, and $\_$ a wildcard denoting exactly one node. We denote by WPO_+ the set $WPO \cup \{\star, \_\}$.*

A "pattern descriptor" is a vector $a \in (WPO_+)^*$, such that any two $\star$-elements in a are separated by at least one page occurence from WPO.

Thus, a pattern descriptor is a vector of page occurences and wildcards. We disallow constructs like $\star\star$ which is identical to $\star$, or $\star\_\star$ which is identical to $\_\star$.

We must now specify when a trail y matches a pattern descriptor a. Intuitively, a page occurence is matched only by itself, a $\_$ is matched by one arbitrary trail node, while a $\star$ is matched by an arbitrary subtrail. We generalize this into a predicate $matches(a, y, k)$ which is true if y matches a up to position k.

Definition 2. *Let a be a pattern descriptor, whose non-wildcard elements are at positions $k_1, \ldots, k_n$. The "navigation pattern with descriptor" a is a graph $navp(a)$. It is built by discovering the trails that contain a subtrail matching a, extracting those subtrails, merging them by common prefix and at the positions $k_1, \ldots, k_n$ and summing up the support values.*

This rather informal definition indicates that the navigation pattern is defined in a constructive way. In the following, we analyze the two steps of the pattern construction process and present an algorithm for each step. Those algorithms are conceptual, though, intended to make the principles of navigation pattern construction clear. The algorithms used in WUM process the Aggregated Log instead of individual trails and are much more complicated.

4.2   The Subtrails Satisfying a Descriptor

A pattern is formed from the subtrails satisfying the predicate $matches(\cdot)$. Hence, we must detect and extract those subtrails from the trails $Trails$. To do so, we first identify the page occurences contained in the pattern descriptor. We then extract the subtrails that satisfy the pattern descriptor up to each page occurence in an iterative way. We show the algorithm in Fig. 5.

Conceptual Algorithm-1: Extracting the subtrails that match a descriptor

Input: *A pattern descriptor a with page occurences at positions $k_1, \ldots, k_n$ and a bag X originally set equal to Trails.*

Output: *A list of bags bag_list(a) of matching subtrails*

Method: *We iterate on the contents of X for $i = 1, \ldots, n$. After each iteration, X contains the trails x for which $matches(a, x, k_i)$ is true.*

1. *From each trail x in X, for which $matches(a, x, k_i)$ is true, we extract the suffix $y = a[k_i] \cdot z$.*
   Those suffixes form a bag Y_i.
2. *We remove from X all trails that do not contribute to Y_i.*
3. *If Y_i (or X) is empty, we return the empty list and quit.*
   Otherwise:
   If $i = n$, we are done and can go to Step 4.
   Otherwise, we continue from Step 1 for $i = i + 1$.
4. *We return the list $< Y_1, \ldots, Y_n >$.*

Fig. 5.

By Step 1 of the first iteration, $X = Trails$. If the descriptor starts with a page occurence (i.e. $k_1 = 1$), we look for this page occurence anywhere in each trail. Otherwise, the wildcards before k_1 determine how many elements prior to $a[k_1]$ a trail may or should have. Non-matching trails are deleted from X.

By Step 1 of iteration i, X is already reduced to the trails that match the descriptor a up to position k_{i-1}. Among them, we select those matching the descriptor up to position k_i; in Step 2, we remove all other trails from X.

For each trail matching the descriptor up to position k_i, we store the suffix starting at $a[k_i]$ in a bag Y_i. Thus, Y_i contains all subtrails that start with a node referring to $a[k_i]$ and originate from trails matching the descriptor up to $a[k_i]$. Note that each trail in X contributes at most one suffix to Y_i: since $a[k_i]$ is a page occurence, it can appear in a trail at most once.

After the last step of our algorithm, X contains the subtrails that match the whole pattern descriptor. The reader may therefore wonder what we need the Y_i bags for. We explain this in a small example.

Example 3. Let $Trails = \{\!\{c, dac, acb, ad\}\!\}$ and let $<(a,1),*,(b,1)>$ be a descriptor. We can directly see that its pattern is $(a,1),3\text{--}(c,1),2\text{--}(b,1),1$. It indicates that from the 3 visitors of a only 1 reached b via c, while a second one stopped at c.

We now use our algorithm to find the trails constituting this pattern. X is initially equal to *Trails*. In the first iteration, it is reduced to $\{\!\{dac, acb, ad\}\!\}$. $Y_1 = \{\!\{ac, acb, ad\}\!\}$. In the second iteration, $X = \{\!\{acb\}\!\}$ and $Y_2 = \{\!\{b\}\!\}$. Now, if we compute the support of each node in the navigation pattern from X, we obtain a value equal to 1 for *all* nodes. To obtain the correct support values, we must build the aggregate tree of Y_1. This is done by the algorithm presented in the next subsection.

It should be noted that the bag Y_i can be directly built from the bag Y_{i-1}, so the computation of X is actually redundant. However, a correctness proof is necessary for this simplification, which falls beyond the scope of this study.

4.3 Constructing a Pattern as a Graph

In Def. 2, we state that the navigation pattern with descriptor a is a graph $navp(a)$. Conceptual Algorithm-1 extracts the subtrails matching the descriptor's parts in an incremental way and stores them in $bag\_list(a) = Y_1, \ldots, Y_n$.

To build the graph, we first merge the subtrails in each bag Y_i on common prefix to form the aggregate tree $aggTree(Y_i)$, as described in 3.3. According to Step 1 of the Conceptual Algorithm-1, all those subtrails start at $a[k_i]$. The aggregation ensures that each element of Y_i that does not contain $a[k_{i+1}]$ but has a common prefix with another element that does is still taken into account when the statistics for the common prefix are computed.

After building $aggTree(Y_i)$, we can safely remove branches that do not satisfy the part of the descriptor between positions k_i and k_{i+1}. We then discard all subtrees rooted at $a[k_{i+1}]$: all subtrees of interest are already contained in $aggTree(Y_{i+1})$. Finally, we connect the affected parent nodes to the root of $aggTree(Y_{i+1})$, which refers to $a[k_{i+1}]$ by definition. The complete algorithm is shown in Fig. 6.

For each aggregate tree $AT_i = aggTree(Y_i)$, this algorithm gradually removes all (sub)branches that do not end at $a[k_i + 1]$. This is done at Step 3(c). Since the traversal of AT_i is postfix, we access the parent after having processed the children. Hence, if the parent of a removed node becomes a leaf, it will also be removed in a subsequent iteration.

Conceptual Algorithm-2: Building the navigation pattern as a graph.

Input: *A pattern descriptor a with page occurences at positions $k_1, \ldots, k_n$*
Output: *The "navigation pattern with descriptor" a, which is a graph navp(a)*
Method:
    1. *We build the bag_list(a) $=< Y_1, \ldots, Y_n >$ by Conceptual Algorithm-1.*
    2. *We form the $AT_1 = aggTree(Y_1), \ldots, AT_n = aggTree(Y_n)$.*
    3. *On each of $AT_1, \ldots, AT_{n-1}$, we perform the following depth-first postfix traversal:*
        (a) We find the next node N of AT_i that is a leaf or refers to $a[k_{i+1}]$.
        (b) If N refers to $a[k_{i+1}]$, then
            — we discard the subtree rooted at N
            — and we link the parent of N to the root of AT_{i+1}.
        (c) We discard N.
        (d) We can now go to Step 3.(a) to find the next N within AT_i.
    4. *We return the linked graph structure as navp(a).*

Fig. 6.

4.4   An Example on the Construction of Patterns

We now explain the above definitions in an example. We use the Trails in Fig. 3.

Example 4. Let $a =< (b, 1), *, (e, 1), *, (f, 1) >$ be the pattern descriptor. To build its navigation pattern, we first build the bag list *bag_list(a)* $=< Y_1, Y_2, Y_3 >$ using Conceptual Algorithm-1. In the following table, we show the contents of Y_1, Y_2, Y_3, as well as the contents of X after each iteration.

    On the table, we have annotated each trail with with the number of times it appears in the *Trails*. Then, a subtrail extracted from it appears the same number of times. We further omit occurence numbers for brevity. This has no side effects, because only the first occurence of b qualifies.

	Trails	X.1	Y_1	X.2	Y_2	X.3	Y_3
(8)	abe	abe	be	abe	e	—	—
(2)	bdbc	bdbc	bdbc	—	—	—	—
(7)	bcegf	bcegf	bcegf	bcegf	egf	bcegf	f
(3)	abef	abef	bef	abef	ef	abef	f
(10)	adb	adb	b	—	—	—	—
(4)	bdbe	bdbe	bdbe	bdbe	e	—	—

In this example, X.1 = *Trails* because all trails contain the element b.

    The aggregate trees and the output navigation pattern built according to Conceptual Algorithm-2 are shown in Fig. 7. The retained branches of the trees are enclosed in lassos.

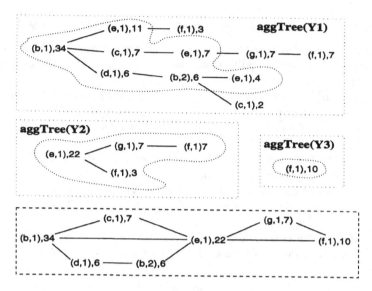

Fig. 7. The aggregate trees and result pattern for descriptor $< (b, 1), *, (e, 1), *, (f, 1) >$

5 Knowledge Discovery Queries

Similarly to [6], we believe that good mining results require a close interaction of the human expert and the mining tool, in which the expert uses her domain knowledge to guide the miner. Therefore, WUM provides a mining query language, MINT , with which the expert can specify the subjective characteristics that make a navigation pattern of interest to her.

5.1 The Mining Language MINT

Specifying the interesting characteristics of a pattern. The notion of interestingness based on beliefs is discussed in [9]: a belief is a rule of the form $A \rightarrow B$, which is expected to be true. The same study proposes mechanisms for the verification of beliefs and the discovery of belief violations *in the context of association rules*. To our knowledge, there is no respective formalism for beliefs on sequential patterns. However, MINT allows the specification of beliefs or belief violations as predicates. Via predicates one can also specify the structure or statistics a navigation pattern should have to be of significance. Thus, besides the classical statistical thresholds, more elaborate criteria are supported.

In particular, the human expert issuing queries in MINT may specify the interesting aspects of the patterns to be discovered in terms of:

Content: The user may specify properties of the content or meta-data of pages that should appear in the navigation pattern. Occurences of pages may be also specified, if the user is interested in discovering cycles.

Statistics: These include the support of a page within the pattern to be built or within the Aggregated Log as a whole, as well as the confidence of a page with respect to a previously accessed page.

Structure: The user may specify the order of the pages, adjacency of visited pages, length of subtrails between pages etc.

For this, MINT supports the notion of "template" for a pattern descriptor. A template is a vector of variables interleaved with wildcards. During query execution, the variables are bound, resulting in one descriptor per binding.

The schema and syntax of MINT queries. The syntax of MINT reminds of SQL. However, MINT is not a conventional query language: Instead of selecting tuples, it discovers patterns. Instead of accessing a database or data warehouse, it is applied on the Aggregated Log presented in subsection 3.3.

In Fig. 8, we show the conceptual schema used for query formulation. This schema reflects our definitions: A navigation pattern is a graph, the nodes of which refer to web pages. The properties of the entities can be used in the query predicates. The primary keys are underlined.

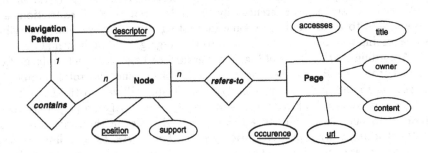

Fig. 8. The schema of the Aggregated Log (using ER-notation)

A navigation pattern is determined by its descriptor. In MINT we specify "templates" for descriptors, i.e. vectors of node variables and wildcards. The statement TEMPLATE a*b AS t specifies that we are interested in descriptors of the form a*b, where a and b are variables. Each pair of nodes that can be bound to a and b results in a descriptor and a navigation pattern satisfying it.

The above template is not very convenient. In data mining, we want to focus the discovery process by statistical thresholds and other interestingness measures. Those measures are applied on the node variables of the template. With the statement NODE AS a b we declare the two node variables for the template a*b above. According to the schema of Fig. 8, we can specify thresholds on the support of those nodes. The predicates:

`a.support >= 1000  AND b.support / a.support >= 0.9`

describe the usual specification of a support threshold (here: 1000 visits to this node) and of a confidence minimum (here: 0.9).

One may notice that the entity **Node** in our schema has no property "confidence", so that the confidence must be described by means of supports. We show our motivation for this decision in a small example:

Example 5. We consider pattern descriptors with three variables:

```
SELECT t
FROM NODE AS a b c, TEMPLATE a*b*c AS t
WHERE b.support >= 1000
AND c.support / b.support >= 0.8
AND c.support / a.support >= 0.6
```

The support of b is the summation of the supports of paths leading from a towards it. The same holds for c in the context of a, b. Hence, the confidence of c is expressed by the second predicate above. The last predicate does not express any confidence but can still be observed as a reasonable measure. Therefore, we have decided for the generic specification of any confidence-like measure by means of arithmetic operations on the support.

Beyond the specification of thresholds for statistical measures, MINT allows restrictions on the pages referenced by the node variables. Such restrictions are appropriate to focus mining to some interesting types of pages only, to refine some mining results or to drill down into the Aggregated Log information.

According to the schema of Fig. 8, we retain for a **Page** some meta-information gained from the HTML-file, the URL of the page and the total number of **accesses** to the page, independently of the trails followed to the page. Since a trail may contain backward moves to already visited pages, a page may occur more than once in a trail. As we cannot model cycles in the Aggregated Log without losing statistical information, we "flatten" cycles by attaching to each page an **occurence** number. This introduces redundancy in the schema shown in Fig. 8. In our implementation, we obviously avoid such redundancies.

5.2 Querying in MINT

A MINT query produces a set of navigation patterns extracted from the Aggregated Log according to the query predicates. In the following, we present the functionality of MINT by means of examples. To make those examples more intuitive, we introduce another Aggregated Log on a fictious site with HTML-pages on middleware. This Aggregated Log is shown on Fig. 9.

Paths between web pages. A generic question on web usage concerns the paths followed between two or more web pages. Usually, only certain types of pages are of interest, e.g. pages on Corba from our example Aggregated Log. Typically, restrictions on the statistics of those paths are also placed, e.g. to discover the paths dominantly or most rarely used. Query **Q1** below constructs the navigation patterns from a page on middleware to a page on Corba, which has been followed by more than 20% of the visitors of the page on middleware.

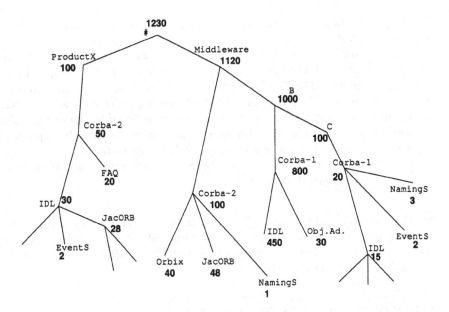

Fig. 9. The Aggregated Log of a fictious example web site

```
SELECT t
FROM NODE AS a b, GRAPH TEMPLATE a*b AS t
WHERE a.title CONTAINS "Middleware"
AND b.title CONTAINS "Corba"
AND b.support / a.support > 0.2
```

By comparing this query to the schema of Fig. 8, we notice that the title is a property of a page, not of the node referring to a page. So, the syntax of MINT hides part of the schema complexity from the user. The result of **Q1** is shown in Fig. 10 and explained below.

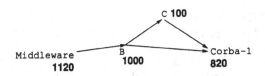

Fig. 10. The result of query **Q1**

Conceptually, the *MINT-Processor* evaluates this query as follows: All nodes in the Aggregated Log referring to Middleware are discovered. The branches from them to a page on Corba are found, thus producing two pattern descriptors, `<(Middleware,1),*,(Corba-1,1)>` and `<(Middleware,1),*,(Corba-2,1)>`.

Descriptors are built incrementally; candidates without corresponding patterns are pruned out at each step.

Next, the pattern for each descriptor is constructed. Instead of applying the conceptual mechanism of section 4 on the trails, the *MINT-Processor* operates on the Aggregated Log [11]: The branches matching each descriptor are extracted from the Aggregated Log and aggregated by merging nodes belonging to common prefixes and nodes referring to the page occurences of the descriptor. The support values of the merged nodes are summed up to compute the support of the resulting node. Then the last predicate of **Q1** is evaluated.

Only the first of the two descriptors above satisfies this predicate. It produces the navigation pattern shown in Fig. 10.

Statistical thresholds. Query **Q1** contained two rather restrictive predicates on the contents of the web pages. If only statistical thresholds are considered, the number of candidate descriptors considered by the *MINT-Processor* is significantly larger. Consider **Q1':**

```
SELECT t
FROM NODE AS a b, GRAPH TEMPLATE a*b AS t
WHERE a.support >= 1000
AND b.support / a.support > 0.7
```

This query produces the navigation pattern of Fig. 10, the navigation patterns (Middleware,1),1120---(B,1),1000, (B,1),1000---(Corba-1,1),800 and some navigation patterns starting at the dummy root node and ending at the node on Middleware or at node B.

Results in Tree or Graph form. "Where do visitors of page a go afterwards?" Some restrictions are often placed on content and support of a and of the subsequent pages, as in the following query **Q2:**

```
SELECT t
FROM NODE AS a b, TREE TEMPLATE a*b AS t
WHERE a.support > 100
AND a.title CONTAINS "Corba"
AND b.support / a.support > 0.5
```

Here, we receive all URLs reached after a page a on Corba, which has been accessed 100 or more times, provided that those URLs have been accessed by more than 50% of the visitors of a. We have however specified that the template should be a TREE instead of a GRAPH. This means that the result will be an aggregate tree.

More precisely, **Q2** is executed as follows: All nodes in the Aggregated Log whose title refers to Corba-1 or Corba-2 are retrieved. All subtrees rooted at each such node are identified, their common prefixes are merged as described in section 3, and the supports of the nodes of the new tree are computed. However, differently from the approach for navigation pattern s, the leaf nodes need not be identical, nor are identical leaf nodes merged together. Rather, the last query predicate is evaluated for each branch of the tree separately.

In Fig. 11, we show the intermediate aggregate trees produced for **Q2** and the tree satisfying all query predicates. At the lower right corner we show the two navigation patterns output by query **Q2'**, which is the same as **Q2** but for using the **GRAPH** option for the template. The different results are caused by the different values of **b.support** in the descriptors for the tree and the graph.

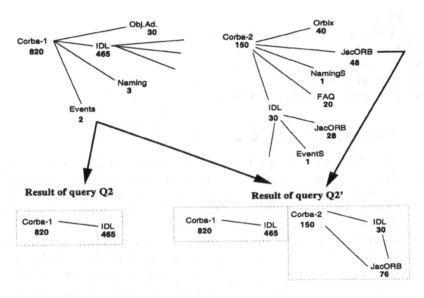

Fig. 11. aggregate trees and graph patterns as query output

The reader may have noticed that if the pages on Corba-1 had not been merged, the path from Corba-2 to IDL would have satisfied the predicates. To avoid this merging, the **TREE** template should be changed into #*a*b, where # indicates that the navigation pattern should start at the dummy root.

Revisited nodes. The study of [12] showed that 58% of accesses in the studied domain were node revisits, also called "recencies". For a given site, this statement can be verified by issuing a query that sums up the support of all revisited nodes and compares it to the total number of accesses. Recall that this number is the support of the dummy node ^. This test is performed in the following query **Q3**:

```
SELECT SUM(a.support) / ^.support
FROM NODE AS a, TREE TEMPLATE #*a
WHERE a.occurence = 2
```

Note that the occurence number must be exactly 2. Otherwise, nodes revisited more than once would contribute to the support summation multiple times.

As can be seen from this query, conventional aggregation of nodes is also permitted. For a template with multiple variables, e.g. #*a*b, grouping would also be of interest: A clause "GROUP BY a" would compute the summation of the supports of all distinct values of b within the context of a given a value. The full syntax is given in the Appendix.

The study of [12] also states that recencies to any *specific* node do not exceed 19% of the total accesses. To find nodes revisited more often than that we can issue query **Q4**:

```
SELECT b
FROM NODE AS a b, TREE TEMPLATE #*a*b
WHERE a.url = b.url
AND a.occurence = 1
AND b.occurence = 2
AND b.support / a.support > 0.19
```

5.3 Complexity of the Mining Process

The *MINT-Processor* is responsible for identifying common patterns in the large aggregate tree of the Aggregated Log, merging them to aggregate graphobjects, computing the node supports and evaluating the query predicates. Any navigation patterns not satisfying the predicates should be recognized and filtered out as soon as possible.

This mechanism can be quite expensive: A query asking for all navigation patterns containing nodes with supports beyond a threshold will imply considering all possible variable bindings. We are working on optimization techniques to alleviate this problem. One of them is to retain for each web page a list of the nodes corresponding to it, thus trading speed for space.

Still, our *MINT-Processor* is de facto faster than a miner operating on web log data [5,3], because of the off line aggregation of weblog information into the Aggregated Log. Moreover, our mechanism can exploit restrictive predicates to avoid building uninteresting navigation patterns. A miner not accepting ad hoc predicates needs a postprocessing module that removes all unnecessarily computed patterns.

6 Related Work

The subject of discovering navigation patterns in web logs has been addressed in the studies of [3, 5, 13]. The "Footprints" tool of [13] focusses on the visualization of frequently accessed patterns and on the identification of pattern *types* that may be of importance [14]. Our work on MINT is complementary to Footprints, since we are interested in ways of formally describing such types.

The studies of [3, 5] focus on pattern discovery. They are both based on the adaptation of an existing miner to the particular problem. More precisely, a preprocessing algorithm groups consecutive page accesses of the same visitor into a transaction, according to some criterion. Then, a miner for association rules or sequential patterns is invoked to discover similar patterns among the transactions. In [5], the association rules' miner has been further customized to guarantee that no feasible patterns are erroneously skipped.

This approach has some drawbacks. First of all, the generic characteristics that make a navigation pattern interesting are different than those making an association rule interesting, and which are studied e.g. in [9]. Interestingness in the mining of sequential patterns is expressed in rather simple criteria on the support/confidence and length of the patterns [7]. Hence, the miners used in [3,5] do not allow an expert to guide the mining process to discover e.g. node revisits, patterns of unexpectedly low support etc.

This problem is alleviated in [5] by the query language, with which the expert can give instructions to the miner. The language of [5] is syntactically similar to MINT but, in contrast to MINT, it is only a front end to an existing miner. Thus, instructions that cannot be understood by the miner must be postponed to a postprocessing phase: the interestingness of some plans cannot be tested prior to this phase. This decreases the overall system performance.

A performance drawback of miners on sequential patterns [1,7] is caused by activating them over the whole set of transactions. By aggregating transactions into an Aggregated Log, WUM guarantees a performance improvement at least linear to the degree of similarity between transaction prefixes in the original log.

Our work is conceptually related to the study of [6] for text mining. A query language is introduced to drive a miner that discovers association rules in document collections. This miner is applied on *aggregated data*, organized in a trie structure [2] in a way similar to our Aggregated Log. The performance gains of using such an aggregated representation are demonstrated in [6].

However, the exploitation of the aggregated information in [2] is different than in WUM: Association rules have no order, so any rule can be discovered by traversing a single subtree of the trie. Web navigation patterns have order, so that the discovery of all matching branches of the large aggregate tree in our Aggregated Log are necessary. Thus, the *MINT-Processor* uses a much more complicated technique than a simple trie traversal.

7 Conclusions

We have presented the Web Utilization Miner, our system for the discovery of interesting navigation patterns in a web site. We have primarily focussed on the MINT query language and its execution mechanism. MINT can be used by a human expert to guide the mining system by specifying the generic structural and statistical characteristics that make a navigation pattern interesting.

WUM is intended for web site authors and administrators who are trying to improve the organization of their web documents and adapt it better to the needs of the information consumers. This applies to research and educational institutions, but also to other organizations, e.g. public authorities providing citizens with environmental information.

Of the modules of WUM, we have implemented the *Aggregation Service* and are now developing the MINT query processor and a simple visualization tool for presenting the discovered navigation patterns to the user. Our current work focusses on the experimentation with WUM, on optimization techniques for *MINT-Processor* to reduce the complexity of pattern discovery, and on the formulation of beliefs for navigation patterns. The *Notifier* module of WUM, intended to periodically execute preprocessed queries, will then be designed to discover belief violations.

References

1. Rakesh Agrawal and Ramakrishnan Srikant. Mining sequential patterns. In *ICDE*, Taipei, Taiwan, Mar. 1995.
2. Amihood Amir, Ronen Feldman, and Reuven Kashi. A new and versatile method for association generation. *Information Systems*, 22:333–347, 1997.
3. Ming-Syan Chen, Jong Soo Park, and Philip S Yu. Data mining for path traversal patterns in a web environment. In *ICDCS*, pages 385–392, 1996.
4. Robert Cooley, Bamshad Mobasher, and Jaideep Srivastava. Grouping web page references into transactions for mining world wide web browsing patterns. Technical Report TR 97-021, Dept. of Computer Science, Univ. of Minnesota, Minneapolis, USA, June 1997.
5. Robert Cooley, Bamshad Mobasher, and Jaideep Srivastava. Web mining: Information and pattern discovery on the world wide web. In *ICTAI'97*, Dec. 1997.
6. Ronen Feldman, Willi Klösgen, and Amir Zilberstein. Visualization techniques to explore data mining results for document collections. In *KDD'97*, pages 16–23, Newport Beach, CA, Aug. 1997. AAAI Press.
7. Heikki Mannila and Hannu Toivonen. Discovering generalized episodes using minimal occurences. In *KDD'96*, pages 146–151, 1996.
8. Peter Pirolli, James Pitkow, and Ramana Rao. Silk from a sow's ear: Extracting usable structures from the web. In *CHI'96* (http://www.acm.org/sigchi/chi96/proceedings), Vancouver, Canada, April 1996.
9. Avi Silberschatz and Alexander Tuzhilin. What makes patterns interesting in knowledge discovery systems. *IEEE Trans. on Knowledge and Data Eng.*, 8(6):970–974, Dec. 1996.
10. Myra Spiliopoulou. The laborious way from data mining to web mining. *submitted for publication*, June 1998.
11. Myra Spiliopoulou, Lukas Faulstich, C., and Karsten Winkler. Discovering Interesting Navigation Patterns over Web Usage Data. In *(submitted for publication)*, 1998.
12. Linda Tauscher and Saul Greenberg. Revisitation patterns in world wide web navigation. In *CHI'97*, Atlanta, Georgia, Mar. 1997.
13. Alan Wexelblat. An environment for aiding information-browsing tasks. In *Proc. of AAAI Spring Symposium on Acquisition, Learning and Demonstration: Automating Tasks for Users*, Birmingham, UK, 1996. AAAI Press.
14. Alan Wexelblat. *Footprints: History-Rich Social Navigation*. PhD thesis, MIT Media Laboratory, Dec. 1997.
15. Karsten Winkler. Realization and testing of a data mining environment for the discovery of user navigation patterns in a web site. Master's thesis, Institut für Wirtschaftsinformatik, HU Berlin, Oct. 1998. to appear on german.

A   The Syntax of MINT

Query structure

```
query::= 'SELECT' selectList
         fromClause [whereClause]
         [groupClause [havingClause]]
```

Specifying the query output

```
selectList ::=  ['DISTINCT'] derivedColumn (',' derivedColumn)*
derivedColumn ::=  (valExpr|aggrExpr) ['AS' columnName]
aggrExpression ::= aggrOp '(' ['DISTINCT'] (valExpr|varName) ')'
aggrOp ::=  'AVG' | 'MAX' | 'MIN' | 'SUM' | 'COUNT'
```

In the current version, aggregates are not implemented, so the groupClause and the havingClause are not supported yet.

Specifying the query template

```
fromClause ::=  'FROM' nodeRef ',' (templateRef)*
nodeRef ::= 'NODE' 'AS' nodeVar*
templateRef ::= [templateType] 'TEMPLATE' template
                ['AS' templateVar]
templateType ::= 'GRAPH' | 'TREE'
template ::= ['#'] [wildcards] (nodeVar [wildcards])*
wildcards ::=  '_' | ('_')* | '*'
```

In the current version only a single template variable is allowed. The default template type is GRAPH. The type TREE is not supported yet.

Introducing predicates

```
whereClause ::=  'WHERE' condition ('AND' condition)*
condition ::= stringCondition | numericCondition
stringCondition ::= columnReference stringCompOp stringLiteral
columnReference ::=  [templateVar '.'] nodeVar '.' columnName
stringcompOp ::=  '=' | 'CONTAINS' | 'STARTSWITH' | 'ENDSWITH'
numericCondition ::= numericExpr numericCompOp numericLiteral
numericExpr ::=  [numericExpr ('+'|'-')] term
term ::=  [term ('*'|'/')] factor
factor ::=  [('+'|'-')] primary
primary ::=  numericLiteral | columnReference
```

In the current version, numeric expressions involve at most two column references and are always linear.

Aggregating and grouping results

```
groupClause ::=  'GROUP' 'BY' groupExpr (',' groupExpr)*
groupExpr ::=  nodeVar | columnRef
havingClause ::=  'HAVING' condition ('AND' condition)*
```

Finding Near-Replicas of Documents on the Web

Narayanan Shivakumar, Hector Garcia-Molina

Department of Computer Science
Stanford, CA 94305.
{*shiva, hector*}*@cs.stanford.edu*

Abstract. We consider how to efficiently compute the overlap between all pairs of web documents. This information can be used to improve web crawlers, web archivers and in the presentation of search results, among others. We report statistics on how common replication is on the web, and on the cost of computing the above information for a relatively large subset of the web – about 24 million web pages which corresponds to about 150 Gigabytes of textual information.

1   Introduction

Many documents are being replicated across the world wide web. For instance, there are several copies of JAVA FAQs and Linux manuals on the net. Many of these copies are exactly the same, while in some cases the documents are "near" copies. For instance, documents may be older versions of some popular document, or may be in different formats (e.g., HTML, or Postscript), or may have additional buttons, links and inlined images that make them slightly different from other versions of the document.

Replication also occurs at a higher level than documents. In some cases, entire servers are mirrored across different countries and updated daily, weekly or on a monthly basis. The Linux Documentation Project (LDP) page with Linux manuals is one such instance, with over 180 mirror servers across the world. In some cases servers are exclusively dedicated to maintaining LDP pages and are therefore exact or near-replicas; in other cases there are several servers that replicate LDP manuals along with other manuals (`http://sunsite.unc.edu` contains manuals on LDP, FreeDOS, JAVA, etc.) In this paper, we concentrate on computing pair-wise document overlap; we can similarly solve the pair-wise server overlap problem if we consider the server to be the union of all documents in the site.

We believe it is useful to identify near-replicas of documents and servers for the following applications:

1. **Improved web crawling:** Until recently, web crawlers [2, 10] crawled the "entire" web. However since the web is growing rapidly and changing even faster, current crawlers are concentrating on crawling some subset of the web that has "high importance." For example, crawlers may only choose to visit "hot pages" with a high *backlink* count, i.e., pages that are pointed to by many other pages [6, 11]. After finishing each crawl, these crawlers will

recrawl the same pages to acquire updates to the hot pages since the last crawl.

When a limited number of web pages are to be crawled, a crawler should avoid visiting near-replicas, especially if they can be efficiently identified based on prior crawls. For instance, by identifying the 25 MBs of LDP pages to be near-copies ahead of time, the crawl can avoid crawling and indexing these pages from the 180+ sites – a potential savings of nearly 4.5 GBs for LDP pages alone!

2. **Improved ranking functions in search engines:** If documents A, B and C are considered relevant (in that order) to a user query, search engines currently[1] rank links to the three documents based on relevance, without regard to the overlap between the documents. However, we believe the "interestingness" of B is lower than C, if B overlaps with A significantly, while C is a distinct result. Similar proposals are being considered for "result reordering" based on overlap in other database contexts as well [7, 8].

3. **Archiving applications:** Since companies are trying to "archive" the web [1], it may be useful for them to identify near-copies of documents and compress these in a more efficient manner. Also finding near-copies is useful in services that avoid the common "404 error" (error for "Document not found" on the web) by presenting an alternate near-copy on the web, or a copy from a web archive [1].

1.1 Related work

Manber considered computing pair-wise document overlap in the context of finding similar files in a large file system [13, 14]. Researchers at the DEC SRC Lab are developing a similar tool to "syntactically" cluster the web [4, 5]. Heintze has developed the KOALA system for plagiarism detection [9]. As part of the Stanford Digital Library project, we have developed the COPS [3] and SCAM [15, 16] experimental prototypes for finding intellectual property violations. All the above techniques use variations of the same basic idea – compute "fingerprints" for a set of documents and store into a database. Two documents are defined to have significant overlap, if they share at least a certain number of fingerprints. The above systems have different target applications, and therefore differ in how they compute fingerprints of documents, and how they define the similarity measure between a pair of documents.

In this paper, we do not propose new notions of document similarity: we use the similarity measures we have been using in our SCAM (Stanford Copy Analysis Mechanism) prototype over the past three years [15, 16]. We primarily concentrate on efficiently solving the "clustering" problem of computing overlap between all document-pairs simultaneously. This problem is especially hard when the number of documents is on the order of millions. The techniques we use to solve this problem are different from the techniques adopted by the above

---

[1] Search engines are beginning to cluster exact copies of documents by computing simple checksums.

work [5, 9, 13, 14] as well as in our prior implementation in SCAM. Our new approach to solving the all-pairs document overlap problem is based on efficiently executing *iceberg* queries [17]. As we will see, our techniques take orders of magnitude less space and time.

2 Computing all-pairs document overlap

Each document is first converted from its native format (e,g., HTML, PostScript) into simple textual information using standard converters on UNIX (such as ps2ascii, html2ascii). The resulting document is then *chunked* into smaller units, such as words, sequences of words, sentences, paragraphs, or the entire document itself. Each textual chunk is then hashed down to a 32-bit fingerprint and stored into the *FPrint-DocID* file, with the following attributes: (1) fprint, which is the hashed fingerprint, and (2) docID, the ID of the document (typically a 32-bit integer).

We define the problem of computing all-pairs document overlap as follows. Produce the *Overlap* lookup table with triplets of the form $\langle d_i, d_j, F \rangle$, if documents d_i and d_j share F fingerprints in common. Since we are interested in cases where there is "significant" overlap between documents, we can restrict ourselves to storing tuples $\langle d_i, d_j, F \rangle$, only when $F \geq T$, for some threshold T.

2.1 Sort-based approach

The simplest approach to computing all-pairs overlap is the "sort-based" approach as follows. (1) Sort the *FPrint-DocID* file on the fprint attribute. (2) Scan the sorted *FPrint-DocID* file: if f_k is a fprint, d_i, d_j are docIDs, and if $\langle f_k, d_i \rangle$ and $\langle f_k, d_j \rangle$ occur in the sorted *FPrint-DocID* file, produce pair $\langle d_i, d_j \rangle$ into file *DocID-DocID*. (3) Sort the *DocID-DocID* file by both attributes, so that all $\langle d_i, d_j \rangle$ pairs, for documents d_i and d_j, are contiguous. (4) Scan the sorted *DocID-DocID* file: if some pair $\langle d_i, d_j \rangle$ occurs more than T times, the document pair is deemed to have significant overlap, and is stored in the *Overlap* lookup table. The above is roughly the approach followed by earlier work in computing all-pairs overlap, including the GLIMPSE system [13, 14], the DEC prototype [5] and in our earlier implementations of our COPS and SCAM prototypes.

The efficiency of the above implementation depends critically on how often fingerprints occur across documents. This is because Step (2) produces a cross-product of all document pairs that share a fingerprint, and subsequent steps process the resulting cross-product. Hence if fingerprints tend to be common across documents, the output may be too large (as we will report in our experiments). In fact, a significant portion of the output from Step (2) consists of document pairs that share one or two (common) fingerprints in common. These pairs will be discarded only in Step (5) when it is recognized that the document pairs do not share more than T fingerprints – until then, these tuples will be stored and sorted, requiring large amounts of storage as well as processing time.

In general, fingerprints that are computed on sequences of words or lines tend to be common, compared to fingerprints computed on paragraph level chunks. On the other hand, similarity measures that use the latter fingerprints tend to be less effective in finding overlap [3, 15, 16]. In applications where the goal is to identify "approximately similar" documents (as in GLIMPSE [13, 14], and in DEC's prototype [5]), the former class of fingerprints tend to be useful due to their efficiency. On the other hand, in applications (like SCAM and COPS [3, 15]) where the goal is to identify document pairs with smaller overlaps, we choose to use the latter class of fingerprints. Hence we need more efficient procedures to compute the *Overlap* table.

2.2 Probablistic-counting based approach

Roughly, our approach to computing the *Overlap* table for a given chunking (such as lines) is as follows. We first compute document pairs that are exact copies using the above "sort-based" procedure, and remove them from subsequent processing. This step is useful in cases when the number of exact copies is very large, since it reduces the work required by the subsequent, less efficient steps. We then chunk up the document and compute fingerprints for the document, and solve the pair-wise overlap problem using "probabilistic counting."

We can implement the above conceptual steps in a variety of ways, depending on our main memory resources. For the rest of the discussion, we assume the following about our main memory: (1) We can maintain the set of docIDs in main memory, along with a small constant number of bytes (about ten) for each docID. This assumption was almost valid in our case and some of our data structures were in fact allocated in virtual memory. However the paging overhead incurred was very small, and we continue to make this assumption in the rest of our discussion. (2) We do not have the main memory to maintain a counter for each $\langle d_i, d_j \rangle$, document pair that share a chunk. (If we did, we can easily count the number of chunks each document pair shares.) We compute the *Overlap* table as follows under the above assumptions of our main memory.

1. *Produce fingerprints:* We compute one fingerprint for each document based on the entire document, and store into *FPrint-DocID-Exact*. We also compute fingerprints based on the chosen chunk, and store into *FPrint-DocID-Chunk*. Sort the *FPrint-DocID-Exact* file, so that docIDs of documents with the same fingerprint are located contiguously.

2. *Remove exact copies:* Scan the sorted *FPrint-DocID-Exact* file: for each d_i that contains fingerprint f_k, maintain in main memory the smallest docID d_j that also shares f_k. (The document with smallest docID is chosen as the "central" document for a set of documents with the same signature.) Finally remove the signatures of non-center documents from *FPrint-DocID-Chunk*, by scanning *FPrint-DocID-Chunk* and producing *FPrint-DocID-Chunk'*.

3. *Computing non-exact overlap:* We use "coarse counting" or "probabilistic counting" as our primary basis for computing the *Overlap* table. Coarse counting is a technique often used for query size estimation, for computing

the number of distinct targets in a relation, for mining association rules and for other applications. The simplest form of coarse counting uses an array $A[1..m]$ of m counters and a hash function h_1. The *CoarseCount* algorithm works as follows: Initialize all m entries of A to zero. Then perform a linear scan of the sorted *FPrint-DocID-Chunk'* file. For each d_i and d_j that share some fingerprint f_k increment the counter $A[h_1(d_i, d_j)]$ by one. After completing this *hashing-scan*, compute a bitmap array $BITMAP_1[1..m]$ by scanning through array A, and setting $BITMAP_1[i]$ if bucket i is *heavy*, i.e. if $A[i] \geq T$. We compute $BITMAP_1$ since it is much smaller than A, and maintains all the information required in the next phase. After $BITMAP_1$ is computed, we reclaim the memory allocated to A. We then compute the *Overlap* table by performing a *candidate-selection* scan of *FPrint-DocID-Chunk'*: for each pair d_i, d_j sharing f_k and with $BITMAP_1[h_1(d_i, d_j)]$ set to one, we add the pair $\langle d_i, d_j \rangle$ to a candidate list F. Finally we remove the false-positives by performing one more scan of the sorted *FPrint-DocID-Chunk'*, and explictly counting the number of fingerprints the document pairs in F share, thereby producing *Overlap*. The candidate-selection scan in this simple coarse-counting algorithm may compute a large F, due to false-positives. We however can progressively remove false-postives using *sampling* techniques, as well as *multiple hash-functions* [17]. In practice, we have seen that by using a small number of hash functions and a small pilot sample, we can remove a large fraction of false-positives for many real-world data sets [17].

The above procedure allows us to avoid explicitly storing the cross-product produced in Step (2) of the "sort-based" algorithm, and the sorting required in the subsequent steps. In fact in many cases, the above approach would finish computing the *Overlap* table, even before Step (2) in the "sort-based" approach terminates [17].

3 Experiments

	Measures / Signatures	Entire document	Four lines	Two lines
Space	Fingerprints	800 MBs	2.4 GBs	4.6 GBs
	Server Map	750 MBs	750 MBs	750 MBs
	URL Map	1.5 GBs	1.5 GBs	1.5 GBs
Time	Read "pagefeed" and compute fingerprints	44 hrs	44 hrs	44 hrs
	Sort *FPrint-DocID*	52 mins	163 mins	7.14 hrs
	Compute all-pairs overlap	45 mins	85 mins	2.42 hrs

Table 1. Storage and time costs for computing *Overlap*.

We used 150 GBs of web data crawled by the Stanford BackRub web crawler [12] for our experiments. This corresponds to approximately 24 million web pages crawled primarily from domains located in the United States of America. We ran our experiments on a SUN UltraSPARC with dual processors, 256 MBs of RAM and 1.4 GBs of swap space, running SunOS 5.5.1. We computed fingerprints of each document for three different chunkings: (1) one fingerprint for the entire document, (2) one fingerprint for every four lines of text, and (3) one fingerprint for every two lines of text. We computed the corresponding *FPrint-DocID* file with these fingerprints, along with a 32-bit integer for the URL and Server. We also maintained a "URL Map" to keep track of the textual URL along with the corresponding numerical identifier. Similarly we maintained a "Server Map." We report the costs in storing the signatures and maps, as well as the time breakdown in computing the *Overlap* table in Table 1, with $T = 15$ and $T = 25$ for the "four line" and "two line" fingerprints respectively. Note that the time to compute *Overlap* for the "four line" and "two line" fingerprints, is the additional time required to compute *Overlap*, after computing the document-pairs that are exact replicas.

In Figure 1 we report the number of replicas for each document for the three chunkings. For instance, about 64% of the 24 million web pages have one exact (darkest bar) replica (itself); about 18% of pages have an additional replica – that is, there are about $\frac{1}{2} * \frac{18}{100} * 24 * 10^6$ distinct pages that have one replica among the other $\frac{1}{2} * \frac{18}{100} * 24 * 10^6$ pages. Similarly, about 5% of pages have between 10 and 100 replicas. As expected, the percentage of pages with more than one replica increases when we relax the notion of similarity from 36% $(100 - 64\%)$ for exact replicas, to about 48% $(100 - 52\%)$ for "two-line" chunks.

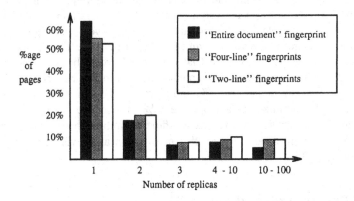

Fig. 1. Document replication on 24 million web pages.

We were initially very surprised by the high degree of replication implied by Figure 1. To understand what data was replicated, we manually examined several highly replicated pages, and identified the following common reasons for such high replication:

1. **Server aliasing:** Several servers have multiple aliases, and therefore different URLs lead to the same page. For instance, www.webcrawler.com has many aliases including wc4.webcrawler.com and webcrawler.com. Hence the BackRub crawler that currently retrieves pages based on URLs, does not in fact recognize the server aliases. Note these are not really copies, but the crawler retrieves these URLs multiple times since the textual URLs appear different. We believe checking the IP address of the machine before crawling may help in a few cases. However in many cases, machines have multiple IP addresses. So in general, detecting server aliasing is a hard problem.

2. **URL aliasing:** Many documents on a server in fact have multiple URLs due to links on the local file system. For instance, the URLs
http://www-db.stanford.edu/~ widom and
http://www-db.stanford.edu/people/widom.html in fact correspond to the same HTML document, with a UNIX link on the local filesystem on the www-db machine from the latter to the former.

3. **Replication of popular documents:** As we mentioned in the introduction, there are several manuals and FAQs that are replicated in many servers across the world. Since many manuals contain several hundreds or thousands of HTML pages, when they are replicated across 10 – 100 sites, they constitute a significant fraction of web pages. In Table 2 we report the five most popular set of pages that were replicated in our data, along with an approximate count of the number of distinct servers they were replicated at.

The knowledge gained from our copy analysis can be used to significantly reduce the amount of work done by a crawler. For example, if a page has 10 copies, on its next crawl the system need only visit and index one of those pages. Using our sample data and assuming we only avoid visiting exact copies, the number of pages to be visited can be reduced by 22%. This is about 33 GB (out of our 150 GB total) of data that does not have to be retrieved, indexed, and stored! If we avoid visiting documents that share 15 or more 4-line chunks, the visited pages can be cut by 29%, and if we avoid documents that overlap by 25 or more 2-line chunks the savings are 33%. In the later case, this is almost 50 GBs less! One can see that the extra effort of finding the near-duplicates (as opposed to exact duplicates) pays off, since we can avoid visiting and indexing 50 - 33 or 17 GB less of data.

4 Conclusion and future work

Web documents are being replicated across servers. In many cases, these documents are *near-copies* of other documents. We considered the problem of efficiently identifying all document pairs on the web that have significant overlap. Such overlap information is useful in a variety of applications including web crawling, improving presentation of search results, as well as in web archiving.

Rank	Description	Approximate number of server replicas
1	TUCOWS WinSock utilities http://www.tucows.com	100
2	Microsoft Internet Information Server 2.0 Manuals http://acctserver.cob.vt.edu/iisadmin/htmldocs/	90
3	UNIX Help Pages http://www.ucs.ed.ac.uk/~ unixhelp/	75
4	RedHat Linux Manual Version 4.2 http://www.redhat.com/support/docs/rhl	55
5	JAVA 1.0.2 API Documentation http://dnaugler.cs.semo.edu/tutorials/API/	50

Table 2. Popular web pages.

We report on the degree of replication among 24 million web documents crawled by the Stanford BackRub crawler.

When we started this research, we were interested in knowing how much of the web was replicated. We later realized that our view of the web was very biased by the set of pages crawled by our specific web crawler. Indeed this is the case for any other commercial or research web crawler. We now believe that the techniques presented in this paper serve as a good "debugger" to evaluate web crawlers. For instance the BackRub crawler currently uses one among many possible heuristics to choose the set of pages to crawl. The statistics we compute however show that the current heuristic crawls pages with multiple replicas, several times. Based on the statistics we computed, the authors of the crawler are currently considering options to improve their current heuristic. One proposal they are considering to avoid server aliasing problems, is to use IP addresses of machines, as well as IP addresses of domains (since a machine might have multiple IP addresses) while choosing which pages to crawl. Indeed the degree of replication after the next crawl based on some improved heuristic may be substantially different!

We would also like to raise a more philosophical question, based on our statistics: does the web really need so many replicas of popular pages? For instance, even if the TUCOWS site is popular, we wonder if the number of accesses across the sites, justifies such a high degree of replication. Also it is especially disturbing that the highly replicated Microsoft IIS manuals, and JAVA 1.0.2 API documentation are in fact ancient, and subsumed by future versions of the manuals. Perhaps the HTTP protocol should start including additional meta-information about documents, so that each page can be optionally tagged with information on what is the "primary" document from which the page was copied. Such information will certainly be useful to crawlers, archivers as well as for notifying users that "more up-to-date" copies can be found at an alternate site.

References

1. Alexa. Alexa technology. http://www.alexa.com.
2. AltaVista. Altavista search engine. http://altavista.digital.com.
3. S. Brin, J. Davis, and H. Garcia-Molina. Copy detection mechanisms for digital documents. In *Proceedings of the ACM SIGMOD Annual Conference*, San Francisco, CA, May 1995.
4. A. Broder. On the resemblance and containment of documents. Technical report, DIGITAL Systems Research Center Tech. Report, 1997.
5. A. Broder, S.C. Glassman, and M. S. Manasse. Syntactic Clustering of the Web. In *Sixth International World Wide Web Conference*, April 1997.
6. J. Cho, H. Garcia-Molina, and L. Page. Efficient crawling through url ordering. In *Seventh International World Wide Web conference*, April 1998.
7. D. Florescu, D. Koller, and A. Levy. Using probabilistic information in data integration. In *Proceedings of 23rd Conference on Very Large Databases (VLDB'97)*, pages 216 – 225, August 1997.
8. L. Gravano and H. Garcia-Molina. Merging ranks from heterogeneous internet sources. In *Proceedings of 23rd Conference on Very Large Databases (VLDB'97)*, pages 196–205, August 1997.
9. N. Heintze. Scalable document fingerprinting. In *Proceedings of Second USENIX Workshop on Electronic Commerce*, November 1996.
10. Infoseek. Infoseek search engine. http://www.infoseek.com.
11. J. Kleinberg. Authoritative sources in a hyperlinked environment. In *Proceedings of 9th ACM-SIAM Symposium on Discrete Algorithms, (SODA'98)*, 1998.
12. S. Brin L. Page. Google search engine/ backrub web crawler. http://google.stanford.edu.
13. U. Manber. Finding similar files in a large file system. Technical Report TR 93-33, University of Arizona, Tuscon, Arizona, October 1993.
14. U. Manber and S. Wu. Glimpse: A tool to search through entire file systems. In *Proceedings of the winter USENIX Conference*, January 1994.
15. N. Shivakumar and H. Garcia-Molina. SCAM: A copy detection mechanism for digital documents. In *Proceedings of 2nd International Conference in Theory and Practice of Digital Libraries (DL'95)*, Austin, Texas, June 1995.
16. N. Shivakumar and H. Garcia-Molina. Building a scalable and accurate copy detection mechanism. In *Proceedings of 1st ACM Conference on Digital Libraries (DL'96)*, Bethesda, Maryland, March 1996.
17. M. Fang, N. Shivakumar, H. Garcia-Molina, R. Motwani and J.D. Ullman. Computing iceberg queries efficiently. In *Proceedings of 24th Conference on Very Large Databases (VLDB'98)*, August 1998.

Author Index

Lecture Notes in Computer Science

For information about Vols. 1–1506
please contact your bookseller or Springer-Verlag

Vol. 1544: C. Zhang, D. Lukose (Eds.), Multi-Agent Systems. Proceedings, 1998. VII, 195 pages. 1998. (Subseries LNAI).

Vol. 1545: A. Birk, J. Demiris (Eds.), Learning Robots. Proceedings, 1996. IX, 188 pages. 1998. (Subseries LNAI).

Vol. 1546: B. Möller, J.V. Tucker (Eds.), Prospects for Hardware Foundations. Survey Chapters, 1998. X, 468 pages. 1998.

Vol. 1547: S.H. Whitesides (Ed.), Graph Drawing. Proceedings 1998. XII, 468 pages. 1998.

Vol. 1548: A.M. Haeberer (Ed.), Algebraic Methodology and Software Technology. Proceedings, 1999. XI, 531 pages. 1999.

Vol. 1550: B. Christianson, B. Crispo, W.S. Harbison, M. Roe (Eds.), Security Protocols. Proceedings, 1998. VIII, 241 pages. 1999.

Vol. 1551: G. Gupta (Ed.), Practical Aspects of Declarative Languages. Proceedings, 1999. VIII, 367 pgages. 1999.

Vol. 1552: Y. Kambayashi, D.L. Lee, E.-P. Lim, M.K. Mohania, Y. Masunaga (Eds.), Advances in Database Technologies. Proceedings, 1998. XIX, 592 pages. 1999.

Vol. 1553: S.F. Andler, J. Hansson (Eds.), Active, Real-Time, and Temporal Database Systems. Proceedings, 1997. VIII, 245 pages. 1998.

Vol. 1554: S. Nishio, F. Kishino (Eds.), Advanced Multimedia Content Processing. Proceedings, 1998. XIV, 454 pages. 1999.

Vol. 1555: J.P. Müller, M.P. Singh, A.S. Rao (Eds.), Intelligent Agents V. Proceedings, 1998. XXIV, 455 pages. 1999. (Subseries LNAI).

Vol. 1556: S. Tavares, H. Meijer (Eds.), Selected Areas in Cryptography. Proceedings, 1998. IX, 377 pages. 1999.

Vol. 1557: P. Zinterhof, M. Vajteršic, A. Uhl (Eds.), Parallel Computation. Proceedings, 1999. XV, 604 pages. 1999.

Vol. 1558: H. J.v.d. Herik, H. Iida (Eds.), Computers and Games. Proceedings, 1998. XVIII, 337 pages. 1999.

Vol. 1559: P. Flener (Ed.), Logic-Based Program Synthesis and Transformation. Proceedings, 1998. X, 331 pages. 1999.

Vol. 1560: K. Imai, Y. Zheng (Eds.), Public Key Cryptography. Proceedings, 1999. IX, 327 pages. 1999.

Vol. 1561: I. Damgård (Ed.), Lectures on Data Security. VII, 250 pages. 1999.

Vol. 1563: Ch. Meinel, S. Tison (Eds.), STACS 99. Proceedings, 1999. XIV, 582 pages. 1999.

Vol. 1567: P. Antsaklis, W. Kohn, M. Lemmon, A. Nerode, S. Sastry (Eds.), Hybrid Systems V. X, 445 pages. 1999.

Vol. 1568: G. Bertrand, M. Couprie, L. Perroton (Eds.), Discrete Geometry for Computer Imagery. Proceedings, 1999. XI, 459 pages. 1999.

Vol. 1569: F.W. Vaandrager, J.H. van Schuppen (Eds.), Hybrid Systems: Computation and Control. Proceedings, 1999. X, 271 pages. 1999.

Vol. 1570: F. Puppe (Ed.), XPS-99: Knowledge-Based Systems. VIII, 227 pages. 1999. (Subseries LNAI).

Vol. 1572: P. Fischer, H.U. Simon (Eds.), Computational Learning Theory. Proceedings, 1999. X, 301 pages. 1999. (Subseries LNAI).

Vol. 1574: N. Zhong, L. Zhou (Eds.), Methodologies for Knowledge Discovery and Data Mining. Proceedings, 1999. XV, 533 pages. 1999. (Subseries LNAI).

Vol. 1575: S. Jähnichen (Ed.), Compiler Construction. Proceedings, 1999. X, 301 pages. 1999.

Vol. 1576: S.D. Swierstra (Ed.), Programming Languages and Systems. Proceedings, 1999. X, 307 pages. 1999.

Vol. 1577: J.-P. Finance (Ed.), Fundamental Approaches to Software Engineering. Proceedings, 1999. X, 245 pages. 1999.

Vol. 1578: W. Thomas (Ed.), Foundations of Software Science and Computation Structures. Proceedings, 1999. X, 323 pages. 1999.

Vol. 1579: W.R. Cleaveland (Ed.), Tools and Algorithms for the Construction and Analysis of Systems. Proceedings, 1999. XI, 445 pages. 1999.

Vol. 1580: A. Včkovski, K.E. Brassel, H.-J. Schek (Eds.), Interoperating Geographic Information Systems. Proceedings, 1999. XI, 329 pages. 1999.

Vol. 1581: J.-Y. Girard (Ed.), Typed Lambda Calculi and Applications. Proceedings, 1999. VIII, 397 pages. 1999.

Vol. 1582: A. Lecomte, F. Lamarche, G. Perrier (Eds.), Logical Aspects of Computational Linguistics. Proceedings, 1997. XI, 251 pages. 1999. (Subseries LNAI).

Vol. 1584: G. Gottlob, E. Grandjean, K. Seyr (Eds.), Computer Science Logic. Proceedings, 1998. X, 431 pages. 1999.

Vol. 1586: J. Rolim et al. (Eds.), Parallel and Distributed Processing. Proceedings, 1999. XVII, 1443 pages. 1999.

Vol. 1587: J. Pieprzyk, R. Safavi-Naini, J. Seberry (Eds.), Information Security and Privacy. Proceedings, 1999. XI, 327 pages. 1999.

Vol. 1590: P. Atzeni, A. Mendelzon, G. Mecca (Eds.), The World Wide Web and Databases. Proceedings, 1998. VIII, 213 pages. 1999.

Vol. 1592: J. Stern (Ed.), Advances in Cryptology – EUROCRYPT '99. Proceedings, 1999. XII, 475 pages. 1999.

Vol. 1593: P. Sloot, M. Bubak, A. Hoekstra, B. Hertzberger (Eds.), High-Performance Computing and Networking. Proceedings, 1999. XXIII, 1318 pages. 1999.

Vol. 1594: P. Ciancarini, A.L. Wolf (Eds.), Coordination Languages and Models. Proceedings, 1999. IX, 420 pages. 1999.

Vol. 1596: R. Poli, H.-M. Voigt, S. Cagnoni, D. Corne, G.D. Smith, T.C. Fogarty (Eds.), Evolutionary Image Analysis, Signal Processing and Telecommunications. Proceedings, 1999. X, 225 pages. 1999.

Vol. 1597: H. Zuidweg, M. Campolargo, J. Delgado, A. Mullery (Eds.), Intelligence in Services and Networks. Proceedings, 1999. XII, 552 pages. 1999.

Vol. 1605: J. Billington, M. Diaz, G. Rozenberg (Eds.), Application of Petri Nets to Communication Networks. IX, 303 pages. 1999.